CHRISTIANITY IN THE
SECOND CENTURY

As a writer who spanned East and West, Tatian was an important figure in second century Christianity. In the first dedicated study for more than 40 years, Emily Hunt examines both his work and his world.

Topics covered include Tatian's relationship with Justin Martyr, the Apologetic attempt to defend and define Christianity against the Graeco-Roman world, and Christian use of hellenistic philosophy. Tatian was accused of heresy after his death, and this work sees him at the heart of the orthodox/heterodox debate. His links with the East, and his Gospel harmony the *Diatessaron*, lead to an exploration of Syriac Christianity and asceticism.

Emily Hunt reassesses scholarly assumptions about heresiology and the Apologists' relationship with hellenistic philosophy, and also traces a developing Christian philosophical tradition from Philo, to Justin Martyr and Tatian's *Oration to the Greeks*, and then within the work of key Syriac writers.

This is an important volume on many levels: a study of a significant Church father, it is also a comprehensive overview of second century Christianity, an exploration of the development of several strands in philosophy, and an insight into the Church in both East and West in a seminal period.

Emily J. Hunt researches first to third century Patristics and the impact of theology on literature. She gained her PhD in Theology from the University of Birmingham in 2000.

CHRISTIANITY IN THE SECOND CENTURY

The Case of Tatian

Emily J. Hunt

Routledge
Taylor & Francis Group

LONDON AND NEW YORK

First published 2003
by Routledge
11 New Fetter Lane, London EC4P 4EE

Simultaneously published in the USA and Canada
by Routledge
29 West 35th Street, New York, NY 10001

Routledge is an imprint of the Taylor & Francis Group

© 2003 Emily J. Hunt

Typeset in Garamond by Wearset Ltd, Boldon, Tyne and Wear
Printed and bound in Great Britain by Biddles Ltd, Guildford and
King's Lynn

British Library Cataloguing in Publication Data
A catalogue record for this book is available from the British Library

Library of Congress Cataloging in Publication Data
Hunt, Emily J. (Emily Jane), 1974–
Christianity in the second century: the case of Tatian/Emily J. Hunt.
p. cm. – (Routledge early church monographs)
Includes bibliographical references (p.) and index.
1. Tatian, ca. 120–173. 2. Theology, Doctrinal–History–Early church,
ca. 30–600. I. Title. II. Series.

BT1720.T25H86 2003
270.1′092–dc21

2002037152

ISBN 0-415-30405-9 (hbk)
ISBN 0-415-30406-7 (pbk)

DEDICATION

TO MY PARENTS, JANE AND DAVE
LANGLOIS, AND MY HUSBAND, LEIGH
HUNT, WITHOUT WHOSE FINANCIAL
AND MORAL SUPPORT I WOULD
NEVER HAVE COMPLETED MY PhD.

CONTENTS

ACKNOWLEDGEMENTS

This book is a revised and extended version of the thesis that I submitted for the degree of PhD in July 1999 at the University of Birmingham. The first three years of my research were funded in part by a scholarship from the Department of Theology, for which I am extremely grateful. My supervisors during this time were Prof. Frances Young and Dr David Taylor, and I would like to thank them both for all the help and encouragement that they gave me during my time at Birmingham.

My thanks are also due to Dr David Parker for his help with the more difficult aspects of Tatian's Greek, and to Kirsten Holtschneider for her help in translating German. I would also like to thank the editorial team at Routledge, and particularly Richard Stoneman, who has always been remarkably prompt at responding to my queries.

English quotations from the Bible are taken from the *Revised Standard Version* (1946; 2nd edn 1971) New York and Glasgow: William Collins Sons & Co. Ltd. Quotations from the Greek New Testament are taken from the Nestle-Aland edition, B. and K. Aland *et al.* (1898; 27th edn 1993) *Novum Testamentum Graece*, Stuttgart: Deutsche Bibelgesellschaft.

Excerpts from Tatian's *Oration to the Greeks* are taken from Molly Whittaker (1982) *Tatian Oratio ad Graecos and Fragments*, Oxford Early Christian Texts, Oxford: Clarendon Press, and are reprinted by permission of Oxford University Press.

Excerpts from *Saint Justin Martyr: The First and Second Apologies* are taken from the Classics of Western Spirituality Series by L.W. Barnard ©1977, and used with permission of Paulist Press, www.paulistpress.com.

Excerpts from Philo's 'On Giants' are reprinted by permission of the publishers and Trustees of the Loeb Classical Library from

Philo: II, Loeb Classical Library Vol. 227, translated by F.H. Colson and G.H. Whittaker (1929), Cambridge, Mass.: Harvard University Press. The Loeb Classical Library® is a registered trademark of the President and Fellows of Harvard College.

Excerpts from Philo's 'Special Laws' are reprinted by permission of the publishers and Trustees of the Loeb Classical Library from *Philo: VIII*, Loeb Classical Library Vol. 341, translated by F.H. Colson and G.H. Whittaker (1939), Cambridge, Mass.: Harvard University Press. The Loeb Classical Library® is a registered trademark of the President and Fellows of Harvard College.

Excerpts from Philo's 'Questions and Answers on Exodus' are reprinted by permission of the publishers and Trustees of the Loeb Classical Library from *Philo: Supplement II*, Loeb Classical Library Vol. 401, translated by Ralph Marcus (1953), Cambridge, Mass.: Harvard University Press. The Loeb Classical Library® is a registered trademark of the President and Fellows of Harvard College.

Excerpts from Sextus Empiricus' 'Outlines of Pyrrhonism' are reprinted by permission of the publishers and Trustees of the Loeb Classical Library from *Sextus Empiricus: I*, Loeb Classical Library Vol. 273, translated by R.G. Bury (1933), Cambridge, Mass.: Harvard University Press. The Loeb Classical Library® is a registered trademark of the President and Fellows of Harvard College.

ABBREVIATIONS

ACW	Ancient Christian Writers. Mahwah: Paulist Press, 1946–.
ANRW	Aufstieg und Niedergang der römischen Welt, ed. H. Temporini and W. Haase. Berlin: De Gruyter, in progress.
Apol	*First and Second Apologies*, Justin Martyr (Barnard 1997).
BJRL	*Bulletin of the John Rylands Library*
CBQ	*Catholic Biblical Quarterly*
ChHist	*Church History*
Dial	*Dialogue with Trypho*, Justin Martyr (Falls 1977).
GCS	Die Griechischen Christlichen Schriftsteller. Berlin: Akademie, 1897–.
HThR	*Harvard Theological Review*
JECS	*Journal of Early Christian Studies*
JEH	*Journal of Ecclesiastical History*
JBL	*Journal of Biblical Literature*
JThS	*Journal of Theological Studies*
JThS (NS)	*Journal of Theological Studies (New Series)*
LCL	Loeb Classical Library. Cambridge, Massachusetts: Harvard University Press, 1912–.
NovTest	*Novum Testamentum*
NTS	*New Testament Studies*
Or	*Oration to the Greeks*, Tatian (Whittaker 1982).
SC	Sources Chrétiennes, ed. H. de Lubac, J. Daniélou *et al.* Paris: Cerf, 1942–.
SCent	*The Second Century*
SP	*Studia Patristica*
STh	*Studia Theologica*
Suppl. VChr	Supplements to Vigiliae Christianae

Suppl. NovTest	Supplements to Novum Testamentum
TU	Texte und Untersuchungen. Berlin: Akademie, 1883–.
VChr	*Vigiliae Christianae*
WS	*Wiener Studien*
ZNTW	*Zeitschrift für die neutestamentliche Wissenschaft*

INTRODUCTION

The second century was a rather curious period in church history. It was a time when Christians were struggling to define themselves, not only in terms of departure from their Jewish roots, but also against the Graeco-Roman world around them. Christianity was still very much a minority movement during this period, forced underground by repeated persecution, and martyrdom was still a frequent reality. Doctrinally a certain amount of fluidity existed, although by the end of the second century concepts of what was acceptable in the mainstream church began to harden and what may have been considered merely 'extreme' in the mid-second century became 'heresy' by its end.

Furthermore, our picture of second century Christianity is somewhat distorted since most of the evidence is presented by Christians who belonged to the stream that was to become known as 'orthodoxy'. Texts that were later considered 'heretical' were suppressed, unless useful, and so the voices of alternative streams of Christianity of this period have been muted.

In this book I hope to help clarify the forces that were acting within second century Christianity by focusing on a figure who is presented as bordering on the heretical. Tatian (c.120–180 CE) was accused by the heresiologists of turning to gnosticism and Encratism in the latter part of his life, but I suspect that this accusation actually characterizes the process of polarization that began at the end of the second century.

Tatian originally came from Assyria,[1] and was born around the year 120 CE of pagan parents. He received a broad Greek education, which included training in rhetoric, and travelled extensively before finally arriving in Rome. At some point he was converted to Christianity through reading the 'barbarian writings' of the Jews.[2] His conversion may have been due to Justin Martyr, whose pupil he became in Rome, but this is uncertain. Whilst in Rome Tatian himself taught a man named Rhodo, who wrote against Marcion.[3]

Following Justin's martyrdom in about 165 CE, Tatian is reported to have turned to the heresies of gnosticism and Encratism, and to have apostatized from the church in Rome.[4] He then returned to the East, where he seems to have vanished into obscurity. Our only information about his life after this point comes from Epiphanius, who tells us that Tatian founded his own school in Mesopotamia around the twelfth year of Antoninus Pius, although it seems likely that Epiphanius was actually referring to the reign of Pius' successor, Marcus Aurelius, which makes the date 172 CE.[5]

Of Tatian's works, only one has been passed down to us in its entirety; the *Oration to the Greeks*. Tatian also wrote a very popular gospel harmony, the *Diatessaron* or *Euangellion da-Meḥalleṭe* (*Gospel of the Mixed*), which was widely used in the East until well into the fifth century, when it was replaced by the four Gospels under the westernizing influence of men like Rabbula and Theodoret.[6] Unfortunately the work itself is not extant, but some of its variants have been determined through careful study of dependent material. This work will be important when we consider Tatian's relationship with Syriac Christianity in Chapter 6.

A fragment of Tatian's treatise *On Perfection According to the Saviour* is preserved for us in a work of Clement of Alexandria.[7] Tatian also wrote treatises called *On Animals*,[8] and *On Problems* which set out 'the obscure and hidden parts of the divine Scriptures',[9] and planned to write a work *To Those who Have Propounded Ideas about God*,[10] none of which have survived.

Thus, our chief witness for Tatian's theology is his *Oration to the Greeks*. This is an apologetic work that has probably survived because of its chronological argument.[11] The *Oration* will form the backbone of my comparison of Tatian with contemporary streams of Christianity, although reference will be made to Tatian's *Diatessaron* in relation to Encratism in Chapter 6, and to the Clementine fragment of *On Perfection* in relation to Pauline exegesis in Chapter 2, and again in relation to asceticism in Chapter 6.

As far as the manuscript history of the current text for Tatian's *Oration* is concerned, it is now widely accepted that the four main extant manuscripts, M, M^bis, P and V, are derived from a missing portion of the Arethas codex, dated to 914 CE.[12] The edition that I will use here is that of Molly Whittaker,[13] although where the text is problematic I will refer to Miroslav Marcovich's edition,[14] which provides a more extensive critical apparatus, and I will suggest an alternative to Whittaker's English translation where necessary.

The question of dating Tatian's *Oration* is somewhat problematic; despite Grant's claim to the contrary,[15] there is no clear chronological evidence within the *Oration* to date this work securely. This is further complicated by the heresiological claim of Tatian's apostasy; if one is determined to claim the *Oration* for orthodoxy a date prior to Justin's death in 165 is necessary, but if one is anxious to see elements of Tatian's heresy in the *Oration*, as indeed is Grant, one will choose a late date.[16] Of course, all of this presupposes that Irenaeus was correct in recording that Tatian left the church and then turned heretic.

Various dates have been suggested for the *Oration*, from the 150s,[17] to the late 170s.[18] However, a passage in Tatian's *Oration*, which Eusebius assumes to refer to Justin's death, may hold the key to dating this work. In Chapter 19, Tatian speaks of the cynic philosopher Crescens attempting to bring the death penalty against both Justin and himself.[19] Eusebius connects this with a passage in Justin, where Tatian's master expresses his expectation of being killed by Crescens,[20] but in citing Tatian Eusebius omits Tatian's reference to himself, interpreting *Or* 19:1 as a record of Justin's death.[21]

Barnard points out this discrepancy in Eusebius, and rightly concludes that Tatian's inclusion of himself in Crescens' death plot suggests that Justin's martyrdom had not yet occurred when Tatian wrote the *Oration*;[22] had Justin been martyred before the *Oration* was written, surely Tatian would have mentioned it in Chapter 19. Thus it seems necessary to date the *Oration* prior to Justin's death, and although it is difficult to date it more precisely, it is likely that Barnard is correct in dating it shortly before Justin's death, at around 160 CE.

Traditionally, Tatian is viewed as an apologist and disciple of Justin Martyr, who turned heretic after his master's death.[23] However, I shall be questioning this assumption, and by tracing Tatian's relationship with various contemporary streams of Christianity I will attempt to place Tatian more accurately within the second century.

My approach in this book is to adopt the *Oration* as the standard document outlining Tatian's theology,[24] and to use it to compare Tatian with the streams of Christianity around him. Thus in Chapter 2 I compare the *Oration* with Valentinian texts; in Chapter 3 I turn to the works of Tatian's teacher, Justin Martyr, and examine how far Justin influenced his pupil; in Chapter 4 I consider the influence that contemporary hellenistic philosophy may have had on Tatian; and finally, in Chapter 6, I compare the *Oration* with later Syriac texts in an attempt to discover whether Tatian influenced the Christianity of his homeland, and if so, how.[25] I shall begin by providing an outline of how second century Christianity relating to Tatian is generally perceived by modern scholarship.

1

CHRISTIANITY IN THE SECOND CENTURY

The nature of second century Christianity is actually quite difficult to pin down with any accuracy. Sources from the second century itself are sparse, and later church historians present partial and often contradictory accounts, which are clearly biased and marked with an agenda of a later time. This confusion is further reflected in modern scholarship, and many different perspectives on second century Christianity have been presented.

Nevertheless, some sort of initial survey is necessary in order to begin the process of locating Tatian within the second century. A comprehensive overview is, of course, impossible within the space of a single chapter; nor would it be appropriate within this context. Thus the following survey of second century Christianity will focus on what is of importance for placing Tatian, and extra weight will be given to issues that are of particular relevance.

Christianity and Judaism

The first significant shift that began to shape early Christianity was its struggle to define itself against its Jewish roots. Christianity had, of course, begun its existence as a Jewish sect which believed that Jesus was the Messiah.[1] It would appear that the first real change in Christianity's evolution began with Paul and his mission to the Gentiles, which is outlined in the Pauline Epistles.[2] Paul's proposal to accept the conversion of Gentiles to Christianity without the enforcement of Jewish conversion requirements[3] seems to have initiated Christianity's development away from Judaism, although it was some time before the consequences of Paul's actions were felt within Palestinian Christianity.

It is difficult to give a date for the split between Christianity and Judaism, and even the way in which the split is defined has been the cause of much controversy amongst Jewish and Christian scholars. The separation itself was gradual, and occurred at different rates in different locations. For instance, in the communities that were particularly receptive to Pauline ideas and where there were few Christians of Jewish descent, the split was probably very quick. However, in Palestine, the heart of Jewish Christianity, the separation was very slow, and some Jewish Christians may never have made the break. In areas where the presence of the hellenized Jews of the Diaspora was strong, the issue of separation becomes very complicated. Moreover, the fact that, besides the *Epistle of Barnabus*, there is very little textual evidence to highlight this development within early Christianity means that our picture of the separation from Judaism is very unclear indeed.

However, something of the parting of the ways can be made out from certain historical events centred on Palestine. In 70 CE, the Temple in Jerusalem was destroyed. This had serious ramifications for Jewish religious life, since religious activity had been centred on the Temple. From a Christian point of view, the destruction of the Temple was interpreted in some circles as a just punishment for the Jewish rejection of Jesus.

Around 85 CE, a benediction against heretics (*minim*) began to be read in synagogues. Although there is still some debate about whether *ha-minim* refers specifically to Christians,[4] it is almost certain that Jewish Christians were included in this anathema. Schiffman has suggested that the purpose of the benediction was not actually to excommunicate Jewish Christians from the Jewish faith (since, according to the halakic concept of Jewish identity, Jewishness was based upon race, not right or wrong belief), but rather to prevent Jewish Christians from functioning as Precentors, since a Christian was unlikely to curse himself.[5] However, the benediction certainly made many Christians feel unwelcome in the synagogues, and there is evidence in the New Testament which suggests that by the end of the first century, Christians were already having to come to terms with their exclusion from Jewish worship.[6]

In the years between 70 and 132 CE, tensions in Palestine began to build, and Messianic and apocalyptic hopes within Palestinian Judaism were high. This culminated in the Bar Kokhba revolt of 132–135. Bar Kokhba was perceived by many Jews as a Messianic figure. The Jewish Christians, who believed that Jesus had been the Messiah, therefore rejected Bar Kokhba and refused to take part in the revolt. As a result, Bar Kokhba and his followers turned against the Jewish Christians, and some were even killed.[7]

The failure of the Bar Kokhba revolt had far-reaching implications for Judaism, and for Jewish Christianity. Jerusalem was taken over by the Romans and renamed 'Aelia Capitolina', and in 135 the Emperor Hadrian issued an edict that banned all Jews from entering the city. This included Jewish Christians, and so the new church that was established in Jerusalem became a Gentile church, which no longer fulfilled the halakic requirements for Jewish identity. From a Jewish perspective, it was at this point that Christianity and Judaism finally split.

The remaining Jewish Christians were very few; following the hostilities of Bar Kokhba and his followers, few converts could be found from within Judaism, whilst Roman enforcement of the prohibition on circumcision after the war discouraged Gentile converts. Thus, rejected by Jews for their Christian beliefs, the remnants of the Jewish Christians of Palestine became increasingly isolated. Irenaeus, who talks of a sect called the 'Ebionites', may attest to their existence at the end of the second century.[8]

Something of the tension between Christianity and Judaism of the mid-second century can also be seen in one of the extant works of Tatian's teacher, Justin Martyr (c.100–165 CE). Justin's *Dialogue with Trypho*, written between 155 and 160 CE, purportedly records a conversation that occurred in Ephesus with a Jew named Trypho, and is part of the 'Adversus Judaeos' tradition of early Christianity.[9] Whether Trypho was real or whether he was a fictional character introduced by Justin, the debate itself clearly represents Justin's attitude to the problem of Christianity's relationship with Judaism.

Trypho is introduced as a 'Hebrew of the circumcision, a refugee from the recent war',[10] and a little later Trypho's companions speak of 'the war waged in Judaea'.[11] The war would appear to be the Bar Kokhba revolt of 132–135. This would place Trypho as an exiled Palestinian Jew, although from the reverence that he shows towards philosophy,[12] Trypho would still seem to be strongly influenced by hellenism.

The main issues that Trypho raises during the course of the *Dialogue* are the Christian rejection of circumcision; their failure to observe the Jewish law, the Sabbath and feasts; and the basic question of Jesus' messiahship and its discrepancy with Jewish expectations (especially Jesus' crucifixion). Justin confronts some of these issues by presenting a spiritualized interpretation of their relevance for Christians; thus the Jewish practice of circumcision is represented in Pauline terms as a circumcision of the spirit, and the Jewish law and covenant is superseded by the new law and covenant of

Jesus.[13] Justin supports his claim to Jesus' messiahship by citing a great quantity of Old Testament prophecy that he claims relates to Jesus.

During the course of this debate, however, Justin mentions his attitude towards Jews and Jewish Christians more directly. When asked by Trypho whether those who follow the Mosaic law would be saved, Justin states:

> They who are obliged to obey the Law of Moses will find in it not only precepts which were occasioned by the hardness of your people's hearts, but also those which in themselves are good, holy, and just. Since they who did those things which are universally, and eternally good are pleasing to God, they shall be saved in the resurrection, together with their righteous forefathers, Noe, Henoch, Jacob and others, together with those who believe in Christ, the Son of God.[14]

When asked whether Jewish Christians would also be delivered, Justin replies:

> But if some [Jewish converts], due to their instability of will, desire to observe as many of the Mosaic precepts as possible – precepts which we think were instituted because of your hardness of heart – while at the same time they place their hope in Christ... then it is my opinion that we Christians should receive them and associate with them as kinsmen and brethren.[15]

Yet despite this apparently tolerant attitude towards Jewish practices, we find some anti-Judaic overtones present in the *Dialogue*,[16] and Justin is particularly damning of lapsed Jewish Christians and of Jewish Precentors who pronounced the benediction against heretics in the Synagogues.[17]

The whole tenor of Justin's attitude towards Judaism in the *Dialogue* is one of patronizing benevolence; the Jews are presented almost as children, unable to remain faithful to God (hence the laws), and for the most part unable to mature to the full faith of Christianity.[18] Justin is clearly conscious of a sharp separation between Judaism and Christianity, and yet he willingly acknowledges Christianity's Jewish roots, and actively seeks to convert Trypho and his friends to the Christian faith.[19]

Christianity and the hellenistic world

Christianity's separation from its Jewish roots necessarily had repercussions for its relationship with the Graeco-Roman world. With the increase in the numbers of Gentile converts the 'Jewishness' of early Christianity began to be lost, but the Gentile converts brought with them a new set of religious and cultural presuppositions, rooted in their hellenistic backgrounds. Clearly Christianity also had to define itself in relation to the Graeco-Roman world.

Christianity's struggle for self-definition was, however, somewhat complicated by the hostile attitude of the Graeco-Roman world. Christianity was perceived as something of a threat to the existing social and political order. On a religious level, Christians were considered disruptive because they rejected the polytheistic system by asserting the supremacy of their own God, and refused to take part in the imperial cult – a refusal that was tantamount to treason.[20]

Although similar behaviour was tolerated in Jews, this seems to be due to the esteem in which antiquity was held; the Jews could appeal to the great age of their religion, which excused them from Graeco-Roman expectations of piety. By the end of the first century, however, the majority of Christians had split away from Judaism, and no longer took part in Jewish religious ceremonies and festivals. They could not therefore benefit from the indemnity extended to the Jews. Moreover, Gentile converts had chosen to abandon the religion of their ancestors in order to join this upstart movement.

The Graeco-Roman response to Christianity in the second century was extremely hostile. Persecutions were both frequent and fierce, and were not only encouraged by the Roman Emperors, but also often initiated by them.[21] Christian executions were ordered without trial and, from the time of Nero, admission to bearing the name 'Christian' was sufficient to merit death. This state of affairs is clearly attested to by Justin Martyr in his second *Apology*. Here he tells the story of a Christian woman whose conversion leads her to reject her previous life, and eventually to divorce her adulterous husband. The jealous husband accuses her of being a Christian, and then turns on her Christian teacher Ptolemaeus. Ptolemaeus is convicted after confessing his allegiance to Christianity, and, together with two Christian bystanders who protest the sentence, is summarily executed.[22]

Thus, second century Christians had a twofold task; they had to defend Christianity against this onslaught from the Graeco-Roman world around them, but on a deeper level they sought to reconcile their Christian faith with their hellenistic roots. The result was a series of apologetic writers who attempted to defend and justify the Christian position, and yet also struggled to define themselves with relation to the hellenistic world. This is exactly what we find in Justin Martyr's *Apologies* and in Tatian's *Oration to the Greeks*.

Since this book is largely concerned with exploring the Christian philosophical tradition in Tatian, we will return to consider the issues surrounding Tatian's relationship to the Graeco-Roman world in detail. In approaching these issues, however, some important distinctions must be made. Both Justin and Tatian, and indeed the other apologists, do not just present us with hellenistic backgrounds; they belonged to the hellenistic world and thus bring a set of presuppositions and expectations to their Christian faith. Whilst we see the apologists actively using elements of Graeco-Roman culture, such as mythology and philosophy, some of their 'use' of hellenistic culture was undoubtedly at a subconscious level. We must therefore be cautious in analysing how the apologists use Graeco-Roman culture, and ensure that we are aware of the subtleties present in the relationship between second century apologists and the hellenistic world.

Orthodoxy and heresy

Perhaps the most significant aspect of second century Christian self-definition is the struggle between 'orthodoxy' and 'heresy'. Traditionally this has been viewed through the eyes of the group that won through and became known as 'orthodox'. The concept of orthodoxy is expressed most explicitly in Eusebius' *Ecclesiastical History*, but can also be seen in Irenaeus and other earlier writings. The view put forward was that 'orthodoxy' was a line of tradition that represented the original apostolic teaching, and thus represented 'authentic' Christianity, whilst alternative streams were considered to be aberrations that deviated from the 'true' Christianity of the orthodox, and were therefore deemed 'heresies'.

This view prevailed until 1934, when Walter Bauer's influential book *Rechtgläubigkeit und Ketzerei im ältesten Christentum* was published.[23]

Bauer's hypothesis

Bauer challenged the traditional view of the relationship between orthodoxy and heresy in an attempt to perceive the situation historically and not through the eyes of the church, which, after all, has a vested interest in the traditional view of orthodoxy. He argued that more diversity had existed within the early church than the traditional view allowed, and that many so-called 'heretical' groups had as much claim to apostolic roots as mainstream 'orthodox' groups did.

Bauer essentially interpreted the struggle between orthodoxy and heresy as the Roman Church's struggle for dominance, driven by political ambitions. Thus he identified 'orthodoxy' with the prevailing stream of Christianity in Rome, which gradually increased its influence during the course of the second century, spreading outwards to Corinth, into Asia Minor and, to a lesser extent, to Philippi and Antioch. Meanwhile, he presents Edessa and Egypt as places where the 'orthodoxy' of Rome had barely touched. As we shall see, during the second century the Christianity of the Orient appears to have been synonymous with the streams of Christianity that were later to be labelled 'heresy'.

Bauer's thesis was revolutionary in its day, which may explain why it took so long before the impact of his work was felt, following the publication of the second German edition in 1964 and the English translation in 1972.[24] The response amongst modern scholars was somewhat mixed. James Robinson and Helmut Koester proved to be the strongest proponents of Bauer's thesis,[25] whilst the work of James Dunn and Elaine Pagels clearly develops from Bauer's understanding of the orthodox/heterodox struggle.[26] More negative responses were presented by Henry Turner,[27] and especially by Jerry Flora, who pointed out that Bauer's German Protestant background had affected his view of Christian history and coloured his appreciation of the position and status of 'orthodoxy' in the early Christian centuries.[28]

Between these extremes, more moderate responses have been put forward, and whilst the significance of Bauer's theory of early Christian diversity is now generally accepted, most scholars have questioned and refined Bauer's understanding of orthodoxy and its development during this period.[29]

Christianity in Rome and Edessa

For my purposes here in presenting a background to the study of Tatian, there are two locations that need to be considered in more detail; Rome, the city where Tatian met Justin Martyr and wrote his *Oration to the Greeks*, and eastern Syria, since this was probably the homeland to which he returned in the early 170s. So I shall now pause to take a more detailed look at the evidence that Bauer and other scholars of early Christianity present for the streams of Christianity in these areas during the second century.

Bauer's understanding of the Roman Church and the spread of orthodoxy from Rome is perhaps the weakest part of his thesis. In *Orthodoxy and Heresy in Earliest Christianity*, Bauer deals primarily with Rome's relationship to other Christian communities and gives no consideration to the nature of Christianity in Rome. He assumes that Rome encountered very little 'heretical' influence until the arrival of Marcion (*c.*144),[30] and that by this time the orthodoxy of the Roman Church was 'firmly set'.[31]

Bauer's representation of second century Christianity in Rome seems somewhat oversimplified. George La Piana, writing some years before the initial publication of Bauer's seminal work, gave a detailed examination of the forces at work within the second century Roman Church.[32] Rome was the political centre of the ancient world; people were drawn to the Imperial city from all over the Empire, and Rome was something of a cultural melting-pot. Far from being secure from heretical advances, it seems likely that the Roman Church had to face these threats head-on. Both Marcion and Valentinus spent a great deal of time in Rome, were accepted as members of the church, and were only later expelled. Indeed, according to Tertullian, Valentinus was at one time even considered as a candidate for the Roman see.[33]

The key to understanding how 'heretical' teachers were able to operate openly within the Roman Church lies in the organization of Roman Christianity. From evidence presented by Peter Lampe,[34] it would appear that Christianity in Rome was fractionalized into several house churches, each with its own leader. Thus many diverse streams of Christianity were able to exist side by side, until the stream that was to become known as 'orthodoxy' began its bid for power at the end of the second century.

Allen Brent has further suggested that the Roman house churches reflect different school communities that used private houses,[35] and this notion may be particularly helpful in understanding how Tatian and his master Justin Martyr operated within the church. Teachers appear to have functioned independently, gathering around themselves a circle of followers. Thus we should envisage several separate, perhaps rival schools situated in Roman house churches.

Thus, a strong diversity appears to have existed within Roman

Christianity. Indeed, a comment made by Justin Martyr in his *Dialogue with Trypho* highlights the tolerance that appears to have existed in the capital in the mid-second century; whilst Justin is rather hostile towards several gnostic groups, and especially towards Marcion,[36] when talking about his belief in the millennium and resurrection Justin states that not all 'pure and pious' Christians share his views.[37]

Clearly, to speak of 'orthodoxy' and 'heresy' in the context of second century Rome is somewhat problematical. Different streams of Christianity appear to have existed side by side, and the notion of 'orthodoxy' was far from fixed. It was only at the end of the second century that things began to change; extremes began to polarize and what had been acceptable in the mid-second century became heretical by the beginning of the third. I suspect that these changes may help to explain Tatian's return to the East, as well as Irenaeus' condemnation of Tatian as a heretic.

The Christianity that Tatian encountered on his return to the East was almost certainly less conservative than that in Rome towards the end of the second century. Indeed, the prevalent streams of Christianity in eastern Syria appear to have been gnostic in outlook. It is perhaps because 'heretical' streams were dominant that it is so difficult to reconstruct second century Christianity in Edessa and the surrounding area.

Our first document, the *Doctrine of Addai*, which purports to be the tale of how Christianity reached Edessa, is clearly legendary.[38] It records correspondence between Jesus and King Abgar,[39] where Jesus' promise to send one of his disciples to Syria is fulfilled when Judas Thomas sends Addai to Edessa.[40] Arthur Vööbus claims that there is a kernel of truth in this document in so far as the *Doctrine of Addai* displays a strong Jewish involvement in Addai's mission to the city of Edessa.[41] Vööbus understands the origin of Christianity in Syria in terms of missionary activity from Palestinian Aramaean Christians, and, judging from the Jewish forms of Scripture and the Rabbinic exegetical traditions that later developed within Syriac Christianity, there may well be some truth in this claim.

However, Bauer insists that it is not necessary to deduce a historical kernel within the Abgar legend at all. He sees the *Doctrine of Addai* as a propagandist work, supporting the orthodox cause in Syria, and argues that it was offered to Eusebius for inclusion in his *Ecclesiastical History* by Bishop Kûnê (fourth century), in an attempt to give some degree of authenticity to the legend.[42]

In fact, firm evidence of an orthodox orientated Christianity in

Syria is difficult to find until the fourth century, when the building of what seems to be the first orthodox church was begun by Bishop Kûnê in 313 CE. Thus Bauer identifies the early fourth century as the period when 'orthodox' Christianity in Edessa was attempting to consolidate its position and lay claim to apostolic roots. This is also reflected in the claim made in the *Doctrine of Addai* that Palût was consecrated at the end of the second century by Serapion of Antioch. Bauer considers this to be a fabrication designed to link the fourth century 'orthodox' Syriac Church to the Apostolic succession of the 'great Church'.[43]

However, the figure of Palût does not himself appear to be fiction; in his cycle of hymns *Against Heresies*, Ephrem (fourth century) complains that the orthodox are known as 'Palûtians'.[44] Not only does this prove that the stream of Christianity that was to become known as 'orthodoxy' was present in some form at the end of the second century; it also strongly suggests that 'orthodoxy' was in the minority, and continued to be so even during Ephrem's time. Indeed, this state of affairs is corroborated by the *Edessene Chronicle*, which mentions only Marcion, Bardaisan, and Mani.

In response to the question of which stream of Christianity was first to arrive at Edessa, Bauer concludes that the chronological sequence favours the Marcionites, and dates their arrival to shortly after 150, whilst the brand of Christianity initiated by Bardaisan had already emerged by 200.[45] He further suggests that, as the first to arrive on the scene, the Marcionites designated themselves as Christians.[46]

In his well-known article 'GNOMAI DIAPHOROI: The Origin and Nature of Diversification in the History of Early Christianity',[47] Helmut Koester corrects Bauer's assumption that the Marcionites were the first to arrive in Edessa. This is in the light of the discovery of the Thomas material found in the Nag Hammadi Library. Assuming the Syriac provenance of the *Gospel of Thomas* and the *Book of Thomas the Contender*, Koester argues that the Thomas tradition represents the oldest form of Christianity in Edessa.[48]

As we have already noted, Vööbus traces the origins of Syriac Christianity to Jewish roots, as too does Brock.[49] Burkitt, on the other hand, has put forward the remarkable suggestion that the apostle Addai of the *Doctrine of Addai* should be equated with Tatian, and that Tatian was the first missionary to bring Christianity to Edessa.[50] Whilst this suggestion seems very unlikely, Burkitt may have been correct in postulating a strong Tatianic influence on Syriac Christianity. Such is the view of Drijvers, who considers early

Syriac Christianity to have been formed by the opposing influences of Tatian and Marcion.[51] Needless to say, I shall return to consider Tatian's relationship with Syriac Christianity in depth later in this book.

So what can we deduce of second century Christianity in eastern Syria? First of all, it is highly likely that the stream of Christianity that was to become known as 'orthodoxy' was barely represented, if at all, until the end of the second century. Marcionism seems to have appeared in the mid-second century, and to have remained strong for some time, whilst followers of Bardaisan were present in increasing numbers from the end of the century. Evidence for the existence of a Jewish Christian stream is limited, although later 'orthodoxy' was certainly heavily influenced by Jewish concepts. The *Gospel of Thomas* and the *Book of Thomas the Contender* may also bear witness to a stream of Christianity that espoused a strongly dualistic view of the world (which was not necessarily 'gnostic'), and is characterized by a heavy emphasis on the Thomas tradition.

Scripture and the development of the canon

The tale of how the Christian canon was formed charts, in part, the struggle between the various streams of early Christianity. Particularly significant, in view of our purpose here in presenting a background to Tatian, is the development of the four-fold Gospel, and the use and appropriation of Paul in gnostic and mainstream circles during the second century.

The earliest Christian Bible consisted of the Hebrew Scriptures. Since Christianity began as a sect within Judaism, this appropriation is hardly surprising. As the church became predominantly Gentile, the Hebrew Scriptures were retained but were interpreted in a Christian way.[52] The issue was probably further forced by Marcion's radical rejection of all things Jewish.

Marcion (*c*.90–160 CE) expressed a deep distrust of the Hebrew Scriptures, which sprang from his conviction that they were in fact the work of the creator god, the Demiurge, who was entirely alien to the Father of Jesus. Marcion therefore rejected the Hebrew Scriptures and much of the Christian tradition (which he regarded as tainted by Jewish influence), and attempted to return to the original teaching of Jesus. He did this by appealing to written documents that he believed to contain older, more authentic material.

Thus Marcion accepted the *Gospel of Luke* as the least Judaized gospel, and then proceeded to strip it of any covert Jewish tendencies. He also included 'seven' Pauline Epistles within his Scriptures.[53] This was probably because Marcion felt that the Pauline material was in line with his own thinking, especially since Paul spoke out against Jewish influence. What Marcion in effect produced was a collection of authoritative Christian writings that may represent the first Christian canon, although this is by no means certain.

The dominant view of scholars today is that it was in response to the Marcionite threat that the mainstream church developed the New Testament canon with which we are now familiar.[54] In the face of Marcion's claim that he taught the original message of Jesus, the church was forced to prove that its tradition also stretched back to Jesus, and in so doing appealed to written documents, investing them with an authority that they did not previously have.

The story of what was included (or excluded) from the canon and why is a lengthy one that stretches far beyond the limits of this brief introductory chapter. Indeed, although many scholars consider the charismatic threat of Montanism to be responsible for the movement towards fixing what was considered canonical,[55] the debate about what was to be included in the New Testament canon continued into the fourth century.

There are, however, two specific areas relating to the canon that must be considered in the context of presenting a background to Tatian. The concept of four Gospels, which is strongly defended by Irenaeus,[56] probably evolved in response to Marcionite use of a single gospel (i.e. *Luke* purged of Jewish influence). However, Tatian would have found this solution unacceptable; whilst the four Gospels produced a rounder picture of Jesus, they also presented conflicting accounts of his life, and that went against Tatian's principle of inner consistency.[57] Possibly drawing on an existing tradition of harmonization,[58] Tatian therefore combined the four Gospels (and possibly elements from one or more Jewish-Christian gospel(s)), and produced the *Diatessaron*, a continuous narrative that harmonized or omitted inconsistencies within the Gospel accounts.

The other area of relevance is the use and appropriation of Paul within second century streams of Christianity. As we have seen, Marcion incorporated ten of the Pauline Epistles into his canon of scripture, and the Valentinians also made extensive use of the apostle's letters, as Elaine Pagels' study of Valentinian exegesis of Paul shows.[59] Paul was clearly popular within Valentinian circles.

The question of what use was made of Paul within non-gnostic circles at this time is more uncertain. There is clear evidence of Pauline usage in the Apostolic Fathers and Polycarp, but scholars have pointed to an increased mistrust of Paul (due to gnostic associations) from the mid-second century; according to von Campenhausen, both Papias and Justin 'pass over Paul in silence'.[60] However, in view of the work of Oskar Skarsaune, who argues that Justin used Paul as a testimony source for Old Testament quotations,[61] the use of the authentic Pauline letters within the stream that became dominant (in a sense the 'mainstream church', although they were probably still not in the majority at this time) is not at all clear-cut.

It has been convincingly argued that the legendary Paul of the *Acts of the Apostles*, the *Acts of Paul* and the Pastoral Epistles is an attempt on the part of the mainstream church to reclaim Paul for 'orthodoxy'.[62] This trend is of particular significance because a study of Tatian's use of Paul and its place within this gnostic/mainstream struggle for appropriation may help to illuminate his relationship with Valentinianism.

Gnosticism

Before we begin the process of placing Tatian within second century Christianity, a brief aside on gnosticism is required. The origin, history and nature of gnosticism have been the cause of much debate in recent years. Whilst I cannot begin to give a comprehensive overview of scholarly opinion, or indeed to outline anything of the gnostic phenomenon itself,[63] I do hope to present those aspects of gnostic studies that are necessary as a background to this book.

'Gnosticism' is the term given to several of the Christian streams that were to become known as 'heretical', including those groups that were led by Basilides and Valentinus.[64] Today it has become something of an umbrella term for a general dualistic movement that devalued the material world and laid a heavy emphasis on mystical knowledge. The use of the term 'gnosticism' is justified by the fact that these streams have certain elements in common that can be called 'gnostic',[65] but the term itself is anachronistic; 'gnostic' groups were originally identified by the name of their leaders, and whilst the claim to 'gnosis' was common amongst such groups, the word was also used by more mainstream Christians like Clement of Alexandria. Modern usage of the term 'gnosticism' seems to spring from Irenaeus' *Against the Heresies*, where the heresiologist attempts to combat 'gnosis falsely so-called'.[66]

Thus 'gnosticism' is a very difficult phenomenon to pin down; if one is to perceive of gnosticism as a unified force, its manifestations seem multifarious and relationships between various gnostic sects are not always obvious. To my mind, modern scholarship has become somewhat bogged down with the issue because it has been attempting to force gnostic-type streams together and expanding what is 'gnostic' to include specific elements, which in context should not be interpreted as gnostic at all. I believe that Robert Grant's treatment of Tatian is one example of such blanket labelling.[67]

Modern interest in gnostic studies has been fuelled by the discovery in 1945 of the Nag Hammadi Library, a collection of thirteen coptic codices, mostly containing previously unknown gnostic texts.[68] Amongst these are the *Gospel of Thomas* and *The Book of Thomas the Contender*, both of which appear to have a non-gnostic, Syriac origin.[69] A rather poor translation of Plato's *Republic* was also found within the Library.

The most debated question in the area of gnostic studies has been whether gnosticism had a pre-Christian or Christian origin. The current dominant view seems to be that it had a pre-Christian, probably Jewish, origin,[70] although an earlier scholarship explored the possibility of Mandean or Iranian origin. This view has been challenged by Edwin Yamauchi and Simone Pétrement, who both argue for a Christian origin.[71] Whilst their arguments are persuasive and point up the ambiguity of the evidence, this is still the minority view.

Another aspect of the question of origins has been the issue of the relationship between gnosticism and Greek philosophy. As we shall see, Middle Platonism displays a marked interest in religious concerns, coupled with a sometimes pessimistic view of the world, and this has raised the question of whether the shift is due to gnostic influence.[72] On the other side of the coin, however, some Nag Hammadi and other gnostic texts display evidence of Platonic influence. The current opinion seems to be that there was only a small influence of gnosticism on Platonism, Numenius being the strongest example, and that although Platonic influence can be found in gnostic texts[73] it was not a fundamental factor in the development of gnostic ideas and does not explain the gnostic world view.[74]

In 1966, a conference was held in Messina on the origins of gnosticism. The conference attempted to define the gnostic phenomenon with more clarity and, in a compromise between the pre-Christian and Christian camps, proposed to restrict the term 'gnosticism' to the developed systems of the second century. It was further suggested that the term 'pre-gnostic' be used to describe pre-Christian elements of gnosticism, and 'proto-gnostic' for early forms of gnosticism that preceded the second century gnostic systems.[75] Whilst criticisms have been made,[76] I believe it constitutes an important step forward in the refining of gnostic studies.

What is gnostic overlaps with other elements, and if we are to clarify the state of second century Christianity we should not merely group all apparently gnostic ideas under the banner of gnosticism. Instead, we should be attempting to separate and analyse the various gnostic-type groups. This involves a more sensitive approach that considers individual contexts and influences.

Tatian and his *Oration to the Greeks*

It is before this backdrop that Tatian's *Oration* must be set. It is an apologetic work, written to justify the position of Christianity in the Graeco-Roman world, and belongs to the stream of hellenized Christianity that emerged after Christianity's divergence from Judaism. Tatian's Scriptures are the 'barbarian writings' of the Jews, but we can be reasonably sure that he read them in a Christianizing way, much as his master Justin did. Tatian also appeals to those Christian writings, and especially to Paul, which, although they still did not possess canonical status, were increasing in authority.

The main issue with which this book is concerned, however, is the question of where Tatian should be placed within the various streams of second century Christianity. As we have seen, Christianity during the second century was very flexible and fluid, and the notion of 'heresy', although developing, was still not set, whilst the notion of 'orthodoxy' did not yet really exist; Christianity, with its many facets, was still attempting to define itself.

My concern here, then, is to question anachronistic labelling of Tatian, and by exploring Tatian's relationship to the Christianity around him, I hope to shed light on this crucial period in Christianity's development.

2

TATIAN AND
VALENTINIANISM

Tatian has been associated with gnosticism since the end of the
second century. Irenaeus (c.130–200 CE) was the first of the church
fathers to condemn Tatian for heresy. In his book *Against the Heresies*
Irenaeus claims that after Justin's martyrdom, Tatian apostatized
from the church and set down his own teaching. According to Irenaeus, this teaching included a myth about invisible aeons, like that
of Valentinus, the rejection of marriage as 'corruption and fornication', and the denial of Adam's salvation, which Irenaeus considered
to be the invention of Tatian himself.[1]

Looking over these charges, it would seem that Irenaeus is accusing Tatian of adherence to Valentinianism as well as Encratism.[2] By
suggesting that Tatian spoke of a myth about invisible aeons
'similar to those of Valentinus', Irenaeus is certainly making it clear
that he considered Tatian to have been influenced by Valentinian
gnosticism, although he does not actually state that Tatian adhered
to Valentinianism.

The second church father to imply Tatian's involvement with
gnosticism is Clement of Alexandria (c.150–215 CE). In *Stromateis*
III.82.2, Clement states that Tatian made a distinction between the
old humanity (i.e. the law) and the new (i.e. the gospel), and that he
considered the law to be the work of a different god and wanted it
abolished.[3]

The charge that Clement is here laying against Tatian is that he
rejected the Old Testament because he considered it to be the work
of the Demiurge.[4] This position is very close to that of several
gnostic groups, and, as we have seen, especially to Marcionism.
Whether Clement has Marcionism in mind or not when making
this statement, it is clear that he is also trying to link Tatian with
the gnostic movement. This is again emphasized later in the

Stromateis, when Clement makes the slightly different claim that Tatian was a Valentinian gnostic.[5]

Hippolytus (*c*.160–235 CE) is the next church father to link Tatian with Valentinianism. He seems largely dependent upon Irenaeus for his account of Tatian's heresy, although in the final book of his *Refutation of all Heresies* Hippolytus elaborates on Irenaeus somewhat when he claims that Tatian considered one of the aeons to be responsible for creating the world.[6]

Likewise, for his description of Tatian, Eusebius (*c*.260–339) is also dependent upon Irenaeus; Eusebius merely repeats Irenaeus' words of *Against the Heresies* I.28. The wording differs slightly, but the content is essentially identical.[7]

Epiphanius (*c*.315–402 CE), on the other hand, embellishes the account found in Irenaeus; he adds some biographical details about Tatian that we find nowhere else, and expands on the information about Tatian's Encratism, although admittedly with a strong bias.[8] Of Tatian's Valentinianism, Epiphanius writes that, like Valentinus, Tatian introduced aeons, principalities and emanations.[9]

Thus there would seem to be a clear progression in the heresiological accounts of Tatian's gnosticism. Irenaeus begins by accusing Tatian of being influenced by Valentinianism, and is closely followed by Hippolytus, Eusebius and Epiphanius, who are clearly using Irenaeus' material. The only church father to offer different information about Tatian's gnosticism is Clement.

In evaluating the heresiologists' picture of Tatian, we must remember that they were heavily biased; they wanted to paint him in the worst possible colours. In Epiphanius it becomes particularly difficult to differentiate between historical fact and heresiological fiction. There was also a practice, initiated by Irenaeus, of presenting genealogies of heresy; the theory was that all heresies derived from the very first heresy, introduced by Simon Magus.[10] So, the heresiologists had an agenda to prove that Tatian's heresy also descended from this common origin. Inevitably, then, the reliability of the heresiologists must be called into question, and their accounts of Tatian's heresy should be proved rather than assumed when considering Tatian's extant works.

The work of Grant

The issue of Tatian's relationship with Valentinianism has been brought into focus particularly through the work of Robert Grant.

Grant argued for a late date for Tatian's *Oration to the Greeks*, around 177 or 178 CE,[11] and, working from the assumption that Irenaeus' claim of Tatian's apostasy following Justin's death is correct, therefore asks whether any of Tatian's Valentinian heresy is reflected in the *Oration*.[12]

First, let us turn to consider terminology in Tatian that Grant regards as Valentinian. Grant claims that Tatian uses terminology from the Valentinian pleromic myth; he asserts that Tatian spoke of 'better aeons' above.[13] This phrase comes from a problematic passage in Chapter 20, where Tatian is talking about heaven:

> For heaven, O man, is not infinite, but bounded and within limit; and above this one are better worlds (αἰῶνες) which have no change of season.[14]

Whilst it is true that the word αἰών is used by the Valentinians as a technical term for the divine emanations and can consequently be translated 'aeon', the word also has much wider meanings; in the New Testament αἰών is primarily used to describe a period of time,[15] but it can also be translated as 'world',[16] and I believe that this is what Tatian intends here. In this passage, he is speaking of the geography of the heavenly realms, and not of divine principles. To translate αἰῶνες as 'aeons' seems to me to make a complete nonsense of the passage.

Grant adduces a further passage in Tatian that he believes to reflect Valentinian emanationism, but in my opinion this evidence is also rather weak. In explaining the process of creation, Tatian speaks of the Logos, who was 'begotten' (γεννηθείς) by God, in turn 'generating' (ἀντεγέννησε) creation.[17] Grant considers this to express the emanation of the Valentinian aeons.[18] However, the usual word used by the Valentinians to express their theory of emanations is προβολή,[19] and in Theodotus language of begetting is actually used exclusively of human generation.[20]

In fact, I suspect that Tatian's understanding of the generation of the Logos is in total opposition to gnostic emanationism. The emanation process outlined in the Valentinian pleromic myths would appear to lessen the divine nature through division. In contrast, Tatian goes to great pains to prove that the Word came into being by partition, not by separation, and is very anxious that the nature of the divine should not be diminished in any way.[21]

Grant also points out that the term συζυγία, which Tatian uses to describe the union between human soul and divine spirit,[22] is another term used frequently by Valentinians.[23] The word 'syzygy' was used by the Valentinian gnostics to describe the return of the pneumatic sparks to the pleroma. It was perceived in terms of a spiritual marriage, and reflected the divine ordering of aeons in pairs.[24] Tatian also uses the term to describe a redemptive process and to express the union between the divine and man, but it is the soul and not a pneumatic spark that is the contribution offered by man. Most significantly, Tatian's union takes place within the body[25] whilst, according to gnostic anthropology, the pneumatic spark must first be released from the prison of the body.

Clearly there are similarities between Valentinian use of the term συζυγία and that of Tatian, but there are also fundamental differences in how the union between the divine and man are perceived. The existence of these differences suggests that Tatian's usage of the term does not imply Valentinian influence.

Inevitably, when Grant comes to consider the divine spirit in Tatian he interprets it as the pneumatic spirit of the Valentinians.[26] Tatian does speak of the human soul retaining a 'spark of the spirit's power', but, as Grant himself admits, Tatian uses the word ἔναυσμα instead of the more usual gnostic term σπινθήρ.[27] Other passages that refer to the divine spirit in the *Oration* do not even imply a Valentinian pneumatic spark. Thus I would suggest that Tatian's use of the concept is purely coincidental, and that this is even apparent in his choice of the word ἔναυσμα.

When Grant comes across Tatian's assertion that there will be a physical resurrection[28] one might expect him to run into difficulties, but he notes that the term which Tatian uses (supposedly σαρκίον instead of σάρξ)[29] is also used by Valentinians, and concludes that the 'fleshly' resurrection in Tatian is a resurrection of the Spirit and soul only.[30] I believe that Grant's interpretation here is wrong. Tatian's protracted explanation at the end of Chapter 6 of how the body can be resurrected if it is destroyed and scattered proves that matter does play a part in his vision of the resurrection. In fact, I consider Tatian's expectation of a 'bodily' resurrection to be a non-gnostic element in his system, and I shall return to consider this in greater detail shortly.

Besides the more general terminological correlations that Grant believes he has found between the *Oration* and Valentinianism, he claims that there are two particular Valentinians whose ideas parallel Tatian's most closely: Ptolemaeus and Theodotus. We know very little of the lives of these Valentinians, except that they were both active in the second century.[31] Ptolemaeus' *Letter to Flora* is presented in full by Epiphanius,[32] whilst a collection of extracts from Theodotus, which in fact include contributions from other anonymous Valentinians, is appended to the *Stromateis* of Clement of Alexandria.[33]

Ptolemaeus does betray some similarities with Tatian; Grant points out that both speak of the 'perfect God',[34] claims that both perceive of God as the sole principle,[35] and identifies a similarity in language when talking of the incorruptible nature of the Father and his law.[36] They both also speak of God as 'the good',[37] and of God being 'ungenerated'.[38]

These last two parallels, which Grant has omitted, may well explain the link between Tatian and Ptolemaeus. 'The good' is an attribute ascribed to divinity in Platonism, and the same is true of the ungenerated and incorruptible nature of the divine, the concept of God as the sole principle, and the notion of the perfection of God.[39] It seems likely, especially in view of the strong philosophical influence on Tatian that I shall be arguing, that these similarities between Tatian and Ptolemaeus are due to a common philosophical background.

Moreover, Grant's assertion that both Tatian and Ptolemaeus speak of God as 'the sole principle of all things' is certainly puzzling, since he goes on to make a distinction between this and the concept in Justin Martyr and Theophilus of Antioch of the Logos as the sole principle. Justin speaks of the Word or Rational Power being begotten of the Father as a beginning before all his works.[40] Meanwhile, Theophilus stresses God's self-sufficiency and existence prior to the generation of the Logos, yet conceives of the Logos as an innate being who is generated along with Sophia, and is called 'Beginning'.[41]

Tatian has a similar view of the generation of the Logos; in Chapter 5, Tatian speaks of God being alone with the 'Word which was in him' in the period prior to creation, and of the generated Word as 'the beginning of the universe'.[42] I see very little distinction between Tatian's understanding of the pre-existence of God and the Word and that of Theophilus; both seem to consider the principle of the Word to be existent in an embryonic form within God prior to its generation, and both call the Logos the 'beginning'. Furthermore, as we shall see, Tatian's understanding of the actual generation of the Logos has much in common with that of Justin.

Why, then, does Grant claim that Tatian understands God to be the sole principle, whilst Justin and Theophilus consider this function to be performed by the Logos? Grant's terminology seems to originate from Ptolemaeus' choice of language; Ptolemaeus explicitly talks of 'one first principle of all'.[43] Precisely what Grant means when using this terminology is not clear, but he certainly seems to be imposing Ptolemaeus' language onto Tatian in *Or* 4:1, and yet ignores *Or* 5:1, with its similarities to Justin and Theophilus.[44] Grant's intention here is clearly to push Tatian away from more 'orthodox' apologists and towards Valentinianism, but his argument falls down because he has failed to take into account other passages in the *Oration*, and a closer study of Grant's supposed distinction in fact proves a greater closeness between Tatian and the two other apologists whom Grant mentions.

Furthermore, Grant's claim that Ptolemaeus' 'incorruptible father' was responsible for the law can not be substantiated since, in the context, the law to which he is referring is in fact ordained by the Demiurge, and not by the 'incorruptible father' at all.[45] Any similarity in phrasing between Ptolemaeus and Tatian's statement about 'the law of the incorruptible Father'[46] is probably pure coincidence.

If we turn to consider the thought world of Ptolemaeus, with its intermediate God, the Demiurge, its dynamic view of evil in the person of the Devil, and its preoccupation with legislation, it becomes apparent that Ptolemaeus' thought world is totally alien to that of Tatian. The majority of the parallels that Grant has identified are due to the influence of philosophy upon both writers.

Similarly, although our second Valentinian, Theodotus, seems to contain parallels with Tatian, these are fairly superficial, and the thought worlds within which both move are entirely alien to each other. Grant claims a large number of correlations between Tatian and Theodotus. He states that Tatian's demonology closely resembles that of Theodotus, that Tatian's 'better earth' is Paradise and is therefore equivalent to Theodotus' fourth heaven, and that much of Tatian's use of Paul is related to a doctrine about baptism and that this parallels Theodotus. Grant also points out a similarity between Tatian's use of the Johannine concept of darkness, and Theodotus' hylic 'Powers of the Left', and extrapolates what he believes would have been Tatian's Christology, and compares this with Theodotus.[47]

In comparing Tatian's demonology with that of Theodotus, Grant does not make it entirely clear what the similarities are. He acknowledges that Tatian's designation of demons as 'robbers' probably originates with Justin,[48] but says that Tatian goes beyond Justin in saying that the demons desired to steal divine status, and that they deceived the souls abandoned by the divine Spirit.[49]

The relationship between Tatian's demonology and that of his master is a question to which I shall return, and whilst it is true that they are not entirely similar it should be remembered that demonology was also a popular philosophical topic, as well as being an issue for Christians and Jews. If I am right in claiming philosophical influence upon Tatian, then it should not be surprising that Tatian chose to discuss the position and influence of demons in his world in a way that is not identical to that of his master.

If we compare Tatian's demonology with that of Theodotus we find that although Theodotus also describes demons as 'robbers',[50] there are some important differences; the word 'demon' is not used to describe these robbers, instead the word 'power' is used, although it is clear that Theodotus is referring to the type of evil being that others might term 'demon'. Theodotus' 'powers' are presented as totally evil beings who constantly fight against the angels, who are servants of God and side with the Valentinians.[51] For Tatian, demons are beings who began existence as angels but lost their status at the fall, and who are capable of good or evil.[52] Evil demons do try to deceive men, and there is some sort of cosmic battle between the demons and man and the powers of good, but it is a rather one-sided affair, since God is all powerful and the antics of the demons are merely tolerated.[53] Therefore we do not find the same kind of ultimate dualism in Tatian that we seem to find in Theodotus.

Tatian speaks of a 'better earth' from which the beings known as 'angels' or 'demons' are cast down following the fall.[54] Grant identifies Tatian's 'better earth' as Paradise, an identification which, although logical, is not evident in Tatian, and then points out that Theodotus calls his Paradise the 'fourth heaven'.[55]

For Grant to imply a similarity between Tatian's 'better earth' and Theodotus' 'fourth heaven' seems totally unjustified. First, Theodotus speaks of men, not angels or demons, being made in his Paradise; second, it is not at all clear that Tatian is referring to Paradise in the same sense as Theodotus; and finally, if Tatian is referring to Paradise, he would have a Biblical basis for this in *Genesis* and Jewish Christian exegesis of *Genesis*. There is no need to extrapolate the concept of Paradise in Tatian, nor to see anything more than common Biblical background and coincidence in Tatian's 'better earth' and Theodotus' 'fourth heaven'.

Grant's association of Tatian's understanding of baptism with that of Theodotus is also unfounded; not only was baptism a common theme in early Christianity, but there are also some more fundamental problems with this comparison. Tatian does not directly speak of baptism, although, as Grant shows,[56] this can be inferred; when talking about man's present state in Chapter 11, Tatian urges the reader to 'die to the world' and 'live to God' (probably an allusion to *Rom* 6:10 and *Col* 2:20), and claims that men have been 'put up for sale because of sin' (probably an allusion to *Rom* 7:14).[57]

It is possible that Tatian is envisaging the act of baptism as the point at which men 'die to the world' and begin to 'live to God', but this is to read into Tatian the use that other early Christians (including Paul) made of this language. However, if Tatian is referring obliquely to baptism, the ritual is only of secondary importance to him here; his emphasis is on man's culpability for his present state and, consequently, his capacity to do something about it.

On the other hand, Theodotus clearly does use Pauline passages to support his doctrine of baptism. There is also one particularly striking passage, which seems to parallel Tatian quite closely, where Theodotus says that those regenerated by Christ 'die to the world, but live to God'.[58] The fact that the sense of Theodotus' citation refers back to the regenerated (i.e. the baptized) indicates that he, at least, is using Pauline material to relate directly to baptism.

Theodotus also appeals to Pauline passages like *Rom* 6:3 and *Col* 2:12, where Paul speaks of baptism as a baptism into Christ's death and therefore resurrection.[59] This in fact hints at the main differences between Tatian's and Theodotus' use of these Pauline passages; Theodotus' emphasis is on baptism as a process which involves dying and rising with Christ, whilst Tatian stresses Paul's cry to reject the old nature,[60] without explicit reference to baptism.

These fundamental differences are pointed up again when we consider the contexts in which Tatian and Theodotus talk of conquering death by death. Grant again implies that this language is used in both with reference to baptism.[61] It is true that Tatian speaks of men overcoming 'death by death in faith',[62] but it is not with reference to baptism; he is again speaking of man's capacity to reverse the consequences of the fall through free will. However, in Theodotus the phrase 'death is destroyed by death' is almost certainly referring to baptism, since the sense of the preceding clause refers to the regenerated ones (i.e. the baptized).[63]

In the light of Tatian and Theodotus' use of Pauline passages,[64] it may be that we should also understand the concepts of conquering 'death by death' differently in both writers; in Tatian overcoming 'death by death in faith' would therefore refer to a rejection of the old life, which is perhaps intended ascetically, whilst Theodotus' destruction of 'death by death' would refer to Christ's saving sacrifice on the cross. The similarity in wording may just be coincidental, and perhaps formulated from 1 *Cor* 15:54, where Paul writes 'death is swallowed up in victory'.[65] Tatian's additional reference to 'death in *faith*',[66] may also have roots in *Heb* 11, where the author speaks of those who have 'died in faith'.

Grant further claims that both Tatian and Theodotus speak of 'the Spirit of God received at baptism as the Image'.[67] He admits that this is problematic, but not for the reason that I would have given; Grant points out that because it is not clear whether the chapter in Theodotus (*Excerpts* 86) comes from Theodotus or whether it has been modified by Clement, the doctrine of the Spirit received at baptism as the Image cannot be ascribed to Valentinianism with any certainty. However, I have identified a more basic problem with this parallel; Tatian does not speak of the Spirit being received at baptism at all. He does see the divine Spirit as the 'image and likeness of God', and perceives the Spirit as able to dwell within men, but I believe that Tatian is referring to the prophets here, and not to the baptized.[68] Moreover, there is a Scriptural basis for everything that Tatian says about the Spirit and its indwelling,[69] which refutes any dependence upon Theodotus and suggests instead a common use of Paul.

However, I do not believe that the point Grant is trying to make here is just that both Tatian and Theodotus use Pauline passages to expound baptismal doctrines; after all baptism was a very common practice in the early church! I suspect that what Grant is actually trying to point up is the fact that Paul was frequently used by the second century Valentinians, and that Tatian's use of Paul in apparently the same method as Theodotus implies a great closeness to Valentinianism.[70] Of course this presupposes several things, not least the assumption that Paul was not used by more 'mainstream' writers in the second century, which, as we have seen, is a popular scholarly misconception. Grant has also presumed that Tatian's use of Pauline material means that he is interpreting Paul in the same way as the Valentinians. As I shall demonstrate in the next section, this is most certainly not the case. I suspect that, in his eagerness to compare Theodotus' use of Pauline passages to describe baptism,

Grant has overlooked the fact that Tatian's understanding of baptism is not at all clear in the *Oration*, and that he has read into Tatian much that he has found in Theodotus.

Grant may be making some of the same assumptions when he discusses Tatian's exegesis of the Johannine passages on darkness and light; the *Fourth Gospel*, with its strong emphasis on dualism, was also particularly popular among Valentinian gnostics.[71] The link that Grant makes is between Tatian's interpretation of darkness as the ignorant soul, and Theodotus' assertion that the hylic 'Powers of the Left' are not formed by the light.[72]

In *Excerpt* 34 Theodotus may be alluding to the Johannine concepts of darkness and light, although there is no need to assume this. He speaks of the Powers of the Left, which are produced first by the mother (i.e. the aeon Sophia), then passed down to be formed by the Demiurge, and are therefore formed without Light.[73] In Theodotus, then, darkness is equated with the 'Powers of the Left', which seem to constitute hylic and some psychic matter.[74]

Meanwhile, Tatian also displays a marked dualism in Chapter 13 of his *Oration*, when he describes man's current condition and his potential for achieving immortality; the soul is saved by the divine Spirit, which is equated with light, whilst the soul that is without the Spirit and ignorant of God is doomed, and is therefore equated with darkness.[75] However, there is no gnostic dualism present in Tatian; all souls are capable of gaining the protection of the Spirit,[76] and darkness (ignorance) is not therefore an inherent and immutable condition. Tatian's use of 'darkness' is not equivalent to the hylic understanding that Theodotus expresses.

Finally, Grant embarks on the task of presenting a reconstruction of Tatian's Christology, and in so doing appeals to Theodotus. First, he takes Tatian's description of the Spirit dwelling in the prophets[77] and transfers this into the Logos indwelling Jesus (the man) as a temple, and then explains that since Christ is 'guarded by the Spirit of God',[78] he is able to see the demons, which is presumably intended as an explanation of Christ's ability to exorcize demons. Then Grant uses information from Theodotus to 'complete' what he believes Tatian would have said about Christ; that he 'awakened the soul and enflamed the spark; for the words of the Saviour are power.'[79]

Grant's methodology here seems somewhat suspect; he is importing material from another writer whose thought world, as we have seen, is not at all close to Tatian. Moreover, Grant has also overlooked the fact that Tatian does actually refer to the Incarnation in his *Oration*; in Chapter 21 he talks about God being born 'in the form of man'.[80] I believe that this is yet another non-gnostic element in Tatian, and again will discuss it more fully later in this chapter.

Grant's aim in introducing this patchy Christology seems to be to push Tatian still closer to Theodotus, and by so doing he finds a way of linking Tatian's spark (which otherwise remains redundant) to the salvation process. Not only does Grant's method seem suspect in this instance, but so also does his agenda. This is even more true in the following paragraph, where he claims to be describing the effect of the Saviour's arrival, but in fact merely strings together several unrelated passages in the *Oration*,[81] some of which are mis-quoted,[82] and some of which merely describe Tatian's understanding of man's eschatological hope.[83] Again, the point behind all this appears to have been to cite a passage from Theodotus which can be imposed upon Tatian's thought world.

The Theodotus presented by Clement of Alexandria is most definitely Valentinian; he outlines something of the pleromic myth, distinguishes between hylic, psychic, and pneumatic levels of being, and yet talks about certain Christian elements[84] that can be easily translated across to Tatian's thought system, provided that he is read in an accommodating way. In short, it would certainly be advantageous to Grant's cause in claiming Tatian to be a Valentinian if he could prove that Tatian stands close to Theodotus ideologically. However, as I have shown, Grant's comparison does not stand up to scrutiny, and although I will acknowledge some superficial parallels between Tatian and Theodotus,[85] I believe that, theologically, the two are poles apart.

It is time now to turn to Chapter 30, one of the most obscure passages in Tatian's *Oration*. It immediately follows on from Tatian's account of his conversion, but its precise relationship with Tatian's conversion is not clear. It reads:

> Therefore now that I have apprehended these things I wish to 'strip myself' of the childishness of babyhood. For we know that the constitution of wickedness is like that of the smallest 'seeds', since it grows strong from a tiny 'occasion', but will die if we obey God's word and do not dissipate ourselves. He held power over our property like a kind of 'hidden treasure'; in digging it up we were covered with dust, but provide the occasion of guaranteeing its posses-

sion. For everyone who recovers his own property wins possession of the most precious wealth. Let this be said to our own people; as for you Greeks what can I say except that you should not abuse your betters, nor, even if they are called barbarians, take this as an occasion for mockery.[86]

Perhaps unsurprisingly, Grant offers a detailed gnostic interpretation of this passage.[87] He understands *Or* 30 to be an esoteric text containing secret doctrines intended only for a select group of Christians, and bases this conclusion on the fact that the chapter is addressed to οἱ ἡμῶν οἰκεῖοι and on the 'mysteriousness of the passage'.[88] The implication of this is clearly to push Tatian closer still to Valentinianism, since Valentinians characteristically taught secret doctrines reserved solely for the pneumatics.

Grant adduces several parallels between *Or* 30 and Valentinianism. As we have seen, Tatian begins this chapter by expressing a wish to 'strip' himself of the 'childishness of babyhood'. Although this use of child terminology may have its roots in Paul, Grant stresses similar language in the *Shepherd of Hermas* and the *Gospel of Thomas*.[89]

Tatian also seems to allude to several of the Matthaean parables; his concept of wickedness as the 'smallest of seeds' may be a reverse of the parable of the mustard seed;[90] he also speaks of 'hidden treasure';[91] and his 'possession of the most precious wealth' parallels the 'pearl of great value'.[92] Grant also points out passages in the *Gospel of Thomas* which parallel these parables in *Matthew*,[93] and further passages from the *Gospel of Thomas* which Tatian may be alluding to in *Or* 30; the notion of digging is present in *Thomas*,[94] as too is the idea that ignorance of the true self is poverty (and therefore that knowledge of the self is wealth).[95]

I suspect that Grant's point in stressing these parallels between Tatian and the *Gospel of Thomas* is to infer use of gnostic material, and I believe that the same is true later in the same article when he points up similarities between the *Gospel of Philip* and Tatian.[96] Although Grant does not go as far as to say that Tatian is dependent upon these gospels, he does conclude that Tatian was 'acquainted with both or with the kind of teaching set forth in both', and then states that Tatian's doctrine in *Or* 30 'is Christian only to the extent that Valentinianism was Christian'.[97]

Clearly, Grant is making a very strong connection between the gospels of *Thomas* and *Philip* and Valentinianism. This is not entirely justified, since both gospels incorporate a sayings tradition and, although Valentinians may have used both, only *Philip* displays strong Valentinian leanings. Moreover, as we have seen, the New Testament canon was far from fixed in the second century, and Tatian's possible use of this non-canonical material does not automatically mean that Tatian himself was a Valentinian. In any case, Tatian may well have been drawn to works like the *Gospel of Thomas* for their asceticism.

Grant then goes on to suggest that Tatian offers an exegesis of the parables in *Matthew* and *Thomas* that is in line with Valentinian and Naasene readings,[98] yet only offers two parallels. Once again, Grant turns to Theodotus and mentions his interpretation of the bad seed in the parable of the wheat and tares,[99] Grant also points out the Naasene exegesis of the hidden treasure, which is internalized.[100] These sparse parallels do not prove that Tatian's exegesis of *Matthew* and *Thomas* is similar to that of the Valentinians and Naasenes.

Grant summarizes his exegesis of *Or* 30 by offering the following paraphrase:

> He wishes to strip off his fleshly or material element and become like infants, the models of gnostic asceticism. For this evil material element is comparable to a mustard seed; it is itself the seed of the devil, and though it grows it will be dissolved again if we obey the Word (Logos) of God and as good seeds do not scatter ourselves; we will be collected by the Logos-Saviour. The Logos-Saviour got power over what belongs to us (our spark) by means of the hidden treasure (the inner man). We searched for this treasure. Although in the course of the search we came under the power of the flesh, we also gave the spirit or inner man the opportunity to exist and to become effective. If we receive the whole of our spiritual nature again as our authentic possession ... we have obtained authority over the most valuable thing there is.[101]

Whilst this paraphrase appears to make sense out of context, it does not explain the relationship between *Or* 30 and Tatian's conversion, and neither do I believe that it rings true with the rest of the *Oration*; there is much in Tatian that goes against this interpretation.[102]

Other interpretations of this difficult passage have been offered.[103] Most notably, Maran claims that the third person singular throughout this passage should be understood to be the Devil,[104] whilst Elze proposes an anthropological interpretation,[105] and further suggests that this passage reflects Tatian's philosophical leanings and is an importation from a work belonging to his pre-Christian phase.[106]

In his article on Chapter 30 of the *Oration*, Bolgiani offers a particularly interesting interpretation of this passage. In Tatian's talk of seeds and hidden treasure Bolgiani also sees allusions to the Matthaean parables of the kingdom, but further suggests that the order in which Tatian uses the parable of the tares and the parable of the hidden treasure reflects his use of a harmonized tradition.[107] He also suggests that *Or* 30 should be considered a reflection following Tatian's conversion account in Chapter 29, and should therefore be interpreted as part of a sequence of thought that runs through Chapters 29–30.[108]

Bolgiani also offers more specific interpretations of details within the text. He sees in the small seeds and the hidden treasure a juxta-position of man's potential to achieve good or evil, an expression of man's free will. When Tatian talks of men obeying God's word Bolgiani makes a distinction between the Logos of God and the word of the Christian message, which he suggests is implied intentionally by Tatian. Bolgiani also suggests that the process of digging is not envisaged by Tatian as an attempt to unearth hidden treasure, but rather as an attempt to bury it, to hide it further.[109]

Whittaker, on the other hand, interprets Chapter 30 within the wider context of the *Oration*. She claims that in this passage Tatian is referring to points that are found elsewhere in the *Oration*. Thus she equates 'childishness' with man's previous state of ignorance (outlined in *Or* 13:1) and the stripping process as a desire to mature. She explains the 'digging' and 'dust' as part of the 'laborious task' of gaining knowledge (again referring to *Or* 13:1), and understands 'property', 'treasure', and 'wealth' to be the sought-after union between soul and spirit (stated in *Or* 15).[110]

Of these interpretations, the one that rings most true for me is Bolgiani's suggestion that Chapter 30 should be understood in rela-tion to Tatian's conversion experience. In the opening sentence of this passage ('Therefore now that I have apprehended these things ...'),[111] Tatian is clearly referring back to the tenets of barbarian wisdom mentioned during his conversion account in Chapter 29. I would therefore agree that the rest of Chapter 30 needs to be understood as an exploration of the consequences of his conversion.

There are, however, some further distinctions I would like to make in interpreting this passage. When Tatian speaks of the constitution of wickedness being like a small seed that grows strong from a small beginning, I suspect that he is not referring to an abstract concept of evil, but rather to the natural human inclination to wickedness, to man's inborn tendency to fall towards matter. This wickedness will be weakened again if men believe in the word of God (i.e. obtain the knowledge of God that is revealed through the prophets), and as long as men do not scatter themselves (i.e. sink back into matter).

When Tatian talks about man's hidden treasure, it may be that he is referring to the spark of the divine spirit.[112] However, the spark appears to play no part in Tatian's soteriology, and I suspect that Tatian may instead be referring to the Spirit embodied in the prophets. If this is the case, Tatian's digging and dust may refer to a need to purify the body in preparation for reception of the hidden treasure (i.e. the Spirit), since Tatian seems to have considered asceticism a prerequisite for prophecy.[113]

Thus I would see the second part of *Or* 30 as a celebration of the salvation that is a direct result of his conversion. Tatian's soul was 'taught by God' through the revelation of the prophets, and he was given 'not something we had never received, but what we had received but had been prevented from keeping by our error'.[114] Here, and throughout Chapter 30 I believe that Tatian is talking of the process that reverses the fall, of redemption – first by receiving knowledge of God, but primarily through regaining the divine union with the Spirit.

Grant's position towards Tatian has changed in his more recent work.[115] He still maintains a late date for the *Oration*, and accepts the heresiologists' claim that later in life Tatian defected to Valentinianism and Encratism, although, since Grant offers such a late date for the *Oration*, Tatian's apostasy seems to be linked to his return to the East, rather than Justin's martyrdom.

When considering the literary form of the *Oration*, Grant suggests that it is a farewell discourse, written to mark his departure from the West, which contains some protreptic material designed to encourage converts to Tatian's Christianity. Grant perceives Tatian as primarily a grammarian and rhetorician, although, in the light of Elze's work, he now acknowledges that Middle Platonism influenced Tatian.[116]

The greatest change, however, has been in Grant's attitude towards Tatian's relationship with Valentinianism in the *Oration*; he acknowledges the existence of non-gnostic concepts, such as God as creator, and the Incarnation,[117] and is generally more conservative in presenting parallels between the *Oration* and Valentinian texts.[118] However, he maintains that *Or* 30 is a secret Christian exegesis, and still suggests, albeit rather more cautiously, that it is Valentinian.[119]

The attitude that although Valentinian influence is difficult to prove in the *Oration*, yet later Tatian's theology acquired a predominantly Valentinian (and Encratite) bent, runs throughout Grant's treatment of Tatian in his work *Greek Apologists of the Second Century*.[120] Clearly Grant has taken something of a backward step in his position towards Tatian and Valentinianism; he no longer seems to consider the *Oration* as overtly Valentinian.

However, despite Grant's more prudent approach to the *Oration*, he still asserts that Tatian became a Valentinian later in life. His only real evidence for this is found in the heresiological reports that I outlined at the start of this chapter, and his only reference to gnostic doctrines later held by Tatian[121] originates from Clement of Alexandria's claim, which can easily be demonstrated as erroneous from evidence within the *Oration*.[122] As we have seen, the claims of the heresiologists were certainly not objective. Moreover, they probably read back later 'orthodox' attitudes to groups in the second century, which were then labelled 'heretical'. If this is the case, perhaps we should be more circumspect in labelling second century figures 'gnostic'.

In his earlier work, Grant's approach to Tatian's relationship with Valentinianism in the *Oration* was rather narrow; in paralleling passages in Tatian with those of Valentinian texts he failed to consider the wider meanings of those passages, or the possibility that such similarities may be due to common backgrounds, such as Scripture or philosophy. In adopting this approach Grant has exposed himself to strong criticism, and his awareness of this fact is reflected in his later work.

Parallels do not in themselves prove direct relationships between texts; it is important to take into account the context of a passage, the way in which it is being used, and where the idea may have come from. It seems to me that highlighting similarities without due consideration to the circumstances surrounding them merely leads to the widening of a field, not to its refinement, and serves to confuse an issue further, rather than offer clarification.

Despite Grant's caution in *Greek Apologists of the Second Century*, he still implies some Valentinian influence in the *Oration* and remains convinced that Tatian later became a Valentinian. I would question this more conservative position, since I consider the *Oration* to belong to a non-gnostic stream of Christianity, which was later erroneously labelled 'Valentinian'.

For the remainder of this chapter I intend to consider some of the issues that Grant has overlooked, and in so doing I hope I will prove decisively that Tatian was not influenced by Valentinianism when he wrote the *Oration*.

Tatian, the Valentinians, and their use of Paul

Grant rightly notes that much of Tatian's doctrine is based on the Pauline Epistles,[123] but he also appears to assume that Paul was primarily appropriated by gnostics during the second century, and that therefore Tatian's use of Paul indicates a Valentinian bias. However, in order to confirm or deny whether Tatian's use of Pauline material actually parallels that of the Valentinians, it is necessary to examine Tatian's interpretation of Paul and to compare it with that of the Valentinians.[124]

Tatian makes several allusions to *Romans*, and even seems to cite from this Epistle. In Chapter 4 of his *Oration*, Tatian argues against pagan nature worship:

> We know him through his creation and 'what is invisible in his power we comprehend through what he has made'. I refuse to worship his work of creation, brought into being for our sake.[125]

In *Rom* 1 Paul is talking about much the same subject,[126] and Tatian seems to have incorporated some of this material into his argument; Tatian even cites from *Rom* 1:20 in the passage above.[127] In *Rom* 1:20 f, the notion that God can be understood through his creation is part of an apologetic argument which is intended to explain why pagans did not turn to God. Tatian turns this meaning around slightly, and uses it to defend Christian rejection of pagan religious practices; he begins by acknowledging the authority of the Emperor and his own civic duties, but argues that man is only entitled to the degree of honour appropriate to humanity, and asserts the supremacy of the Christian God.[128]

Tatian may also make use of *Rom* 1:26 and some of the ideas in *Rom* 1:21–23. *Rom* 1:26 expresses God's abandonment of those who turn from him.[129] Something similar happens in *Or* 7:3 when, banished from life with the Word, the demons are 'given up to their own stupid folly',[130] although clearly the identity of those being abandoned by God shifts to include the demons in Tatian. There may also be a parallel in the reason for this abandonment; in *Rom* 1:23, we are told that those who are abandoned exchange 'images resembling mortal men or birds or animals or reptiles' for God. This is clearly a reference to pagan idolatry. In Tatian, men and angels are banished for attributing divine status to the arch-rebel.[131]

If Tatian is making use of Paul here, he is obviously manipulating the passages to incorporate them within the context of the fall. In *Rom* 1 Paul is referring to pagan rejection of God outside of a fall context, and abandonment is not solely due to idolatry.[132]

Tatian also used passages from *Rom* 6:10 and 7:14, which we considered earlier in relation to parallels with Theodotus. Thus it is clear that Tatian made direct use of *Romans* in his *Oration*, and that he used passages from this Epistle to underpin his own arguments. His exegesis of *Romans* is fairly simple; he does turn the sense of the Pauline passages he uses to fit his own point, but his interpretations are fairly literal, and he does not resort to allegory or symbolism for his explanations.[133]

Paul's *Epistle to the Romans* was also used by Valentinians. However, their exegesis was quite different to that of Tatian; the principle of Valentinian exegesis was that the Pauline Epistles contained a hidden doctrine that could only be unlocked through interpretation based on a secret tradition which had been passed on orally from Paul to his Valentinian followers.[134] Therefore Valentinian exegesis of *Romans*, and indeed all the Pauline Epistles, is characteristically symbolic; they attempt to glean Paul's message to the elect from a letter which they believe is pitched at psychic Christians. Thus much of their interpretation involves explanations of passages in Paul that appear to be contradictory to their own worldview.

As we have seen, Tatian understood *Rom* 1:19–25 to refer to pagan nature worship. According to Valentinian exegesis of this passage, however, it was only on a literal, psychic level that Paul was understood to warn against pagan idolatry; on a symbolic, pneumatic level, they believed that Paul's warning was directed against worshipping the Demiurge.[135]

Rom 1:20, where Paul asserts that God can be perceived through his creation, proved to be somewhat problematic for the Valentinian exegetes, since they attempted to separate the supreme God from the creation process entirely. As we have seen, Tatian uses this verse to defend Christian rejection of pagan nature worship, but there are some important presuppositions about God that underpin his argument; Tatian believes that the one transcendent God is the creator of the world.

The Valentinians inevitably found problems with this verse because in their system of belief, the supreme, transcendent God did not create the universe; the creation was the result of the fall of the aeon 'Sophia' (Wisdom), and frequently involved a second creator god, the Demiurge. So we find Theodotus explaining that Sophia created the Demiurge in the image of the Father,[136] and the Marcosians that the Demiurge created the cosmos in imitation of 'the infinite, eternal, immeasurable, and timeless nature of the Ogdoad on high.'[137] Both of these interpretations explain how the divine can be perceived in a world whose very existence was totally alien to the supreme God.

Tatian makes rather less use of 1 and 2 *Corinthians* than he did of *Romans*; he appears to make only two direct allusions to these Epistles, although there are a number of ideas and phrases in Tatian that are paralleled in 1 and 2 *Corinthians*. Tatian's first direct allusion is in Chapter 15, where he states:

> The bond of the flesh is the soul, but it is the flesh which contains the soul. If such a structure is like a shrine, 'God' is willing to 'dwell' in it through the 'spirit', his representative.[138]

This passage, with its language of the body as a temple within which the Holy Spirit may dwell, reflects three related passages in Paul; 1 *Cor* 3:16; 6:19; 2 *Cor* 6:16.[139] In the original Pauline contexts, these passages refer to moral ethics. In view of Tatian's own asceticism, it is likely that he interpreted them in an ascetic way, although it is not explicit in his *Oration*. Tatian uses the passage in explaining what he means by the 'divine image and likeness'; if the body is like a shrine God's spirit will dwell within it, and such indwelling makes man the image of God.[140]

Direct use of a further passage in 1 *Corinthians* is attributed to Tatian by Clement of Alexandria. Clement reports that in his work *On Perfection According to the Saviour*, Tatian states:

> 'Agreement conduces to prayer. The common experience of corruption means an end to intercourse.' At any rate, his [i.e. Tatian's] acceptance of it is so grudging that he is

38

really saying No to it altogether. He agreed to their coming together again because of Satan and because of weakness of will, but he showed that anyone who is inclined to succumb is going to be serving two masters, God when there is agreement, and weakness of will, sexual immorality, and the devil when there is not. He says this in his exegesis of the Apostle.[141]

The passage that Clement claims Tatian to be interpreting is clearly 1 *Cor* 7:5.[142] Since Tatian's work *On Perfection According to the Saviour* is no longer extant, it is impossible to verify whether Clement has understood Tatian correctly here. However, in view of Tatian's ascetic interests, it is certainly credible that Tatian interpreted Paul in this way. If this does reflect Tatian's exegesis of 1 *Cor* 7:5, clearly Tatian took Paul's recommendation for periods of continence within marriage a step further than the Apostle himself did.

I shall now turn to discuss less definite parallels between Tatian and 1 and 2 *Corinthians*. In refuting Grant, we have already met the problematic passage in Chapter 30, where Tatian writes:

> Therefore now that I have apprehended these things I wish to 'strip myself' of the childishness of babyhood.[143]

Child terminology is frequently used by Paul in 1 *Corinthians*,[144] and it is possible that Tatian is drawing on this Pauline language. However, it is difficult to draw any firm conclusions about the relationship between Tatian's child terminology and these passages in Paul because of the problems of interpretation and translation that exist in connection with *Oration* 30. As Grant points out, Valentinians were also fond of child terminology, and used it to express the purity of Valentinian asceticism.[145] However, it seems to me that Tatian is rejecting the child state in favour of greater maturity – an idea much like that of Paul in 1 *Cor* 13:11.

Tatian may also be appealing to 2 *Cor* 5:2–4 when he uses putting on clothing as a metaphor for gaining immortality in Chapter 20:

> But we have learnt through prophets what we did not know, who being convinced that the spirit in conjunction with the soul would obtain the heavenly garment of mortality – immortality – used to foretell all that the rest of the souls did not know.[146]

There is an important distinction to be made here between Tatian's use of clothing imagery and that of Paul; Paul's desire to be 'further clothed' is the only part of the metaphor that Tatian uses. Tatian sees immortality, in the form of union between soul and spirit, as the 'heavenly garment'. There was a strong tradition of clothing imagery within Syriac Christianity,[147] and the question of Tatian's relationship to that tradition is one that I shall return to in Chapter 6.[148]

1 *Corinthians* was also used extensively by Valentinian exegetes, although use of 2 *Corinthians* appears to have been more limited. Once again, their exegesis of these Epistles is markedly different to that of Tatian.

Tatian's exegesis of Paul's idea of the body as a temple in which the spirit dwells has no direct parallel within Valentinian exegesis, although Pagels offers Heracleon's interpretation of the temple in *John* 2:13–15.[149] The Valentinians believed that a divine spark existed within the pneumatics, but the notion of the Holy Spirit dwelling within the human body must have been totally repellent to them.

Similarly, there are also no direct Valentinian parallels to Tatian's reported reading of 1 *Cor* 7:5. As we have seen, in the exegesis that Clement presents, Tatian's interpretation of Paul is very literal and he places further stress upon the value of continence. It is likely that the Valentinians would also have understood 1 *Cor* 7:5 to refer to sexual ethics on a psychic level,[150] but there is much evidence to suggest that on a pneumatic level Valentinians interpreted marriage symbolically, understanding it to represent the redemptive union between the pneumatic and her divine partner.[151] It is therefore reasonably safe to assume that Valentinian exegesis of 1 *Cor* 7:5 would not have broken off at a mere moral teaching of sexual ethics.

There is also evidence that Valentinian exegetes used the Pauline passage that Tatian may allude to when using clothing imagery. The author of the *Gospel of Philip* claims that it is necessary to take off the flesh to inherit the kingdom of God, and speaks of the garments that are to be put on in the kingdom of heaven.[152] To compare this with Tatian's use of clothing imagery, there is no evidence in the *Oration* that the flesh needs to be taken off before the garments of immortality can be put on; the divine spirit is the heavenly garment of immortality, and prior to the fall men possessed the spirit whilst still part of the material world and therefore in the body.[153] It would therefore seem that, in using clothing imagery, Tatian places an entirely different emphasis on the relationship of man with the body to that of the Valentinians; according to Tatian, immortality is worn in addition to the body.

Tatian may also make limited use of *Galatians*, although as I have identified only one parallel this is by no means certain. In Chapter 13, Tatian may echo *Gal* 4:8 when he relates how the fallen soul, abandoned by the spirit, searches for God and turns instead to worshipping demons:

> The soul kept a spark, as it were, of the spirit's power, yet because of its [i.e. the soul's] separation it could no longer see things that are perfect, and so in its search for God went astray and fashioned a multitude of gods, following the demons and their hostile devices.[154]

In *Gal* 4:8–9, ignorance of God leads to man's enslavement to inferior beings, 'weak and beggarly elemental spirits' who 'by nature are no gods'. Paul seems to be referring to pagan gods here in much the same way as Tatian does,[155] since for Tatian the demons are equivalent to the pagan gods.[156]

However, Tatian uses this concept of ignorance leading to pagan worship in a different timeframe to Paul. In *Galatians*, ignorance of God was the common experience of his audience before their reception of Paul's Christian mission, and *Gal* 4:8–9 seems to be a warning against slipping back into pagan worship. However, in the *Oration* ignorance of God is a result of the fall and a direct consequence of the soul's separation from the divine spirit, and the duration of that ignorance is from the time of the fall to the revelation of the knowledge of God through the prophets.[157]

The Valentinians appear to have made rather more use of *Galatians* than Tatian, and also seem to have offered exegeses of *Gal* 4:8. In a fragmentary passage in the *Gospel of Philip*, the author refers to 'powers' that wish to prevent man from being saved.[158] Meanwhile, Theodotus considers these powers to be the astrological bodies that govern fate, and constantly battle against men, and claims that the Lord (i.e. Christ) comes to rescue mankind from them.[159] However, both of these references seem far too vague to offer a comparison with Tatian.

Moving on to consider Tatian's use of *Ephesians*, once again we find only vague references, which suggests the use of parallel concepts rather than direct dependence. In Chapter 16, Tatian uses the imagery of armour when describing man's battle against the power of demons and the matter which they manipulate:

> Armed with the 'breastplate' of 'heavenly spirit' he will be able to protect everything it encompasses.[160]

Similar terminology occurs in *Eph* 6:14, and in 1 *Thess* 5:8.[161] Although conflict imagery was popular in the early church, in terms of both persecution and the ascetic's battle to overcome the body, what is significant in Tatian's use of this imagery is that he speaks of the breastplate of 'heavenly spirit'. This is clearly not a moral virtue like 'righteousness' or 'faith', such as we find in *Eph* 6:14 and 1 *Thess* 5:8. To relate it to Tatian's teaching, he is speaking of the protection that union with the divine spirit offers.

In describing the soul's relationship with the spirit Tatian uses the imagery of darkness and light:

> In itself it [i.e. the soul] is dark and there is no light in it, and so the saying goes 'The dark does not comprehend the light'. For the soul did not itself preserve the spirit, but was preserved by it. The light comprehended the dark, in that the light of God is Word, but the ignorant soul is darkness.[162]

Although in this passage Tatian seems to be primarily using a passage from the *Fourth Gospel*,[163] Paul uses the same imagery of darkness and light in *Eph* 5:8.[164]

Ephesians was very popular amongst the Valentinians. According to Pagels, the Valentinians understood *Ephesians* as an exposition of pneumatic redemption.[165] As far as comparing their exegesis of *Ephesians* with that of Tatian is concerned, vague references do appear to be made to 6:14 and 5:8.

Theodotus refers to *Eph* 6:11 f, and even cites *Eph* 6:16, attributing this passage to 'the Apostle'.[166] However, Theodotus uses this section of *Ephesians* when talking about Christ's temptation in the desert,[167] and does not directly refer to the breastplate imagery of *Eph* 6:14.

The Valentinians also took on board the light and darkness dualism of *John* and *Eph* 5:8. Theodotus describes Jesus as the light, although he apparently also cites from *Phil* 2:7,[168] whilst the author of the *Gospel of Truth* perceives Jesus as the light that enlightens those in darkness.[169] As was the case with *Galatians*, these parallels are too vague to provide a comparison between Tatian's use of Paul and that of the Valentinians.

Tatian's use of *Hebrews* is rather more certain, since he seems to cite *Heb* 2:7 directly in Chapter 15, where we read:

> But after their loss of immortality men have overcome death by death in faith, and through repentance they have been given a calling, according to the saying; 'since they were made for a little while lower than the angels.'[170]

Although the author of *Hebrews* is in turn citing from *Psalm* 8:5,[171] from the form of Tatian's quotation we can be reasonably confident that Tatian is citing from *Hebrews*.[172] The meaning of the passage has also changed as it has passed from *Psalms* to *Hebrews*, and from *Hebrews* to Tatian. The original subject in *Psalm* 8:5 is mankind, and whilst the author of *Hebrews* turns this to refer to Christ, Tatian understands the verse to refer to men who repent.[173]

Tatian's use of this citation is also quite different; he reads it in the context of the fall. For Tatian, men have been made 'lower than the angels' by their loss of immortality at the fall, but they can regain their former state through reuniting with the Spirit.[174] Thus the fall was not intended to be permanent, and man's current state will persist for only 'a little while'.

The Valentinians also used *Hebrews*; Pagels points out that the Valentinian exegetes read the theme of the superiority of the new covenant over Israel's old covenant as symbolizing the supremacy of the pneumatic relationship with God over against that of the psychics.[175] Unfortunately, there is no extant exegesis of *Heb* 2:7 to compare with that of Tatian.

Inevitably, not all of the passages that Tatian uses in Paul are also interpreted by the Valentinians, but from those that are it becomes clear that Tatian's exegesis of Paul is very different to that of the Valentinians. Tatian's exegesis is fairly literal,[176] and he tends to extract passages, using them as proof texts to illustrate the point he is making. In complete contrast, Valentinian exegesis of Paul is far more allegorical, and perhaps even esoteric; they draw out a hidden meaning behind the texts which is intended solely for the elite.

As we have seen, Valentinian exegetes also present a 'psychic' exegesis of Paul that is intended for ordinary members of the church. If we compare the Valentinian 'psychic' reading of *Rom* 1:19–25 with that of Tatian, we find that the two correspond.

In her article 'The Valentinian claim to esoteric exegesis of *Romans* as basis for anthropological theory', Pagels draws out the distinction that she claims the Valentinians made between psychic salvation and gnostic redemption. She concludes that the Valentinian anthropological framework was a modified theory of election, which the Valentinians claimed to be Pauline (extracted from a gnostic exegesis of *Romans*); those who are termed 'hylic' are elected to reprobation, those who are termed 'pneumatic' are elected to redemption, whilst the 'psychics' are not elected to either and stand provisionally in the middle between the alternative elections to grace and reprobation.[177]

Moreover, Pagels identifies two different soteriological processes for 'pneumatics' and 'psychics'; the 'pneumatic', being elected, is saved through faith and grace, whilst the 'psychic' is saved by faith and works. She distinguishes these processes as 'pneumatic redemption', and 'psychic salvation'.[178]

The parallel between the 'psychic salvation' Pagels identifies, and Tatian's salvation of the soul is extremely striking. In both, the soul (or 'psychic') has free will, and is able to choose salvation. Both require a certain amount of grace; for Tatian, the soul needs to attain knowledge of God, which is revealed by the divine spirit through prophecy, for the Valentinians, it is the pneumatics who make 'psychic' salvation possible.

The Valentinians understood the 'orthodox' church to belong to the psychic level. Thus many of the Scriptural interpretations that they held to be 'psychic' were in fact the common interpretations of ordinary Christians. Tatian's use of Paul does not go beyond the psychic, which strongly suggests that he is closer to the mainstream traditions of second century Christianity than to the Valentinians.

Before I move on to discuss non-Valentinian elements in Tatian's *Oration*, a brief aside on Tatian's relationship to the Pastoral Epistles is needed. As we saw in Chapter 1, the Pastoral Epistles appear to have been used by the mainstream church in an attempt to reclaim Paul from the gnostics. It is almost certain that the Pastoral Epistles were in existence by the time of Tatian; both Polycarp and Theophilus appear to have known them,[179] and Jerome claims that Tatian rejected *Timothy* whilst retaining *Titus*,[180] which suggests that he must have known both. Thus, we must ask whether there is any evidence that Tatian used the Pastoral Epistles when writing the *Oration*.

There are, in fact, some similarities between the *Oration* and the

Pastoral Epistles. For example, Tatian's concept of the 'knowledge of truth' is paralleled in both 1 and 2 *Timothy*.[181] Evidence that such terminology was used within mainstream circles is important because, of course, the concept of knowledge was vital within gnostic streams. However, the context in which the author(s) of 1 and 2 *Timothy* use this phrase bears scant resemblance to that of Tatian, who uses the concept within his own theory of salvation.

A further example is found in Chapter 20, where Tatian speaks of a light inaccessible to men.[182] This is paralleled in 1 *Timothy*, where the author writes of an 'unapproachable light'.[183] Moreover, in both writers the concept is used to describe heaven.

A comparison with *Titus* throws up only one parallel; both refer to a saying, reputedly coined by Epimenides, which reflects the philosophical notion of the Liar's Paradox.[184] Since it is likely that both writers may have come across this saying from other sources,[185] this parallel does not prove that Tatian used *Titus*.

In view of the vagueness of this parallel, and the evidence in Jerome, we cannot conclude with any certainty that Tatian used 1 and 2 *Timothy* or *Titus* in the *Oration*. What is significant, however, is the fact that the concept of 'knowledge of truth' is found within an apparently anti-gnostic stream of Christianity. This raises interesting questions about Tatian's relationship with anti-gnostic streams within second century Christianity. Does Tatian's non-Valentinian exegesis of Paul belong to an anti-gnostic stream of tradition? Should his *Oration* be understood as part of the process of reclaiming Paul?

Non-Valentinian elements in Tatian's thought

Having, I hope, proved that Tatian's exegesis of Paul is not Valentinian, I shall now turn to consider the wider context of the *Oration*, and point out the non-Valentinian elements that are present in Tatian's thought.

God as creator of matter

One of the major characteristics of Valentinianism is the anti-cosmic standpoint that the world was not created by a supreme God, but was the result of the fall of the aeon Sophia. Sophia, striving after the unknown father in ignorance and error, attempted to create without her pleromic partner, which led to the creation of the world and the imprisonment of the pneumatic spark within matter.

Thus for the Valentinians the creation of the material world was a mistake, and matter was therefore inherently evil and alien to God.

In contrast to this Valentinian rejection of divine involvement in creation and the consequent devaluation of matter, Tatian believes that the world has been created by the one supreme God. He calls his God 'creator',[186] and tells us that matter has been produced and shaped by God.[187]

Tatian maintains his God's transcendence by introducing the Logos as the instrument through which God creates.[188] It is important to note that here, the Logos does not perform the creative act autonomously; God works through the Logos and is himself ultimately responsible for creation. In involving the Logos in creation Tatian is pushing the boundaries between God and matter further apart, but this is because of the transcendence he attributes to God, and not because matter is absolutely alien to God.

In Chapter 17, Tatian intimates that matter is not inherently evil. He argues strongly against man's use of drugs, since he believes that matter was not intended for this purpose, and that drugs were concocted and used by demons in order to turn men away from God.[189] He states that 'the demons used things in the world for doing mischief and the form of the evil derives from them and not from the perfect God'.[190] This suggests that the 'things in the world', the herbs and roots (i.e. matter) that make up drugs, are not in themselves evil, although the use to which the demons put them is.

Tatian further states that if God had provided drugs for man, he would have been responsible for creating evil. However, Tatian does not believe that this is possible because God created everything that is good.[191] Since elsewhere Tatian clearly states that God created matter,[192] he is probably underlining, in his awkward and condensed style, the fact that matter itself cannot be evil.

So here we find an undeniably non-Valentinian view of matter and its creation. For Tatian, God was directly responsible for creation, and the creation of matter, through the actions of his Word.[193] Matter is not inherently evil or alien to God, because as a perfect being he is incapable of creating anything evil. The evil that exists in God's creation is due to the actions of men and demons, and therefore ultimately springs from the free will with which they were endowed from the moment of creation.[194]

The physical reality of the incarnation

The Valentinian understanding of Christ was docetic. Since Valentinians espoused an anti-cosmic dualism, it was unthinkable that the heavenly redeemer should sink to the level of matter by taking on human flesh. Thus, according to Hippolytus,[195] the Italian branch of Valentinianism taught that Christ had a psychic body,[196] which the pneumatic seed entered at baptism, whilst the Oriental branch considered Christ's body to be purely pneumatic.

However, Tatian seems to offer a corporeal understanding of Christ. There is only one reference to the concept of the Incarnation in the *Oration*, and although the name of 'Jesus' or the title 'Christ' is not mentioned, it can be safely inferred from what he says that it is indeed the Incarnation of Christ to which Tatian refers:

> We are not fools, men of Greece, nor are we talking nonsense when we declare that God has been born in the form of man.[197]

Although it is possible to interpret the notion of God being born in the 'form' of man as a docetic expression, it is clear from what Tatian goes on to say about the Greek gods assuming human bodies that the form of man taken on by God at the Incarnation is a solid, physical body, not something that only appears to be human flesh.[198]

Thus Tatian's understanding of the Incarnation is in complete contrast to Valentinian views, and the little that we learn from his *Oration* of Tatian's Christology disproves Grant's claim to a Valentinian interpretation of Christ.

A physical resurrection

There is a strong tendency in Valentinianism to devalue the human body. Valentinians divided men into three races: the hylic, the psychic, and the pneumatic. The pneumatic, spiritual men are those who possess a spark of the divine, and form an elite class who will return to the pleroma, leaving the hylic and most of the psychic behind.[199] The hylic are considered to be worthless, the malformed results of a fall from the divine. So the Valentinians held a very negative estimation of the body, which was considered to belong to the hylic level of existence, and the flesh becomes a prison from which the spirit must escape. The thought that the human body might take part in the salvation process would have been totally abhorrent to the Valentinian mind.

Yet Tatian clearly states his belief in a physical resurrection:

> For this same reason we are convinced that there will be a bodily resurrection after the universe has come to an end.[200]

The reason Tatian gives for a bodily resurrection is God's creation of matter; this passage follows directly on from the end of Chapter 5, where Tatian is speaking of matter being created by God. I believe the connection that Tatian is making between Chapters 5 and 6 is that since man's body is part of matter and part of creation, so it also takes part in the resurrection at the end of the world.

As we have seen, Grant considers Tatian's resurrection to entail only the 'fleshly element' of man (i.e. the soul), but this claim does not stand up to closer inspection. At the end of Chapter 6, Tatian speaks of how the body can be resurrected if it is torched, drowned, or shredded by animals:

> If fire consumes my bit of flesh, the vaporized matter is still contained in the world. If I am annihilated in rivers and seas, or torn to pieces by wild beasts, I am still stored up in a rich lord's treasuries. The poor, impious man does not know what is stored up, but God the ruler, when he wishes, will restore to its original state the substance that is visible only to him.[201]

In view of this, how can Tatian's 'bodily resurrection' exclude the physical matter that is scattered in this way? Moreover, Tatian clearly states that both soul and body are involved in the resurrection,[202] and at one point he even claims that the flesh is immortal – although since this occurs in a passage where Tatian is refuting various hellenistic schools, I suspect what he means is that the flesh has just as much potential to become immortal as the soul.[203]

Evidently, Tatian does assert a physical resurrection, despite Grant's claims to the contrary, and not only does this run against Valentinian perceptions of salvation, but it also implies that Tatian placed a certain amount of positive value on the body. This is also reflected in *Or* 15:2, where Tatian speaks of the divine spirit dwelling within the bodies of suitable men,[204] and also in his understanding of the original state of man in union with the divine spirit.[205]

Salvation open to all

As I have intimated when talking of the Valentinian division between hylic, psychic, and pneumatic, Valentinian redemption is characteristically limited to the pneumatics who possess a spark of the divine, and possibly extends to a few psychics in some circles. Thus Valentinian soteriology belongs primarily to the elite, and the majority of people are expected to perish.

In Tatian, however, salvation is available to everyone.[206] This is so because of his firm insistence on free will; he believes that the first men fell through their own choice in following the arch-rebel,[207] but that free will also enables men to reverse the fall.[208] Since all men have free will, all men therefore have the potential to turn to God and to achieve salvation.

If we consider how Tatian's salvation is possible, we find further distinctions from Valentinianism. The fulfilment of the redemptive process is, for Tatian, the reunion of human soul and divine spirit.[209] It is not an escape from an evil world, but rather a fulfilment that emulates man's original state, when his possession of the divine spirit whilst in the body meant that he could be part of the material world and at the same time above it.[210]

This union of divine spirit and human soul already occurs within the prophets, and the spirit comfortably dwells within the human body.[211] It is through the prophets that salvation is made possible, through revelation of the knowledge of God, and from what we learn of resurrection in Chapter 6 it is clear that Tatian does not expound a realized eschatology but a future one; that salvation is not immediate, but will occur after the resurrection.

There is a correlation between Tatian and Valentinians in that both claim that 'knowledge' is necessary for salvation, but this was a common idea in the second century. Clement of Alexandria speaks of Christian gnosis,[212] and Irenaeus is distinguishing gnostic 'knowledge' from mainstream 'knowledge' when he speaks of 'gnosis falsely so-called'.[213]

Conclusion: Tatian, not Valentinian

Grant's claim for Valentinian influence on the *Oration* cannot be substantiated; although superficial similarities exist, such as Tatian's emphasis on revelation and his understanding of 'knowledge' as the means of achieving salvation, there is much in the *Oration* that runs counter to Valentinian ideology. As we have seen,

Tatian's exegesis of Paul bears very little resemblance to that of Valentinian exegetes, whilst his inclusion of several non-Valentinian ideas in the *Oration* suggests that Tatian's thought world, at least at the time when he wrote the *Oration*, was not based on Valentinianism.

Earlier in this chapter, when presenting the heresiological association of Tatian with gnosticism, I outlined Clement of Alexandria's alternative claim that Tatian rejected the Old Testament as the work of the Demiurge. The fact that this can also be shown to be erroneous supports my rebuttal of Grant, and reinforces my argument that Tatian should not be understood as a Valentinian.[214]

In discussing Tatian's relationship with Valentinianism, however, we must also consider the issue of how representative the *Oration* is of Tatian's later theology. As we have seen, the heresiologists claimed that in later life Tatian turned to Valentinianism and Encratism, and that after Justin's martyrdom he apostatized from the church and returned to the East. Whilst I acknowledge that a person's belief system is rarely stagnant, I think it is important to question the perspective of the heresiologists.

Justin died as a martyr around the year 165 CE. For those mainstream Christians, like Irenaeus, who were anxious to trace a line of 'orthodox' teaching back to the time of the Apostles, Justin's association with the 'heretic' Tatian (if indeed he was widely considered to be a heretic at that time) must have been embarrassing. Thus Tatian's return to the East provided the heresiologists with an opportunity to distance Justin from Tatian.

To consider events from the opposite perspective, however, it is also possible that Tatian left Rome because he disagreed with the direction the mainstream Roman Church was taking. It would certainly seem that as the stream that was to become known as 'orthodoxy' struggled for dominance, the western church became increasingly conservative in outlook.[215] In which case, perhaps Tatian's return to the East offered a convenient means for developing western orthodoxy to reject the extreme asceticism that permeated the East, by claiming that Tatian took with him the Encratite heresy. The association with Valentinianism was perhaps part of Irenaeus' genealogy of heresy, linking Encratism with the 'heresies' that had gone before.

Furthermore, even if we were to assume that the *Oration* only represents Tatian's belief system prior to Justin Martyr's death, there is a strong principle of internal consistency running throughout the *Oration* that argues against a sudden conversion to Valentinian tenets. This principle of internal consistency was central to Tatian's understanding of Christianity, and is most clearly seen in his presentation of Christianity as 'the truth'. It was certainly a key factor in his composition of the *Diatessaron*.[216]

3

TATIAN AND JUSTIN
MARTYR

We know from various sources that Justin Martyr was the teacher of Tatian,[1] and it therefore stands to reason that Justin probably exerted a certain amount of influence over his pupil. However, the influence of Justin is an area that many scholars of Tatian have passed over quickly, perhaps anxious to disassociate Justin from reports of Tatian's later heresies. In fact I suspect that a comparison of Tatian's ideas with those of Justin may prove him to be far closer to his master's world view, and the Christian tradition behind it, than that of the Valentinian traditions. In discussing Tatian's relationship with Valentinianism in Chapter 2, Tatian's use of Pauline material was considered, so in evaluating the relationship between Justin and Tatian I will first consider Justin's use of Paul and make a comparison by referring back to that earlier discussion. Other common Christian sources will then be studied before I turn to examine the similarities between Justin and the *Oration*.

Use of Christian writings

At first glance, Justin's use of Pauline material seems to be rather limited;[2] he cites or alludes to Paul in only a handful of passages, and does not, like Tatian, seem to incorporate Pauline ideas into his thought. However, as we shall see, two scholars have suggested that Justin uses Paul in other ways.

In Justin's first *Apology*, there are only two passages that may contain reflections of Pauline texts. In 1 *Apol* 3, Justin says that those who have learnt the truth but fail to do what is righteous are 'without excuse' before God.[3] This seems to be an echo of *Rom* 1:20–21, where Paul claims that those who know God and do not honour him are also 'without excuse'.[4] Likewise, we find an echo of

Heb 3:1 in 1 *Apol* 12, where Jesus Christ is called the 'Apostle of God'.

Justin's *Dialogue with Trypho* yields a few more such examples. The first group of passages reveals key words or phrases that seem reminiscent of Paul. In *Dial* 35, Justin states that there will be 'schisms and heresies'. This seems to refer to 1 *Cor* 11:18, where Paul speaks of 'divisions' amidst the Corinthian Church. The 'gifts from the Spirit of God', which we encounter in *Dial* 88, also recall the passage on 'spiritual gifts' in 1 *Corinthians* 12, whilst Justin's reference to the 'man of apostasy' in *Dial* 110 is highly reminiscent of 'the man of lawlessness' of 2 *Thess* 2:3. Finally, we turn to *Dial* 120, where Justin speaks of Isaiah being 'sawed in half'. This may be an echo of *Heb* 11:37.

The next example of parallels between Justin and Paul is in Justin's use of the Pauline notion of circumcision. In *Dial* 12, Justin tells the Jews, that they need 'another circumcision', and again in Chapter 18 he speaks of the 'true circumcision'. These two passages clearly reflect the Pauline concept of a second and over-riding circumcision of the heart, beyond the physical circumcision of the Jews. It is hardly surprising that such a concept should be utilized in the *Dialogue*, since this is essentially a critique of Judaism.

The closest parallel between Justin and Paul is found in *Dial* 27. Here he berates the Jews for their behaviour, and cites several Old Testament texts:

> And He exclaims: 'All have turned out of the way, they are become unprofitable together. There is none that under-standeth, no not one. With their tongues they have dealt deceitfully, their throat is an open sepulchre, the venom of asps is under their lips; destruction and misery are in their paths, and the way of peace they have not known'.[5]

In *Rom* 3:11–17 Paul also cites these passages, which are from *Psalms* 14:1–3; 53:1–3; 5:9; 140:3; 10:7, and *Isaiah* 59:7–8.[6] It seems highly significant that Justin chose to use these particular passages together, and clearly some connection exists between *Dial* 27 and *Rom* 3:11–17.

Thus at first glance Justin's use of Paul seems fleeting; apart from the longer passage in *Dial* 27, the other instances in Justin that echo Paul are merely single words or phrases that may have acted as key words or concepts common in the early church. However, the issue of Justin's use of *Romans* as a testimony source in *Dial* 27 may prove a more direct link between Justin and the Pauline passages.

In his book *The Proof from Prophecy*,[7] Oskar Skarsaune suggests that Justin used Paul's collection of Old Testament quotations as a testimony source. Skarsaune has discovered several correlations between Paul's citations of Hebrew Scripture in *Romans* and those of Justin, and suggests that these correlations form a definite pattern; he claims that there are two blocks in Justin's *Dialogue* where citations of Hebrew Scripture similar to those cited in *Romans* are concentrated, the first from Chapters 17–47, and the second from Chapters 114–119. Not all of the instances Skarsaune puts forward as evidence can be used to prove that Justin is directly dependent on *Romans*, but there are two instances that are actually textually identical.[8]

Skarsaune has also collected material from 1 *Corinthians*, *Galatians*, and *Ephesians* which contain similar Scriptural quotations to those in Justin. Of these three Pauline letters, *Galatians* in particular contains similar citations to those found in Justin.[9]

Skarsaune concludes that Justin knew the Pauline corpus, especially *Romans* and *Galatians*, and made use of the Pauline Epistles as a source for proof texts. Thus, according to Skarsaune's hypothesis, Justin would have used *Rom* 3:11–17 as a collection of Scriptural quotations, which he incorporated into his *Dialogue*.

Skarsaune's argument is certainly persuasive, and presents second century use of Paul in a fresh light. However, as far as a comparison of Justin's use of Paul with that of Tatian is concerned, Skarsaune's analysis of Justin's exegesis proves to be largely irrelevant; despite the reverence Tatian expresses for the Hebrew Scriptures in his conversion account, his allusions to the Old Testament are very sparse.[10]

There would also seem to be little correlation between Justin's direct use of Paul and that of Tatian, since Tatian uses none of Justin's allusions to Paul. Although we should remember that we have a comparatively limited quantity of material from Tatian in relation to that available from Justin, we must conclude that no direct relationship can be found between Tatian's use of Paul and that of Justin.

Before we move on to discuss Justin and Tatian's use of the gospels there is a further usage of Paul by Justin, which has been suggested by Ragnar Holte. In his article on Justin's spermatic logos theory, Holte suggests that Justin has translated Paul's doctrine on natural revelation into the terminology of contemporary philosophy.[11] His justification for this hypothesis is based on Paul's statements concerning the involvement of the pre-existent Christ in creation, and on what Holte terms 'a degree of salvation, existing from the beginning of the world, but revealed only through Christ'.[12]

In support of this latter concept, Holte points to passages in 1 *Corinthians* and *Ephesians*. However, the closest that any of these passages comes to Justin's intuitive spermatic logos is the 'secret wisdom' of 1 *Cor* 2:6–13, which is imparted by the Spirit of God to the mature. I can find no evidence of the existence of this wisdom in the world of men prior to the coming of Christ, and its bestowal only upon Christians suggests an exclusivity that is not present in Justin.

However, the biggest problem with Holte's argument is that, as we have seen, Justin's links with Paul are fairly weak. Although Justin clearly knew some of the Pauline Epistles, and especially *Romans*, there is no evidence to suggest that Paul exerted much of an influence over Justin's thought world.

As we noted in Chapter 1, the New Testament canon was not set until beyond the end of the second century. Hence at the time of Justin and Tatian there was no such thing as a 'canonical' gospel, and a certain amount of textual fluidity still existed. In any case, for Justin and Tatian 'Scripture' meant the Hebrew Bible (in its Greek form) and was considered of greater importance by both than the various contemporary Christian writings that were in circulation in the second century. That this is so is witnessed by Justin's heavy emphasis on Old Testament prophecy and its fulfilment in Christ, and Tatian's claim in Chapter 29 of the *Oration* that it was through reading the ancient 'barbarian writings' (i.e. the Hebrew Scriptures) that he was converted to Christianity.

However, both Justin and Tatian did make use of gospel traditions. In his first *Apology* and his *Dialogue*, Justin refers to a gospel source called the *Memoirs of the Apostles*, and even gives 'gospels' as an alternative name for the *Memoirs* in 1 *Apol* 66. The exact nature of these *Memoirs* is unclear; it may be that this was a name used to designate the material held within the Synoptic Gospels,[13] but some of the citations Justin claims to take from the *Memoirs* seem to be harmonized from two or more gospel accounts, and it has been suggested that Justin's *Memoirs* may themselves have been a harmonized form of the Gospels.[14]

Tatian, on the other hand, makes no mention whatsoever of gospel traditions in his *Oration*, although he may allude to two passages in *Matthew*, one in *Luke*, and cites from the prologue to the *Fourth Gospel*.[15] However, we know from patristic evidence that one of Tatian's other works was the *Diatessaron*, a gospel harmony combining the four 'canonical' Gospels with one or more Jewish-Christian gospel(s).[16] Although there are no surviving copies of Tatian's original *Diatessaron* and its descendants have been corrupted and vulgatized, Diatessaronic variants can be pieced together to create a picture of what Tatian's *Diatessaron* might have been like. Petersen has suggested that there is some degree of textual agreement between Diatessaronic variants and Justin's *Memoirs*, and concludes that Tatian may have used the *Memoirs* in composing his *Diatessaron*.[17]

However, whilst the importance of the Hebrew Scriptures outweighed that of the developing New Testament canon, the emphasis that Justin and Tatian placed upon Christian philosophy overshadowed both. This will become clearer as I go on to consider Justin's influence on the *Oration*.

A comparison between Justin and the *Oration*

Justin Martyr, like Tatian, was one of the apologists of the early church. Tatian's *Oration* has much in common with Justin's *Apologies*, both in style and content, since all three works were written in defence of Christianity before a hostile Graeco-Roman world. Beyond this there are also strong similarities between the world views and ideas of both, which become most evident in the fact that both present Christianity as the 'true philosophy'.

Conversion stories

Let us begin this comparison by examining the conversions of Justin and Tatian. Both give accounts of their own conversions. Tatian's is found in *Or* 29, whilst Justin gives two such accounts, one in 2 *Apol* 12 and the other in the opening chapters of his *Dialogue*.

In his second *Apology*, Justin seems to suggest that it was the behaviour of Christians that made his opinion of Christianity become favourable. He says that while he was a Platonist he heard the slander levelled at Christians and discounted it, as their bravery in the face of death impressed him.[18]

Justin's second conversion account is much lengthier.[19] He begins by describing his disillusionment with various contemporary philosophical schools during his search for truth, claiming that he turned from Stoicism to Peripateticism to Pythagoreanism, and finally to Platonism.[20] Then Justin describes a long conversation with an old man. This conversation takes the form of a philosophical dialogue, and the old man eventually persuades him that there is a greater philosophy than that of Plato. The philosophy that the old man then presents to Justin is Christianity, but it is a Christianity that is deeply rooted in the Hebrew Scriptures and the prophecy contained within them.[21] Thus the starting point for Justin's conversion in his *Dialogue* account is rational debate, and Christianity, grounded in Old Testament prophecy, becomes the ultimate philosophy.

The existence of these two accounts in Justin has led to a debate over their historicity.[22] However, if we examine the context in which these accounts occur, it is not necessary to consider them incompatible with each other; Justin's second *Apology* and his *Dialogue* were written with different aims in mind. His second *Apology* is essentially a defence of Christian values and behaviour in the face of Graeco-Roman persecution. It is therefore perfectly natural that in this particular work Justin mentions the influence the exemplary behaviour of Christian martyrs had upon his interest in Christianity.[23] Meanwhile, in the *Dialogue*, Justin is holding a quasi-philosophical debate with the Jew Trypho, and his aim in this work is to prove the supremacy of Christianity over both Judaism and Greek philosophy. In this context it was again appropriate for Justin to incorporate an account of his own experience of contemporary philosophy, albeit in a somewhat stylized manner.

Parallels between Justin's conversion account in the *Dialogue* and a denouncement of philosophy by the rhetorician Lucian has also led some scholars to suggest that Justin's second account is merely a literary device.[24] Whilst it cannot be denied that this account contains overtones of literary convention, I do not consider it necessary to discount its historicity entirely.[25] The most compelling reason for this is the clear evidence of Middle Platonic influence upon Justin's thought.[26]

Like Justin's second account, Tatian's conversion account also begins with a search for 'truth'. Having expressed his disillusionment with Greek culture and religious practice, Tatian states that he began to seek how he could 'discover the truth'.[27] The 'truth' that Tatian discovers is contained within some 'barbarian writings', and these 'barbarian writings' are in fact the Hebrew Scriptures. Thus, like Justin, Tatian is converted through being introduced to

the Hebrew Scriptures. However, whilst Justin is verbally introduced to the prophets of the Scriptures by the old man, Tatian's
conversion is due to the quality of these Scriptures:

> The outcome was that I was persuaded by these because of
> the lack of arrogance in the wording, the artlessness of the
> speakers, the easily intelligible account of the creation of
> the world, the foreknowledge of the future, the remarkable
> quality of the precepts and the doctrine of a single ruler of
> the universe.[28]

Thus the conversion stories of Justin and Tatian are not identical.
Indeed, on the surface, they seem very different. Whilst Justin
speaks of following various philosophical schools, Tatian places his
conversion within the wider context of disillusionment with Greek
culture, although we know from elsewhere that this rejection also
included a rejection of Greek philosophy.[29] Nor is there an 'old
man' involved in Tatian's conversion. Yet there are still some extraordinary similarities between the two conversion stories that cannot
be dismissed lightly.

Both Justin and Tatian convert to Christianity through their
introduction to the Hebrew Scriptures. Elsewhere we learn that
both consider the authors of the Scriptures (for Justin the prophets
and for Tatian Moses) to be older than the Greek philosophers.[30]
They therefore present the Hebrew Scriptures as an alternative literature that supersedes the classics. Both also take a search for 'truth'
as the basis for their conversion. Such a concept, I believe, belongs
within a philosophical context, and points up the concern of both
with philosophical matters. This preoccupation is also emphasized
by the logical and rational way in which both Justin and Tatian discover Christianity.

Graeco-Roman culture

Greek culture underwent something of a revival in Roman society
between 50–250 CE,[31] and interest in all things Greek would have
been at a peak during the lifetimes of Justin and Tatian. Moreover,
both writers came from hellenized areas,[32] which meant that
Graeco-Roman culture was their common heritage, and it therefore
plays an important role in the works of both.[33] On the one hand
they are anxious to reject this culture in favour of Christianity, and
this is especially true of the myths about the Graeco-Roman gods,[34]

whilst on the other Graeco-Roman culture also becomes an instrument used in the attempt to convince pagans (and, of course, reassure pagan converts) of the truth behind Christian claims. As apologists, Justin and Tatian are forced to defend Christianity before the Graeco-Roman world, and use Graeco-Roman culture (both consciously and subconsciously) in order to do this.

Both Justin and Tatian were particularly hostile towards Graeco-Roman mythology. This is of course because such myths related the essential elements of the traditional religion. Yet they were still capable of using mythology to defend Christianity. Both Justin and Tatian do so by citing myths that mirror Christian stories and concepts. For example, in Chapters 21 and 22 of his first *Apology* Justin underlines the parallels between the Christian story of Jesus and Greek stories concerning the sons of Zeus; the Word is compared with Mercury, 'the announcing word of God'; Christ's crucifixion is paralleled with the manner in which Zeus' sons died; the virgin birth is compared with Perseus' conception; and Christ's healing actions are likened to those of Aesculapius.

Similarly, Tatian also uses Greek myths to defend the Incarnation. In Chapter 21, he writes:

> We are not fools, men of Greece, nor are we talking nonsense when we declare that God has been born in the form of a man. You who abuse us should compare your own stories with our narratives . . . When you repeat stories like this, how is it that you mock at us?[35]

Of course implicit in this usage is a criticism of Greek mythology, as well as a truth claim about the reality of the Christian stories. The general sense of the argument in both Justin and Tatian runs along the lines of: 'you may relate fanciful stories about your gods, incited by demons, yet you mock us when we relate the same kind of stories that are actually true!' However, although the aim of our two apologists in using this argument is the same, different tactics are used to achieve it.

Tatian's approach to rebutting Greek mythology is fairly direct; he points up contradictions in the behaviour of these beings who are supposedly immortal, and repeatedly mocks them.[36] Proof of the powerlessness of the Greek gods is extracted from myths detailing weakness or inappropriate behaviour. Repeatedly Tatian points to examples in Greek mythology where gods commit incest or rape, or even just behave sexually (and therefore presumably in a mortal way).[37] This particular element of criticizing sexual behaviour evidently reflects an ascetic perspective, and I shall return to this shortly.

Justin's attack on mythology, meanwhile, is rather more focused. There is an element of derision in much of his criticism, but he tends to be a little more subtle in his attacks. For instance, perhaps riled by the frequent demands made by pagans that Christians prove the truth of their religion,[38] Justin turns this around to demand proofs of the myths preserved in the classics, and then explains that Christians can prove demons to be responsible for these myths.[39]

It is in proving that these myths were invented by demons that Justin offers his most inspired attack on Graeco-Roman mythology; he quite simply claims that the mythology recorded in the classics is an imitation of the prophecies concerning Christ in the Hebrew Scriptures.[40] Of course this claim presumes that the Scriptures were written before the time of Homer and the other poets,[41] but it also implicitly rejects the stories of the gods used earlier in his *Apology* to defend Christian claims.

It is very difficult to see the overall argument that Justin uses when considering elements of his thought in this disjointed manner. Justin's overall argument is in fact very methodical and coherent; he begins by using parallels in mythology to convince readers not to disbelieve Christian claims, and then knocks down those myths by saying that they are imitations of details given in Scripture that prophesy about Christ.[42]

Another related area of Graeco-Roman culture that Justin and Tatian attack is that of religious practice. Religious belief within the Graeco-Roman Empire, and indeed throughout the ancient world, was characteristically polytheistic. As a monotheistic religion, Christian rejection of the pagan deities was inevitable. In particular Justin and Tatian attack idolatry and the oracular traditions,[43] but their whole treatment of the pagan gods as demons who are far inferior to the supreme Christian God is a degradation of the traditional religion.

In their attack on pagan religion early Christians undoubtedly drew upon their Judaic roots, but by the second century our philosophically minded apologists were also able to use a tradition within hellenistic culture itself; from before the time of Socrates, the Greek philosophers had offered a moral critique of the traditional religion. Moreover, as we shall see, the Middle Platonists had developed a philosophical system that envisaged an absolute supreme being and often identified intermediary daemons as the gods of traditional religion. It was therefore easy for apologists like Justin and Tatian to incorporate these ideas and use them in their attacks.

Christians also rejected the formal act of offering sacrifices, which was used throughout the ancient world and was also practised by the Jews. The presentation of sacrificial offerings had formed part of Jewish worship from the earliest period in Israel's history. By claiming that the Mosaic law was designed specifically for 'hard-hearted' Jews and therefore had no relevance for Christians,[44] early Christianity was rejecting the practical act of sacrifice common to Jews and pagans. Precedents for this criticism of Jewish sacrifice can, of course, be found in many of the Old Testament prophets, who advocated awareness of the spiritual dimensions of such rituals. Christians merely took this spiritualization one step further and internalized the sacrificial concept. Most notably, sacrificial terminology was used by Christians to refer to Christ's crucifixion.[45]

Philosophy is the most significant area of Graeco-Roman culture with which Justin and Tatian are concerned. This is perhaps inevitable in light of the emphasis that they place on a 'Christian Philosophy'; in order to present their listeners with the 'true philosophy' (i.e. Christianity), both Justin and Tatian must use hellenistic philosophy and prove its inadequacies.

Tatian's relationship with hellenistic philosophy will be discussed in detail in Chapter 4, so here it is only necessary to outline his basic approach. On the surface, Tatian is extremely hostile towards Greek philosophy. He attacks philosophers on three levels; he criticizes various philosophical doctrines and the behaviour of certain philosophers, and finally he denounces the contradictions and quarrels between the different philosophical schools. However, on a deeper level I believe that Tatian does make use of hellenistic philosophy, but it is not obvious since he does not consciously use hellenistic philosophy to validate Christian claims as Justin does.

Justin's relationship with hellenistic philosophy is very interesting indeed. As we have seen, in the opening chapters of his *Dialogue with Trypho* Justin claims to have experimented with several branches of hellenistic philosophy before turning to Christianity. The precise relationship between Justin and hellenistic philosophy has been the subject of much debate.[46] The most significant study has been that of Carl Andresen, who carried out a philological investigation of the terms used by Justin.[47] He discovered that Justin frequently uses terms that are characteristic of Middle

Platonism, and concluded that the main influence upon Justin was Middle Platonic.

Although still influential, Andresen's thesis has been challenged – most notably by Holte, who has highlighted the influence which the *Fourth Gospel*, Paul and Philo had upon Justin,[48] and by Hyldahl, who, basing his theory on Justin's attitude to philosophy in the opening chapters of the *Dialogue*, claims that there is no continuation between Platonism and Christianity, and that Justin rejects hellenistic philosophy entirely.[49] Current scholarly opinion, according to Nahm, seems to envisage a partial assimilation of Middle Platonism, which had no 'adverse effect' on the content of Justin's Christianity.[50]

Besides the incorporation of Middle Platonic terms and concepts, Justin also appropriates the figure of Socrates in his defence of Christianity. Part of the purpose of Justin's *Apologies* is to censure the unjustified persecution of Christians. Because they rejected both the pagan gods and the practices of Judaism (which were respected because of their age), Christians were frequently denounced as atheists. This was, of course, also a charge that was made against Socrates at his trial. It is therefore no surprise that Justin should compare the situation the Christians found themselves in with that of Socrates, one of the most respected of the ancient philosophers.[51]

However, Justin also attacks hellenistic philosophy in his attempts to prove the supremacy of Christian philosophy. Justin's method of attack is very similar to the one he uses in dealing with Greek myths; he begins by paralleling elements that hellenistic philosophy has in common with Christianity, then levels criticism at contemporary philosophy, and ends by claiming the Christian philosophy to be superior. This progression is very clear in Justin's first *Apology*, and plays a key role in Justin's argument.

Justin opens his first *Apology* by attempting to defend the Christians from false accusations and subsequent persecution. He does so by appealing to the Emperor and his camp on philosophical grounds.[52] Thus, initially, Justin is anxious to find common ground between Roman philosophy and the Christian Philosophy. His first allusion to Plato is no doubt even intended to flatter the addressees (i.e. the Roman Emperors):

> For even one of the ancients said somewhere: 'Unless both rulers and ruled love wisdom, it is impossible to make cities prosper.'[53]

The next allusion we find to Plato is in Chapter 8, and it is used in exactly the same way as Justin used the parallels between Greek myth and Christian claim in 1 *Apol* 21 and 22; Justin cites the Platonic theory that Rhadamanthus and Minos would judge the wicked, and then compares this with the Christian concept of judgement.[54] Thus the parallels between Plato's doctrines and those of the Christian philosophy are used as a justification for Christian claims.

The same thing is happening in Justin's next allusion to hellenistic philosophy in Chapter 20, where he compares the Platonic theory of the creator ordering the world and the Stoic conflagration with Christian doctrines. Here, however, the tone of address has shifted radically; Justin still uses parallels with philosophy to demand acceptance of Christian doctrines, but he is beginning to assert that Christian doctrines are superior to those of the philosophers. Thus, Christianity becomes 'more complete and worthy of God'.[55]

When Justin next mentions Plato, in Chapter 59, we find that a further shift has occurred. Here Justin accuses Plato of plagiarizing from the Hebrew Scriptures when he said that God created the Universe by changing formless matter. Likewise, in the following chapter Justin accuses Plato of borrowing from Moses in his *Timaeus*, when the philosopher talks of placing a 'Chi' in the Universe.[56]

Thus we can trace an argument running through Justin's first *Apology*, which begins with gaining the respect of the addresses, as one philosopher to another. Justin then outlines similarities between their philosophies, which then develops into a claim that the 'Christian philosophy' holds more truth. Finally Justin adopts a more hostile approach, when he accuses hellenistic philosophers of plagiarism.

In Justin's second *Apology*, his attack on hellenistic philosophy is less subtle and more limited. In Chapter 7, when Justin launches a direct attack upon Stoicism, he criticizes the Stoic doctrine of metamorphosis, and the notion of fate. And in Chapter 13 Justin again states his belief in the superiority of Christianity over Greek philosophy when he says that he strives to be found a Christian because the teachings of hellenistic philosophers, poets and historians are not 'in every respect equal' to the teachings of Christ.[57]

Justin's attack upon philosophy, and indeed upon Graeco-Roman culture in general, is concentrated entirely in his two *Apologies*. This should not surprise us since these works focus on the Graeco-Roman world in an attempt to defend Christianity, whilst the *Dialogue*, by contrast, is concerned with the relationship between Christianity and Judaism.

Since Tatian's *Oration* is also concerned with defending Christianity before the Graeco-Roman world, it is difficult to argue that the parallels in Justin and Tatian's use and rejection of Graeco-Roman culture are anything more than the standard approach used in this kind of apologetic material.[58] The main difference between Justin's approach to Graeco-Roman culture and that of Tatian is that Justin uses the culture in a much more structured way, especially in his first *Apology*, skilfully weaving it into his argument. Justin also uses quotations from works of Plato, whereas Tatian merely alludes to him loosely. This seems to suggest that Justin had more direct contact with the works of Plato than Tatian, and may in fact reflect their backgrounds if Tatian did come from Mesopotamia, and not just western Syria.

Asceticism

Asceticism, in all its many varieties, was very popular in the second century. Not only was it prevalent amongst so-called 'heretical' sects like Montanism, Encratism, Valentinianism and some other gnostic-type schools, but it was also present within the stream that became known as orthodoxy. Moreover, asceticism was particularly strong in the East.

One of the charges brought against Tatian was that he founded, or at the very least adhered to, an eastern sect of extreme ascetics known as Encratites.[59] Because Tatian's alleged Encratism has close links with Syrian Christianity, I shall return to consider Tatian's asceticism in Chapter 6. However, even the briefest of comparisons between Tatian's asceticism in the *Oration* and that of his teacher reveals something quite extraordinary in view of the heresiologists' accusation of Encratism.

Tatian's ascetic beliefs are scarcely noticeable in his *Oration*; besides four passages which may reflect ascetic considerations,[60] the rest of his ascetic 'hints' we find only implicit in his arguments against Greek culture. Justin, meanwhile, reflects a far stronger ascetic bent in his works. He repeatedly refers to chastity and temperance,[61] and in his first *Apology* Justin praises those Christians who are 60 or 70 years of age and have retained their virginity.[62]

Justin's asceticism actually seems stronger than Tatian's, when his pupil's theology can only be viewed through the *Oration*. If asceticism was a major part of second century belief, this raises the question of why Tatian should be condemned for Encratism after leaving Justin's care, or indeed why he should be condemned at all.

Ideas

Up to this point I have mainly been concerned with general aspects of correlation between Justin and Tatian, but it is not just their world views that overlap; in several places concepts converge as well.

The concept of free will is central to the theology of both Justin and Tatian; their understandings of the fall, of the existence of demons, and of man's capacity to achieve salvation all revolve around their insistence on the existence of free will. According to Justin and Tatian, both men and angels were created with free will.[63] It is this ability to choose between right and wrong that leads to the fall, to the existence of demons[64] and, ultimately, for Tatian, to the possibility for man's redemption.[65]

However, Justin and Tatian place slightly different emphases on free will in their approaches to the issue of why free will was introduced in the first place. For Justin the choice of good or evil and the end result of that choice are part of the *status quo*, as a kind of cause and effect. Because free will exists, the sinner is culpable and the righteous are worthy of reward.[66] Tatian goes one step further than his master here, in claiming that the end result of mankind's choice (i.e. punishment or reward) is itself the reason why free will was introduced.[67]

The chief difference, however, between Tatian's view of free will and that of Justin is a matter of anthropological theories. For Tatian, despite his inherent divine spark, man is unable to choose the good without divine aid (by the Spirit acting through the prophets). He seems to see unaided man as naturally inclining downwards into sin.[68] Justin, however, through his spermatic logos theory, already places divine aid within man's grasp in the form of the seminal word.[69]

What is significant, in the light of the emphasis Justin and Tatian place on their 'Christian Philosophy', is the fact that free will was also an issue with which their contemporaries within hellenistic philosophy were grappling.

The same is also true of demonology. Both Justin and Tatian have prominent demonologies that play an important part in their thought. The concept of 'demon', which they share, can be traced back to two roots, the first being Greek, and the second Semitic. As we shall see in Chapter 4, hellenistic philosophers understood a daemon to fulfil several different functions: for some 'daemon' was the word used to describe the souls of the deceased; for others daemons acted as messengers, carrying supplications from men to the divine, and oracles down; whilst for others still the daemons corresponded to the gods of Graeco-Roman religion.

In Greek thought, daemons are not inherently evil; they are merely supernatural beings, and occupy a neutral position that allows them to act in ways that we might subjectively consider 'good' or 'evil'. However, it must have been convenient for our apologists that one understanding of the term 'daemon' equated these supernatural beings with pagan gods, and by incorporating the negative meaning of 'demon' found within most streams of Judaism, they could turn the Greek concept to a purely negative sense.[70] Inevitably, implicit in this negative understanding of the word is a rejection of Graeco-Roman religion, and both Justin and Tatian make full use of this.[71]

Hellenized Jewish writers (e.g. Philo) used the concept of 'demon' in broadly the same way as the Greeks, whilst others, assuming a negative connotation of the concept, preferred the notion of a purely evil spirit. The existence of demons was explained in various ways: in 1 *Enoch* 6:15–16 these evil beings resulted from the intercourse of angels with women; in 2 *Enoch* 29:4 f they are the product of an angelic fall; in the *Life of Adam* 12–17, they are angels who have rebelled through jealousy over man's status; according to *b. Sanh.* 109a, they are the souls who were punished for their involvement in building the tower of Babel; and finally in *Aboth* 5:6 and *Midrash Rabbah, Genesis* 7,5,5d, such evil beings were specifically created by God.[72]

In his second *Apology* Justin gives an account explaining the existence of demons, which is very similar to the account in 1 *Enoch* 6; he states that angels were appointed to look after mankind, but abused this position by begetting children, the demons, on human women.[73]

Tatian's explanation for the existence of demons differs from that of Justin; where Justin sees demons as the offspring of fallen angels and human women, Tatian understands them to be the fallen angels themselves. In this Tatian follows a tradition that is also present in Philo; Philo understands angels and demons, as well as souls, to belong to the same class of being.[74] However, on the whole Tatian's perception of demons is more negative than that of Philo, and in

Tatian a figure appears who is almost entirely responsible for the fall:

> Then came one who was cleverer than the rest because he was first-born, and men and angels followed along with him and proclaimed as god the traitor to God's law ... Because of his transgression and rebellion the first-born was appointed a demon, along with those who had followed his example.[75]

This figure is presumably an angel, since he is later appointed a 'demon', and it seems likely that he fulfils a Satan-type role.[76] This concept is not developed further in Tatian, although we do find a similar figure in Justin.[77]

There is one last correlation between the demonologies of Justin and Tatian which I shall outline here. In Chapter 18, Tatian uses a metaphor which he says originates from Justin:

> The most admirable Justin was right in pronouncing that demons are like bandits, for just as bandits are in the habit of taking men prisoner and then releasing them to their families on payment, so too those supposed gods visit men's bodies and then in dreams create an impression of their presence and order their victims to come forward in sight of all. When they have enjoyed the eulogies they fly away from the sick, terminate the disease they have contrived, and restore men to their previous state.[78]

Although Justin does not use this metaphor in his extant works, from Tatian's claim it seems likely that he did use it elsewhere. The fact that Tatian seems to cite Justin at all is very significant in establishing the relationship between Tatian and his master; the existence of this passage shows an awareness of Justin's work, and is solid evidence of the connection between Justin and Tatian.

There is a great deal more that Justin and Tatian have to say independently about demons. Since I shall return to consider Tatian's demonology in Chapter 5, it is unnecessary for me to repeat that material here. Both Justin and Tatian present a great quantity of material about demons and, whilst their ideas may diverge in several places, it is clear that demonology was a live issue for them.

Both Justin and Tatian also make use of the philosophical

concept of the Logos. The concept of the Logos, which most commonly means 'Reason' or 'Word', originated within Stoicism, and was also taken on by some Platonists.[79] However, Christian writers as early as the author of the *Fourth Gospel* had already appropriated the Logos, and so we should probably associate Justin and Tatian's use of the term with the Logos tradition already present within Christianity, rather than tracing it directly to hellenistic philosophy.[80]

Before I proceed to compare Tatian's concept of the Logos with that of Justin, it is important to justify such a comparison, since both use the concept in different ways. Tatian uses the concept of the 'Logos' to explain the divine act of creation, just as he uses God's spirit as the power responsible for prophetic activity.[81] Both Logos and spirit have specific roles and functions for Tatian. Justin, however, uses a variety of terms to describe how God acts amongst mankind, and these would seem to be interchangeable:

> I shall now show from the Scriptures that God has begotten of Himself a certain rational Power as a Beginning before all other creatures. The Holy Spirit indicates this Power by various titles, sometimes the Glory of the Lord, at other times Son, or Wisdom, or Angel, or God, or Lord, or Word ... Indeed, He [i.e. the Power] can justly lay claim to all these titles from the fact both that He performs the Father's will and that He was begotten by an act of the Father's will.[82]

In demonstrating the way in which this Power was begotten Justin uses the metaphors of speech and fire, which we also find in Tatian.[83] Although this is significant in itself, and I shall return to consider these metaphors shortly, I believe that this parallel use of metaphors also suggests that Tatian would have understood Justin's 'rational Power', with its multiplicity of titles, to be the same entity as his own 'Word'.

In both Justin and Tatian, the Logos becomes necessary because of their insistence on a transcendent God;[84] the Logos enables them to express divine immanence without compromising divine transcendence. The Middle Platonists we shall come across in the next chapter were also faced with this dilemma. They used several different ideas to express this immanence, only one of them being the Logos.[85] In Justin and Tatian, the Logos, or 'rational Power', is given the role of mediator between God and mankind. The Logos not only becomes the instrument of creation,[86] but also, in Justin, the means by which God communicates with mankind.[87]

In turning to consider the precise relationship between God and his Logos we are once again confronted by the metaphors of speech and fire, which are used by both our apologists to express how the Logos came into being. In *Dial* 61, Justin writes:

> But does not something similar happen also with us humans? When we utter a word, it can be said that we beget the word, but not by cutting off, in the sense that our power of uttering words would thereby be diminished. We can observe a similar example in nature when one fire kindles another, without losing anything, but remaining the same, yet the enkindled fire seems to exist of itself and to shine without lessening the brilliancy of the first fire.[88]

Meanwhile, in Chapter 5 of his *Oration*, Tatian writes:

> He [i.e. the Word] came into being by partition, not by section, for what is severed is separated from its origin, but what has been partitioned takes on a distinctive function and does not diminish the source from which it has been taken. Just as many fires may be kindled from one torch, but the light of the first torch is not diminished because of the kindling of the many, so also the Word coming forth from the power of the Father does not deprive the begetter of the power of rational speech. I speak and you hear: yet surely when I address you I am not myself deprived of speech through transmission of speech, but by projecting my voice my purpose is to set in order the disorderly matter in you. Just as the Word begotten in the beginning in turn begot our creation by fabricating matter for himself, so I too, in imitation of the Word, having been begotten again and obtained understanding of the truth am bringing to order the confusion in kindred matter.[89]

These metaphors are very similar indeed, and perhaps if they were unique to Justin and Tatian we would be forced to conclude direct influence. However, these metaphors can be found elsewhere; they are used by Philo,[90] Tertullian,[91] and also by the Neopythagorean philosopher Numenius of Apamea.[92] Whilst the use of these metaphors in Justin and Tatian is not sufficient to prove direct dependence, the increasing weight of accumulative evidence suggests that Tatian was influenced by Justin in his inclusion of them. In fact, I strongly suspect that these metaphors had been handed down to Tatian as part of the Christian philosophical tradition.

However, there is a vital difference between Justin's treatment of the Logos and that of Tatian; in the *Oration* the Logos remains as the agent of creation and appears to have no further contact with man, but Justin speaks of the Logos becoming incarnate in Christ.[93] It is, of course, difficult to reach any firm conclusions about Tatian's understanding of the relationship between the Logos and Christ, since his allusions to Christ are rather sparse in the *Oration*, and the evidence presented here clearly does not offer a full picture of Tatian's theology.[94] It is possible that the genre of the *Oration* and its intended audience may have been a factor in Tatian's exclusion of Christological themes.

We now move on to consider another aspect of our apologists' Logos theology; the spermatic logos. Justin's spermatic logos theory was something of an innovation. We can find antecedents for this theory in Stoicism,[95] Middle Platonism,[96] and especially in Philo,[97] but Justin's interpretation was something quite new.

Justin believed that whilst Christ encapsulated the whole Logos, all men possessed within them a seed of the divine logos. It was this spermatic logos that he believed enabled philosophers of the past to see the truth in part.[98] What was new about Justin's concept of the spermatic logos was that it combined a spiritual interpretation with the notion that its existence within man provided a glimpse of divine realities. Meanwhile, his understanding of Christ as the Logos who reveals the whole truth to man makes Justin's theory unmistakably Christian.[99]

For our current concern of comparing Justin and Tatian, the key question is whether there is any hint of Justin's distinctive spermatic logos theory in Tatian. The answer may be held in some of the most problematic passages of his *Oration*.

In Chapter 12, Tatian speaks of two different kinds of spirit; the soul, or material spirit, and the divine spirit, which is the 'image and likeness' of God. In the beginning men were endowed with both, but at the fall the divine spirit abandoned the soul, leaving only a spark (ἔναυσμα) of the spirit's power with man.[100] As we saw in Chapter 2, Grant has suggested that this term contains gnostic overtones, but could Tatian's 'spark' not rather be related to the divine 'seed' of Justin's spermatic logos theory?

Unfortunately, Tatian's precise understanding of ἔναυσμα is

rather ambiguous. The word occurs only once in Chapter 13 of the *Oration*, and does not appear to be a technical term, as it is introduced somewhat hesitantly by 'as it were' (ὥσπερ). If we turn to consider Tatian's soteriology, we find something even more bemusing. Tatian's theory of salvation revolves entirely around the prophetic revelation of knowledge of God (or the truth) and the consequent bestowal of the divine spirit. His theory has nothing whatsoever to do with possession of a divine spark; without direct aid from the spirit, men incline down towards matter, presumably with the divine spark in tow.[101]

If man's 'spark' is made entirely redundant in Tatian's system, why does he include it at all?[102] Could Tatian's 'spark' be a reflection of Justin's spermatic logos theory, weakened by his strong emphasis on man's helplessness without the more direct intervention of God through prophecy? Such an explanation is certainly possible.

Finally, we turn to consider how our two apologists viewed the beginning and end of the world. Both Justin and Tatian give only brief outlines of their cosmologies. Justin cites the creation account in *Genesis* in both the first *Apology* and the *Dialogue*. In the first *Apology* he uses the Biblical account to prove that Plato plagiarized from Moses,[103] whilst in the *Dialogue* he uses *Genesis* 1:26–28 to argue for the existence of the Logos.[104] Clearly Justin's reference to *Genesis* in these two instances is necessitated by his line of argument, and tells us very little about the position of Scripture in his cosmology.

However, Justin also speaks of God forming the world out of shapeless matter,[105] and of God 'ordering' the world,[106] which suggests philosophical influence. This impression is strengthened by his understanding of the generation of the Logos and its function as agent of creation, which we noted earlier. Although Justin uses the Biblical creation account in his cosmology, his understanding of creation appears to be grounded within Middle Platonic philosophy.[107]

The cosmology that Tatian presents in his *Oration*, meanwhile, displays no direct dependence upon the Biblical account, and seems to revolve instead around philosophical concepts. Since I shall be looking at Tatian's cosmology in greater depth in Chapter 5, I will only mention those elements directly relevant to a comparison with Justin here.

As we saw earlier in discussing the Logos, Tatian uses the same metaphor as Justin in articulating the generation of the Logos and its involvement in creation. Furthermore, in Tatian we find a more explicit description of creation as an ordering of matter.[108] However, in his cosmology Tatian goes one step beyond his master in that he conceives of a creation out of nothing.[109]

If we turn to consider eschatology, we find further points of contact between Tatian and his master. Both Justin and Tatian believe that there will be a day of judgement,[110] and that when this time comes a physical resurrection will occur.[111] They also both believe that there will be a final conflagration to mark the end of the world.[112]

However, there are also some significant distinctions between the eschatologies of Justin and Tatian. Justin's eschatology is, in fact, quite complex, and we find several apparently conflicting elements; Justin repeatedly states his belief in the two advents of Christ,[113] yet elsewhere expresses millenarian views.[114] Furthermore, in his *Apologies*, Justin's emphasis would appear to be on the individual,[115] which may again reflect philosophical influence, since this is also the emphasis found within Middle Platonism. As Barnard has pointed out, these concepts are not necessarily contradictory providing that they are understood in contextual terms,[116] and they lend Justin's eschatology a richness that is missing in Tatian's.

Tatian's eschatology displays none of the apocalypticism of Justin; it is, once again, a primarily philosophical presentation. As we shall see, Tatian's understanding of salvation revolves entirely around the individual, and he appears to make no distinction between realized and future concepts of eschatology.

The areas of cosmology and eschatology are inevitably interwoven; origins and endings seem to go hand in hand. Yet what is interesting as regards 'placing' Tatian in the second century is the tendency of various groups within early Christianity to gravitate towards either cosmology or eschatology; the Valentinians and other gnostic-type groups focused upon cosmology, whilst the Montanists appear to have concerned themselves more with apocalypticism and the descent of the heavenly Jerusalem upon Pepuza.[117] Justin and Tatian seem to belong somewhere in the middle of this spectrum; they both give brief descriptions of their cosmology, and proceed to focus primarily upon eschatology and salvation theories. Clear philosophical influences can also be traced in the cosmologies and eschatologies of both writers.

Conclusion : the extent of Justin's influence upon Tatian

Partly in response to Grant's methodology in assessing Tatian's relationship with Valentinianism, my focus in this study has not been on the use of parallel terms in Justin and Tatian. Instead I have concentrated on more general correlations in attitude and thought in an attempt to present a more rounded and accurate picture of the relationship between Justin and Tatian.

The number of parallels between Justin and Tatian's *Oration* are, in fact, considerable. Although the parallels may not be sufficient individually to prove direct influence, I believe that the weight of accumulative evidence strongly suggests that Justin exerted a substantial amount of influence over his pupil. At any rate, Tatian certainly has more in common with his master than he does with the Valentinians, and I believe that some of Tatian's purportedly 'Valentinian' tendencies can be explained in reference to his teacher.[118]

In the course of this chapter we have also repeatedly noticed the influence of hellenistic philosophy upon Justin and Tatian. Philosophy seems to be a key element in understanding the ideas of both writers, especially since both Justin and Tatian present the teachings of Christianity as a philosophy.[119] Clearly, the influence of philosophy needs to be investigated in depth if we are to place Tatian correctly within the second century, and so the next two chapters are devoted to examining Tatian's relationship with hellenistic philosophy, and the Christian philosophy that he and his master espoused.

4

TATIAN AND HELLENISTIC PHILOSOPHY

Tatian's relationship with hellenistic philosophy is an interesting issue, although it is also rather complicated. This is because, on the surface, Tatian is extremely hostile towards all things Greek in his *Oration*, and his hostility seems to leave no room for the kind of incorporation of philosophical terms that we find in Justin. However, as we have seen, Tatian clearly makes use of several philosophical concepts in his *Oration*. Thus the question that confronts us in considering Tatian's relationship with hellenistic philosophy is how he reconciles these apparently contradictory elements in his thought.

In the second century, hellenistic philosophy was part of a common heritage bequeathed upon well-born sons by the Graeco-Roman education system, and philosophy permeated the intellectual atmosphere of the second century in an almost popularized form. In assessing Tatian's relationship with hellenistic philosophy, it is therefore important to establish the kind of intellectual background to which Tatian would have been exposed. I intend to do this in the first section of this chapter by pointing up the kind of questions that second century philosophers were asking, and exploring how representatives of key philosophical schools were answering those questions in Tatian's time.[1] In doing this, I have only used those second century texts that have a bearing on issues discussed or implicit in Tatian.

Hellenistic philosophy in the second century

Middle Platonism

Disillusioned with conventional Greek piety, and heavily influenced by the Science and Mathematics of his day, Plato (427–348 BCE) developed a philosophical system that incorporated a need for morality and a sense of order with current mathematical principles. However, it is difficult to establish a consistent system of thought in Plato's work because he was constantly criticizing his own ideas and answering questions in fresh ways. There are many contradictions in his work, and Plato's followers reflect this diversity.

However, the most important Platonic concept for our period is Plato's theory of Ideas, which was interpreted in the second century as a theory of a higher plane of existence above the visible. The lower level was corporeal and changeable, belonging within space and time, and its quality of existence was that of 'Becoming' (i.e. it was generated). The higher level was non-corporeal and immutable, existing beyond spatial and temporal limits, and its quality of existence was that of 'Being' (i.e. it was ungenerated). The latter, Plato called the realm of intelligible Forms or Ideas; the true reality that the visible world merely mirrored. Whilst Plato's focus was primarily on the realm of Ideas, within Middle Platonism, the emphasis shifted to consider the relationship between the realm of Ideas and the created world. This shift in emphasis was probably due to an increasing interest amongst Platonists of this period in religious concerns.

In view of the emphasis Middle Platonists placed on the relationship between the realm of Ideas and the visible world, it should come as no surprise that Plato's cosmology was also of particular interest during this period. In the *Timaeus*, Plato describes in the form of a creation myth how a 'Demiurge' produced the lower world as an inevitably flawed reflection of the higher world. His concern in producing this myth was to suggest what was, in his view, the most likely explanation for why the world is as it is. It was not intended as a literal account of creation, but rather as a symbolic story, demonstrating what he considered to be the essential elements that make up the world. It was certainly not envisaged as a temporal creation, although, as we shall see, later Platonists were to interpret it in this way.

In his creation myth, Plato postulated three essential elements to the universe:

1   The Forms or Ideas, which present the pattern from which all things are modelled.
2   The Mind, which is mythologized in the *Timaeus* as the Demiurge. The Mind is the ordering force, which takes the chaotic third element and imposes Form upon it.

3   The chaotic material upon which the Mind imposes Form. Essentially this element is completely irrational, constantly moving in a disorderly manner. Because it receives the imprint of the Forms, Plato called this element the 'Receptacle' or 'Nurse of Becoming'.

The Middle Platonist movement belongs to the time between the first century BCE and the start of the third century CE. As we shall see, prior to our period Platonism was marked by a strong scepticism. Middle Platonists moved away from this towards a more dogmatic position, and tended to concentrate on metaphysics and theology. However, there is no standard for the doctrines of Middle Platonism; Middle Platonists held widely divergent views. Yet their attention was focused on particular questions.

The nature and activity of the supreme principle became an important issue in this period. A transcendent God was sometimes equated with the Platonic higher world, and Plato's Ideas were sometimes understood to be thoughts in God's mind. For some Middle Platonists the Demiurge of the *Timaeus* became a second, active God; for others the Demiurge merged with the Stoic Logos and became the active divine element involved with the world, thus providing a function of immanence for the transcendent (and passive) first principle above. For others still, Plato's world soul provided a further divine element.

Daemons were also entities much discussed in this period; they were subordinate beings, capable of good and evil, who permeated the cultural system of the Graeco-Roman world. The Middle Platonists tended to see them either as permanent, static beings who were intermediaries between God and man, or as the souls of men oscillating between the two qualities of existence. Following Stoic, and in particular Chrysippus', insistence on determinism, the question of the relationship between free will and providence also became important within Middle Platonism.

The solutions to these questions differed widely among the Middle Platonists, but the basic questions remained the same. Perhaps part of the reason why they held such different views was the wealth of material with which they were faced. Besides Plato's own openness to interpretation, Platonists of this period also borrowed widely from other schools; Platonists were often drawn either to Stoicism or to Peripateticism, and Pythagoreanism also became an influence, making its presence most keenly felt within Neopythagoreanism – a movement that we shall consider shortly, and which some scholars would group with Platonism.

There are five important figures representing Middle Platonism in the second century. These are Plutarch, Atticus, Alcinous, Apuleius, and Maximus of Tyre.

Based in Chaeroneia in Boeotia, Plutarch (c.45–125 CE) wrote prolifically, and not only on philosophy. He wrote a series of biographies[2] and a number of philosophical and reflective essays, collected today under the title of *Moralia*.[3] For my purposes here, only a handful of essays in the *Moralia* are relevant: *Isis and Osiris*; *The E at Delphi*; *The Obsolescence of Oracles*; *On Moral Virtue*; *On the Sign of Socrates*; Book Nine of *Tabletalk*; *On the Face in the Moon*; and *Concerning the Procreation of the Soul as Discoursed in Timaeus*.

The key to understanding Plutarch's philosophy is to remember that he presents a truly pluralistic vision of religion, mingled with a strong dualism and a keen interest in etymology and mathematical symbolism.

Like all Platonists of this period, Plutarch is concerned with the question of the nature and activity of the divine. His supreme being evidences all of the transcendent characteristics of a God conceived of in Platonic terms. God is the Good, and he is One.[4] God is Being, and is therefore eternal and immutable, belonging outside of time.[5] Yet Plutarch also seems to reconcile the Platonic concept of a Monadic supreme being with his belief in the existence of the traditional gods. He does this partly by introducing a class of 'demigods', who are equivalent to the gods in Homer and in Egyptian myth, but he clearly perceives a higher class of gods that belong within the sphere of the supreme being.[6]

To permit mediation between his transcendent God and man, Plutarch uses daemons to act as go-betweens. Plutarch's demonology is complex, and may even seem contradictory. As we have seen, he presents a class of demigods, properly called 'daemons', and these function as intermediaries – an 'interpretative and ministering class' – who convey supplications upwards and oracles downwards.[7]

Elsewhere Plutarch says that daemons are disembodied souls, yet he also speaks of guardian daemons attached to individual souls.[8] Perhaps we should not understand 'daemon' in Plutarch's system to refer to a specific category of entity, but rather as a wide-ranging term for those whose qualitative existence is somewhere between the corporeal and the divine.

Returning to the question of divine immanence, we find that this is also expressed in *Isis and Osiris* by the figure of Osiris, who seems to represent the Logos.[9] The Logos' chief function here would seem to be in expressing Plutarch's cosmogony. The creation of the world is described in *Isis and Osiris* in the form of a myth, using the figures of Osiris as Logos, Isis as matter or nature, and Horus, their offspring, as the created result.[10] Plutarch also expresses these figures in terms of two of the elements Plato envisaged the universe to be composed of. Osiris corresponds to the Form, which is imposed upon matter, and Isis to matter itself, the 'Nurse' or 'Receptacle'.[11]

There are other demigods described in this myth, but the only other key figure is Typhon. Typhon is a mischief maker, and is presented in direct opposition to Osiris.[12] He represents everything that is harmful and destructive in nature, providing Plutarch's dualistic system with an evil principle. Typhon's existence is necessary because Plutarch understands God to be Good, and therefore incapable of producing evil.[13] Thus Plutarch argues that nature, the pre-existent matter, must have contained evil from the start.[14] The conclusion of this line of thought is the introduction of a disorderly world soul, whose inclination towards chaos opposes the divine intention for order.[15] If we turn to Plato's three elements, we find that in fact Typhon corresponds to the disorderly motion present within matter. Plutarch is the first philosopher to propose such an entity, and seems to have derived the existence of a disorderly world soul from his interpretation of Plato.[16]

Thus the disorderly world soul was present within pre-existent matter, and entered the world at creation. Here we come across another new development in Plutarch's thought; the temporal creation of the world. He takes Plato's creation myth in the *Timaeus*, and seems to translate it into a reality.[17] Repeatedly Plutarch appeals to Plato for these innovative ideas, highlighting just how open Plato's works are to diverse interpretations.

Plutarch's psychology is also rather interesting. His composition of man is not unusual; he separates body from soul, and divides the soul itself into rational and irrational, identifying the rational part as Intellect and asserting that the rational should rule the irrational.[18] Where Plutarch seems to differ from convention is in placing the rational part of man, or his Intellect, outside of the human body. For Plutarch, a man's rational self, the part that contains the essential identity of self, is only partially resident within the human body. He describes the Intellect as a 'buoy' attached to a man's head and supporting as much of the soul 'as is obedient and not overpowered by the passions'.[19] This rational part of man float-ing externally is in fact what Plutarch terms a man's daemon.

After death, man's soul is freed from the body, and his fate depends upon his obedience to his daemon during life. Plutarch believed that man went through a series of reincarnations until the soul (by which I think he means the rational soul) reached a point where contact with one's daemon was possible.[20] Then a process of divinization began.

Plutarch tells us that after death good souls are conveyed, along with their mind, to the moon.[21] Then a second separation occurs between mind and soul;[22] the soul is left to dissolve into the moon as the body dissolves into the earth, and the mind moves forward alone to the sun, which is evidently intended to be the divine. The whole process can then begin again when the sun sows mind into the moon, which, cementing the divine and the corporeal, produces new soul-bodies, endowed with daemons.[23]

Finally, Plutarch also attempted to deal with the free will/ providence issue. According to Book Nine of *Table Talk*, he envis-ages a combination of destiny and free will; men are free to choose the course of their lives, but destiny is the force that allows a good life to those who choose correctly, and a bad life to those who choose incorrectly.[24]

Atticus (*c*.140–185 CE) was the leader of Platonism in Athens during the latter part of the second century, and may have been the first Chair of Platonic Philosophy, which was set up in 176 CE by Marcus Aurelius. His only surviving work is an anti-Peripatetic work preserved in Eusebius, although Proclus records Porphyry's criticism of Atticus' commentary on the *Timaeus*, from which Atticus' philosophy can also be gleaned. Various other smaller frag-ments have also been identified.[25]

Our knowledge of Atticus' philosophy is necessarily biased, since our main source is his polemical tract against the Peripatetics. Thus his prime concern seems to be to deny any Aristotelianisms in Pla-tonism, resulting in a shift towards Stoicism not present to the same extent in his predecessors.

However, Atticus inevitably retains the Platonic idea of a transcendent God, and equates the Demiurge of the *Timaeus* with the Good.[26] He also seems to push this supreme God above Plato's realm of Ideas; Proclus records Atticus' reasoning that if the Demi-urge is encompassed by the Intelligible Living Being (i.e. the realm of Ideas) he cannot be perfect, since the partial living beings are imperfect. Yet if the Demiurge is not encompassed, the realm of

Ideas is not absolute; Atticus therefore concludes that the supreme God must belong beyond this realm.[27]

If the transcendent supreme God belongs not only above the visible world but also above the realm of Ideas, intermediary powers are even more important within Atticus' system. In a stoicized understanding of the world soul, Atticus explains how nature and providence combine, in the notion of a cosmic soul, to order matter.[28] In his cosmogony, Atticus sets forward the idea that before the creation of the cosmos, disorderly matter existed, along with a disorderly soul (the disorderly world soul of Plutarch), and he also seems to claim, along with Plutarch, a temporal beginning of the cosmos.[29]

Atticus' psychology, meanwhile, is rather more difficult to decipher, since he seems to offer slightly contradictory accounts: in his anti-Aristotelian work Atticus seems to claim that the soul is entirely immortal,[30] yet Proclus records that Atticus held only the rational part of the soul to be immortal.[31] Dillon suggests that these two views need not be mutually exclusive, since Atticus' assertion that the soul is immortal is primarily a polemic against the Aristotelian notion that only the Intellect is immortal, and should therefore be perceived as a radical representation of Atticus' views.[32]

Finally, we do come across the issue of providence in Atticus when he grapples with Aristotle in his anti-Peripatetic work. He argues against Aristotle's rejection of providence, and claims that God's providence is an active element in the world.[33]

Alcinous is our third Middle Platonist. Although formerly identified with Albinus,[34] modern scholarship is now moving towards a separation of these two figures.[35] We know very little about Alcinous, and so scholars have been unable to date Alcinous' life any more precisely than to the second century. However, his one extant work, *The Handbook of Platonism*, is extremely useful for my purposes here; it gives clear, concise summaries of Middle Platonic doctrine on a whole range of topics.

Alcinous' divine principle is, not surprisingly, an absolutely transcendent being. God is entirely above human forms of classification,[36] and thus it is difficult for men to contemplate him. However, Alcinous presents three methods through which man can conceive of God:

1   Through abstraction; by considering the attributes of God, and what he is not, some sort of understanding about his nature can be reached.[37]

2 Through analogy; by comparing the relationships between perceived things and God, man can begin to grasp God's relationship with the world.[38]

3 Through intuition; by contemplating perceptible versions of
divine attributes, one's intellect is led to a perception of the
divine, thus presenting a more direct path between man and
God.[39]

These methods entail a kind of translation of heavenly things into
earthly, visible terms, which can then be understood by men. God's
immanence is barely expressed within Alcinous' thought, and this
'translation' of the heavenly to the earthly would seem to be the
only way in which man can relate to God.

Not surprisingly, many of the attributes that Alcinous assigns to
his supreme God are familiar ones; God is the Good, he is incorporeal and unchanging, eternal, ineffable and perfect.[40] He also
describes God as the Beautiful, Truth and Father.[41] Alcinous clearly
speaks of the Forms of the higher realm as 'eternal and perfect
thoughts of God'.[42] We also come across Aristotelian influence in
Alcinous' appropriation of Aristotle's unmoved mover, and in his
talk of potentialities.[43]

God's immanence is not expressed by a 'Logos' power in Alcinous' thought. God himself is directly responsible for creating the
world, bringing order to pre-existent disorderly matter and model-
ling it on the realm of Ideas.[44] Alcinous delegates the creation of
man and the other earthly creatures to the 'created gods' (alterna-
tively termed 'daemons'), removing his transcendent divine principle from direct interaction with man, and thus satisfying the need
for space between corporeal and incorporeal inherent in Platonic
concepts of God.[45]

Alcinous emphatically rejects the notions, found in Plutarch and
Atticus, of a temporal creation of the world and a disorderly world
soul moving against God. For Alcinous the world is constantly in a
state of 'becoming', and the world soul is ordered by God.[46]

Alcinous understood man to be constructed of four main parts;
body, irrational 'appetitive' soul, irrational 'spirited' soul, and a
rational, immortal soul.[47] Each part of the soul had a particular
position in the body; to prevent contamination the rational soul
resided in the head, whilst the irrational 'spirited' soul (which produces emotions such as anger) belonged to the heart, and the irrational 'appetitive' soul to the lower abdomen, particularly the
liver.[48] The daemons were responsible for producing the irrational

parts of the soul, whilst the supreme God contributes the rational, immortal part. Punishment for men who failed to control their irrational parts was reincarnation, first into the body of a woman, and then into that of a wild animal, whilst the reward for those whose rational soul did achieve dominance was a return to their 'kindred star', which God had originally assigned to each soul at creation.[49]

On the problem of free will versus providence, Alcinous attempts to reconcile free will with fate by introducing the Aristotelian concept of potentialities. He argues that fate works as a consequence of an individual's action; an individual can choose to do something, incorporating the idea of free will, but what follows that action is essentially fated.[50] Alcinous therefore argues that before an action is taken, there are two potential 'fates'; the true and the false.

Our fourth figure representing Middle Platonism in the second century is Apuleius of Madaura (c.123–161 CE). He was primarily a rhetorician, whose subsequent education at Athens brought him into contact with philosophy. Several of his works survive, his most famous being the *Metamorphoses* (Changes of Shape), perhaps better known as the *Golden Ass*. This novel, along with two philosophical treatises, *On the God of Socrates* and *Plato and his Doctrine*, are the only works of direct relevance here.[51] The latter is essentially a handbook of Middle Platonism in the same vein as that of Alcinous, and so is once more especially useful for my purposes in this chapter.

The way in which Apuleius confronts the questions of divine nature and activity is somewhat different to that of the Middle Platonists we have encountered so far. He divides divinity into three classes of gods. The first is the transcendent supreme God of Platonism.[52] He is described as incorporeal and infinite, One, and ineffable and invisible.[53] He is also lord and author of everything, the creator and craftsman of all, and father and architect of the divine world.[54] Apuleius also presents a chasm between God and man that can only be traversed with difficulty, and he may conceive of the Ideas as thoughts in the supreme God's mind, since he speaks of them as the model that God used for things present and future.[55]

The second class of divinity that Apuleius envisages is that of the celestial gods, which he evidently equates with planetary and astral powers.[56] These gods are incorporeal, eternal, and good, and are separated from man through the intervention of the third class of gods.[57] The third class is a step further from the supreme God towards man, and these gods perform an intermediary role, and would seem to be daemons; Apuleius says that there are intermediary divine powers, called 'daemons' by the Greeks, who convey men's prayers up and their rewards and punishments down.[58] Thus for Apuleius the daemons perform the function of divine immanence, and the hierarchy of divinity actually shifts down to include them as a third class of gods. The direct intervention of these intermediary gods is very clearly expressed in narrative form at the end of Apuleius' novel the *Golden Ass*, when Isis intervenes to return Lucius to his natural human form.[59]

The nature of Apuleius' daemons is likewise halfway between God and man. He speaks of five characteristics of daemons; they are animated beings, possessing a rational mind and feelings, an aerial body, and an eternal existence. The latter of these they share in common with God, the first three with man, and the fourth, an aerial body, belongs to them alone.[60]

Apuleius also identifies some daemons as the souls of men, and distinguishes three types of daemon:

1   The human soul within the body.
2   The human soul after it has left the body.
3   Daemons liberated permanently from the body.[61]

Apuleius assigns this third type of daemon to each man as a witness and guardian, watching every action and thought, like the conscience. It is the job of a man's daemon to condemn or acquit a man during judgement, depending upon that man's actions during life.[62] Although Apuleius presents the daemons in an intermediary role, carrying messages from God to man and *vice versa*, he is clearly not concerned to protect God from contact with the world during creation. Matter, for Apuleius, is pre-existent and raw, capable of receiving the forms and being shaped by God. In his section on 'two essences', Apuleius conceives of creation as the organisation of matter by God.[63]

On the question of whether creation was temporal or not, Apuleius seems to admit that it was, but adds that because God was responsible for its generation the world is therefore essentially permanent.[64] Meanwhile, Apuleius' world soul does not seem to have been a disorderly soul within pre-existent matter at all, since he speaks of it as the oldest of all things that have been born.[65] Furthermore, he describes the world soul as perfectly good and wise, animated by an eternal and spontaneous movement, and moving other immobile and inert natures itself.[66]

We have already come across Apuleius' anthropology in part whilst discussing daemons, since for Apuleius the souls of men were daemons. Man's soul is therefore immortal,[67] and he divides the soul into three parts, the same three parts in fact that we have already encountered in Alcinous:

1   The rational principle, which is situated in the head and rules the other two parts of the soul, and also the body.
2   The irrational emotional principle, positioned in the heart.
3   The irrational passionate and appetitive principle, which is baser than the other irrational principle, and belongs within the lower abdomen.[68]

It is possible to draw some further conclusions about Apuleius' understanding of man; if the rational part of the soul rules the rest, a man's soul would seem to be termed a 'good daemon'; if a man's soul is bad (i.e. not ruled by its rational part), it is punished by being refused a home and forced to wander in exile.[69] Beyond this, Apuleius does not seem concerned to explore the state of man and his relationship with the divine.

Apuleius does turn to the issue of providence, but actually seems to deny man's autonomy. He defines providence as divine thought acting on the world, and destiny as the means by which that divine thought is accomplished, a divine law.[70] Free will is not a consideration here.

Our final Middle Platonist is Maximus of Tyre (c.125–195 CE). Very little is known about Maximus, other than that he travelled to Rome at least twice, and lectured there during the reign of Commodus (c.180–191 CE). His one surviving work is a collection of 41 discourses, *The Philosophical Orations*, which are primarily concerned with ethics but also touch on theology and psychology. For my purposes here, only six of the *Orations* are of interest; *Oration* 5 – *Whether one should pray*; *Orations* 8 and 9 – *On the Daemon of Socrates*; *Oration* 10 – *On Learning and Recollection*; *Oration* 11 – *Who is God according to Plato?*; and *Oration* 41 – *Good being the work of God, whence comes evil?*

In *Oration* 11, Maximus presents us with Middle Platonic interpretations of God. He opens this *Oration* by stressing the difficulties involved in exploring the divine nature. His God is transcendent and monadic, and although he refers to God as father and creator, Maximus seems to perceive the Supreme Being primarily in relationship to man. Thus God is described as the perfect intellect, and the relationship between the divine intellect and its kindred element in man (i.e. the soul) is probed.[71]

Despite his references to God as father and creator, Maximus does not outline any cosmological theories, and so we have no idea of how the process of creation could have been achieved without breaching the transcendence of Maximus' God. However, in his final *Oration*, which deals with the problem of evil, Maximus seems to describe the process of creation as a Platonic ordering of pre-existent matter by a 'good Craftsman'.[72]

In the last few sections of *Oration* 11 Maximus goes on to consider man's search for knowledge of God in greater depth, and in so doing seems to reflect a tradition that we have already come across in Alcinous. For Maximus, the initial step towards exploring the divine nature would seem to be contemplation of God's works and worship of his offspring, the heavenly bodies and daemons; he claims that something of God can be seen in the beauty of the created world because God is the source of this beauty.[73]

However, Maximus believes that a higher level of perception is possible, and describes how, by distancing itself from the 'things below' and using Reason, the human intellect can reach out beyond the corporeal and grasp something of the divine. It is the soul's intimate connection with God that enables this level of understanding to be reached.[74]

At the end of *Oration* 11, Maximus describes how a hierarchy of beings exists between God and man.[75] These beings are daemons, and perform an intermediary function. In *Orations* 8 and 9, Maximus gives a fairly lengthy account of the position and nature of daemons. According to Maximus, daemons belong to a race of secondary immortal beings, who exist between earth and heaven. The daemons are less powerful than God but more powerful than men, and so act as servants to the divine and as overseers to men. It is the daemons who communicate with men on behalf of the gods.[76]

In exploring the nature of daemons, Maximus explains why they are able to act as intermediaries. He divides all ensouled beings into five categories: emotionless and immortal, immortal and emotional, emotional and mortal, irrational and capable of perception, and ensouled but incapable of perception. He believes God to be emotionless and immortal, daemons immortal and emotional, men emotional and mortal, animals irrational and capable of perception, and plants ensouled but incapable of perception. It is the shared properties of immortality and susceptibility to emotion that, according to Maximus, make communication between the daemons and God, and the daemons and man possible.[77]

Maximus then goes on to consider why the daemons are immortal, and reveals his belief that daemons are disembodied souls who, freed from the body, are able to perceive the divine. They rejoice in their new level of existence but feel pity for those souls still trapped within the corporeal, and so seek to help them.[78]

Maximus' understanding of man is hinted at in several of his *Orations*. He gives only two divisions to man, body and soul, although he may have envisaged a further division to the soul, since in *Oration* 11 he says that only the best part of the soul is capable of understanding God whilst in the body.[79] However, he does seem to claim that the whole soul is immortal, so this distinction may be false.[80] Maximus has a high estimation of the soul; as we have seen, he perceives the essence of the soul to be a diminished form of the divine Intellect.[81]

Maximus' understanding of the body, meanwhile, is surprisingly negative; it is presented as a hindrance to the vision and comprehension of the soul. At death the soul is freed to perceive divine truths, and life within the body is described by Maximus as a dream.[82]

Finally, Maximus also attempts to tackle the issue of providence and free will. In *Oration* 5 he affirms the existence of providence, destiny and fortune, without really defining these terms or explaining how they influence men.[83] Meanwhile, in *Oration* 41 he strongly asserts the existence of free will and even claims that man's free will is partly responsible for the existence of evil in the world.[84]

However, in *Oration* 13 Maximus seems to attempt to reconcile these apparently conflicting elements in his thought. This *Oration* is concerned with justifying the existence of free will in the face of the reality of divine prophecy. Maximus' basic argument is that prophecy binds the autonomy of man to the workings of fate, and to illustrate this point uses the interesting imagery of a slave who, of his own free will, chooses to follow his captors.[85]

Neopythagoreanism

The term 'Pythagoreanism' is used to denote the lifestyle and doctrines attributed to Pythagoras (*c*.550–500 BCE). We have very little reliable information about the earliest stages of the movement, but Pythagoras' 'school' would seem to have been a way of life rather than a philosophical institution. We also know that mathematics was of great interest to early Pythagoreans, and that Plato was influenced by them in this.

In the first century CE there was a revival of the Pythagorean school (which is often called Neopythagoreanism), although in fact these philosophers took much of their philosophy from Plato, claiming that he had been a pupil of Pythagoras and that he was himself a Pythagorean. Thus Neopythagoreanism is essentially a branch of Platonism, which is distinguished only by a greater concern with religious matters and a deep reverence for numbers.

Numenius of Apamea (c.150–200 CE) is the most notable Neopythagorean of the second century. He seems to accept Plato as a follower of Pythagoras, incorporating Platonic concepts into his avowedly Pythagorean system. Numenius' treatise *On the Unfaithfulness of the Academy to Plato*, although also containing criticisms of other schools, points up a dissatisfaction with developments of Plato's thought, and he clearly feels that he is presenting the true Platonist/Pythagorean view. Of his works, *On the Unfaithfulness of the Academy to Plato*, *On the Good*, *On the Secrets of Plato*, and *On the Incorruptibility of the Soul* are extant in rather fragmentary form, whilst some of his ideas are recorded by such figures as Porphyry and Proclus.[86]

Numenius does seem to take on board Plato's theory of Ideas,[87] but is evidently more preoccupied with the related concepts of Being and Becoming.[88] Numenius divides the divine into three, the first being the Supreme God, the second the Demiurge, and the third a lower aspect of the Demiurge.

The first God is Being, and again we come across Platonic terminology in describing this transcendent God. He is the Good and he is One; as Being, he is eternal, immutable, and identical, and he is also Intellect. Numenius does not present his first God in terms of an Aristotelian 'unmoved mover', but rather as a stationary being whose stability is reliant on its inner motion.[89] This first God is turned inwards, concentrating entirely on himself, and cannot therefore be divided; nor can he be involved in the work of creation, although Numenius does describe him as the 'father' of the Demiurge.[90]

It is the second God, the Demiurge, who is responsible for creation, and in his involvement with matter, the Demiurge is divided to provide Numenius with a third God. Numenius uses the analogy of the relationship between a farmer who plants the seeds and the cultivator who tends them to express his understanding of the relationship between the Supreme God and the Demiurge. The Supreme God provides the souls, whilst the Demiurge distributes them and watches over them. Numenius uses another analogy to describe the Demiurge's relationship with the world; here he is compared with a helmsman steering his ship.[91]

Because of the Demiurge's contact with matter, he does not share the same perfect nature that belongs to the Supreme God. The Demiurge is the principle of Becoming, not Being, who imitates the Supreme God.[92] Likewise the Demiurge is not the Good, but is good through the will of the Supreme God, and thus by participation in the Good.[93] In *Fragment 20*, when Numenius speaks of the models of Ideas, he seems to suggest that the good of the Demiurge is in fact the Idea of the Good, since only the Supreme God is the Good itself. This strongly implies that Numenius understands the Ideas to be related to the Demiurge only, and that the Supreme God in fact dwells above the Platonic realm of Ideas.

In a passage in his *In Timaeum*, Proclus misleadingly claims that Numenius' third God is 'creation' – i.e. the created world itself. It is clear, however, that Proclus was mistaken in this. Numenius' third God is a lower aspect of the Demiurge, which is more intimately connected with the world, and through which the Demiurge performed the creation process.[94] So the third God is essentially performing the function of divine immanence. It may be that Numenius intended to equate, at least in part, his third God with the world soul,[95] but his third God still remains a part of the Demiurge, and not part of the created world.

In Numenius' understanding of Creation, matter is pre-existent in a disorderly state, and it is through the ongoing ordering of this chaos that creation would seem to take place.[96] However, other than the involvement of the third God, this is as much as we can learn of Numenius' cosmology. He does not directly mention the creation in the extant fragments, nor is there any evidence to suggest that he understood a temporal creation of the world.

Of matter we learn a little more. It is constantly changing; Numenius calls it a 'fiery, unstable river'.[97] He also argues that matter is infinite, indefinite, irrational, and incomprehensible, requiring the maintenance of the incorporeal.[98] Matter is clearly seen in terms of the multiplicity of the Indefinite Dyad. Furthermore, Numenius also speaks of a maleficent world soul, which he seems to understand as the disorderly force present in pre-existent matter, and which he probably considers to be the cause of evil.[99] This disorderly world soul may also correspond to the irrational soul within men.

Numenius understands man to be composed of body (matter) and two souls; one irrational (and possibly material) and the other rational.[100] As we have already seen in his metaphor of the farmer and the cultivator, Numenius considers the first God, the supreme God, to be responsible for producing the souls of men.[101] From *Fragment* 41 it would seem that he understood the nature of these souls to be identical to that of the divine, and all other incorporeal things. He also describes the descent of the souls in a rather mystical way, through the planets and stars, and the embodiment of a soul is described as a misfortune.[102] Once more, we find a conflict between the rational and the irrational, although in this case they are not just parts of the same soul, but separate souls in themselves.

In man's relationship with God, the rational soul would appear to bridge the gap between corporeal and incorporeal in Numenius' system. We are told by Proclus that Numenius considered the soul to be a 'mathematical entity', mediating between the physical and the intangible.[103] We know from *Fragment* 14, where he speaks of science as a gift from the divine, and from his metaphor of an isolated fishing boat in *Fragment* 2, that for Numenius knowledge is central to any interaction between man and the divine. Interestingly, in describing how knowledge is passed on without diminishing the giver, he uses the same metaphor that both Justin and Tatian use of the generation of the Logos.[104]

Finally, one must assume, from the ongoing involvement of the Demiurge in ordering the world, that Numenius believes in the existence of divine providence. He certainly makes no attempt to assert the free will of man in the extant fragments.

Aristotelianism

The greatest distinction between the philosophy of Plato and that of his follower Aristotle (384–322 BCE) was that Aristotle rejected the notion that Plato's Ideas existed beyond this visible world. Instead, Aristotle believed that the corporeal world contained both matter and Forms, and that therefore reality could be perceived through the senses.

By the second century CE, however, we find that distinctions between Peripateticism and Platonism have blurred, and that a degree of synthesis has occurred. In thinkers like Aristocles (second half of the second century), this even extends to attempts to reconcile Plato's full theory of Ideas with Aristotle. However, the main contribution of Aristotelians in this period was in commentating on Aristotle's many works. For my purposes here in investigating Aristotelian solutions to the issues with which Tatian is concerned, the majority of second century Peripatetic texts are irrelevant. The Aristotelian treatise *On the Cosmos* and Alexander of Aphrodisias' *On Fate* are the only exceptions.

The Aristotelian treatise *On the Cosmos* was probably written during the first or early second century CE. It is attributed to Aristotle, but is almost certainly pseudepigraphal. The author of *On the Cosmos* takes Aristotle's concept that the primary realities can be perceived through the senses as his starting point, and tackles the issue of divine nature and activity through an exploration of the cosmos.

He retains elements of the idea of a transcendent God. God is described as invisible, most powerful, most beautiful, and immortal, and we are told that it would be unbecoming for God to be too involved with earthly things.[105] However, God's immanence is more directly expressed by God's 'power' rather than through intermediary beings. Indeed, the author even claims that it is the nature of the divine to penetrate everything, the degree of penetration being proportional to the distance of a thing from God.[106] This brings us to God's position within Pseudo-Aristotle's world system.

Since within Aristotelian thought Plato's Forms exist within the cosmos, as a kind of pattern for matter, there is no higher realm to which God's existence can be pushed. Instead, the author of *On the Cosmos* places God within the cosmos, but in the highest and first place – in the ether beyond the stars. The author equates this upper region with Olympus, and, as we shall see, identifies the gods as the supreme God.[107]

In *On the Cosmos*, God is described as 'the cause that holds the world together', 'the preserver of all things', and 'the creator of everything in this cosmos'.[108] From his lofty perch above the stars, the divine principle exerts his power over the cosmos through motion, which is passed down from the element nearest to him towards earth. The magnitude of God's power lessens as it passes down this chain, so that the bodies nearest to him are most influenced. Thus the author speaks of the constancy of the stars, sun and moon,[109] whilst the earth and its inhabitants, being the furthest removed from God, receive less of God's power, are therefore less ordered in motion, and seem weak and full of confusion.[110] Meanwhile, God himself is established in the immovable, and moves and directs all things.[111] The author is thus clearly presenting us with Aristotle's concept of the unmoved mover.

Pseudo-Aristotle reconciles his concept of God with the Greek pantheistic system by identifying the gods with the supreme God.

He also expands his view of divinity to include abstract ideas; necessity, destiny, and fate. He clearly wishes to include all things within the supreme God, since God is the cause of everything.[112]

We should not be surprised to find that in this work, man's autonomy is not an issue; God controls everything, and therefore man has no free will. However, the author does set forward a theory on fate; he suggests three fates, based on Aristotle's dynamic theory of time. These three fates are past (which is irreversible), present (which is being worked), and future (which is to be spun), and God controls these threads.[113]

Alexander of Aphrodisias (fl c.200 CE), in the introduction to his treatise *On Fate*, claims to be the 'principal exponent' of Aristotle. He was certainly influential, and at the end of the second century probably held the Peripatetic chair of philosophy in Athens, which had been established in 176 CE by Marcus Aurelius. Alexander is chiefly remembered as a commentator, and although in his commentaries he believes that he is merely expressing Aristotle's philosophy, he is in fact beginning a process of systematization that was to become very influential within Peripateticism.

Besides his many commentaries, Alexander also wrote several monographs. Of these, I shall only be concerned here with his anti-stoical work, *On Fate*.[114] In this treatise, Alexander sets down the Aristotelian doctrine of fate and free will in opposition to the strictly deterministic position of the Stoics.[115]

Despite attacking Stoic determinism, Alexander readily accepts the existence of fate and, in his strongly analytical style, explores the nature and activity of fate. He concludes that the workings of fate can be found in the things that come to be by nature, and claims that fate and nature are the same thing.[116]

However, Alexander allows for the existence of free will within his system by claiming that some things happen that are contrary to both nature and fate. The prime example Alexander gives is that of Socrates who, in the face of a physiognomist's negative appraisal, declared that through philosophy he had become better than his nature.[117] Thus it would seem that, for Alexander, philosophy offers man an element of free will; through the discipline of philosophy, a man can overcome his nature and thereby also his fate.

Cynicism and Roman Stoicism

Cynicism was not strictly speaking a philosophy, but rather a way of life. The name 'Cynic' is derived from the word κύων, meaning 'dog'. In the ancient world the dog and its behaviour in public symbolized everything that was distasteful, but the Cynics took it to be shameless and 'in accordance with nature'. They lived ascetic lives, holding that the traditional values were not true values, and claiming that the only thing that mattered was virtue, which they defined as life lived according to nature. Thus they were moralists, but essentially, through their behaviour, Cynics were reacting against the *status quo* and flouting traditional conventions.

Since Cynicism was not a conventional philosophy, it had no interest in the usual concerns of philosophy, and had no formal body of teachings. So although Cynicism was popular in the second century CE, nothing was written concerning its doctrines (since it had none). However, both Tatian and Justin mention the cynic Crescens,[118] and it is clear that they both had direct contact with second century Cynicism.

Zeno of Citium (334–262 BCE), the founder of the Stoic school of philosophy, was heavily influenced by Cynicism, and his philosophy was essentially a combination of the Cynic way of life mixed with a doctrinal system, influenced by the older Greek traditions. Thus Stoicism took morality as its basis, but still concerned itself with questions about the universe and man's knowledge of it.

The chief characteristic within Stoic thought is a materialistic understanding of the divine.[119] For the Stoics the divine element was not pushed above the corporeal world, as amongst the Platonists, nor to the edge of the cosmos, as amongst the Aristotelians. In Stoicism, the divine element formed an essential and supremely immanent part of the created order; it was understood to be corporeal, permeating matter. Thus the divine element combined with matter as the individual soul in men, and as the cosmic world soul within all material things. For the Stoics divinity was entirely immanent, and the universe thus formed one living organism.

The Stoics used many terms to express the interaction of the divine element in the universe. One that is of particular interest for its appropriation and use within Christian philosophy is the Logos. By 'Logos', the Stoics meant the rational force that structures and organizes the universe. Since the divine permeated everything, they believed that a small part of the Logos, the spermatic logos, was planted within all things by the divine Logos. This spermatic logos contained a blueprint for everything that an individual or thing would become, such as an embryo's soul.

With the exception of two notable figures,[120] the Stoics also espoused a theory of periodic conflagration. According to Stoic cosmology, the origin of the universe begins with a cosmic fire. The cosmic fire turns into vapour, which in turn changes into moisture. Part of this moisture remains as water, part condenses to form earth, and part vaporizes again to produce air. From air, fire is produced. A period of existence is played out, and then the conflagration occurs, and everything is reabsorbed into the cosmic fire. The process begins again when the restored cosmic fire again changes into vapour.

Thus we are confronted with an all-consuming cosmic fire, which heralds the end of one cycle of existence but the beginning of another, which in turn will be terminated by the same cosmic fire. The Stoics also believed that each cycle of existence produced the same people, the same events, and therefore a history that repeated itself eternally. In view of this it should come as no surprise that the Stoics placed a very strong emphasis upon fate, and, since God is so merged with the universe, upon providence.[121] Non-Stoics frequently understood the Stoic position to be entirely deterministic, but in fact attempts were made to include an element of free will.

Stoicism proved to be very popular within the Roman Empire, but by the second century CE the Stoic movement was on the wane. There are two main figures within our period, sometimes called 'Roman Stoicism', who represent the Stoic position: Epictetus and Marcus Aurelius.

Epictetus (c.55–135 CE) was born a slave and was freed following Nero's death, having belonged to one of Nero's administrators. The only major extant work we have outlining his philosophy is a series of lectures, the *Discourses of Epictetus*, recorded by one of his pupils.

As a Stoic, Epictetus believed that man's soul is divine, and that man is part of the divine principle. Thus the emphasis when considering God shifts to include that divine element in man. When Epictetus speaks of the nature of God as good, it necessarily follows that man must have the potential to be good too. Likewise, when he claims that the gods are 'pure and undefiled', he adds that man's reason tries to make the human body as clean as possible, in imitation of the gods.[122] The result is that Epictetus has very little to say directly about the divine nature and activity. He speaks of men as having been 'begotten of God', but does not elaborate on creation or the divine role in bringing it about, although one may safely assume a Stoic cosmology. Neither does Epictetus say anything about the nature of divine existence, although he does refer to God as the father of gods, which suggests a secondary level of divine beings.[123]

It should now be clear that the Stoic emphasis in tackling questions about God is very different to that of the two schools we have met so far. For Aristotelians, divine realities can be perceived in the world around us, whilst for Platonists, a philosopher must reach beyond the visible world to comprehend God. However, for Stoics, the quest for the divine turns inwards to man's soul, and external questions (such as what God is and what he does) become largely irrelevant. The only thing that Epictetus is anxious to prove is that the divine exists and is involved in human affairs, and this he does by listing examples of God's providence in ordering things.[124]

Epictetus also has surprisingly little to say about the nature of man. He considers man to be composed of two parts, body and rational soul (i.e. divine spirit), but does not really define either. He also claims that the purpose for man's existence is to be a 'spectator' and 'interpreter' of God, and presents the possibility of free will for those who accept what they cannot change, but are free to alter what they can.[125]

The rest of what Epictetus says about man (and there is a great deal) is concerned with morals and how a man should behave. Indeed this seems to be the primary concern of the *Discourses*, although it is not relevant here. For Epictetus philosophy was primarily about man's knowledge of himself, and questions of physics were only relevant in so far as that they showed men how to live.

Our second Roman Stoic, Marcus Aurelius (121–180 CE), was Emperor from 161–180 CE, and is directly addressed by Justin Martyr in his first *Apology*.[126] His only extant work is a collection of twelve books entitled *Meditations*, which are essentially private reflections.[127]

Like Epictetus, Marcus Aurelius also believes that man possesses a portion of divinity. He affirms that the gods exist and are involved with men's lives, but again his focus when contemplating the divine is inwards.[128] He too is concerned with moral issues, but although much of the material in his *Meditations* is concerned with how men should behave, he also has much to say about subjects closer to this field of study, such as man and the cosmos.

Marcus Aurelius understands a three-fold division of man: body (sense perceptions), vital spirit (impulses), and mind (doctrines). The good man is ruled by reason and therefore lives justly, preserving his divine element from the body and inappropriate behaviour.[129] For Marcus Aurelius, this in itself is the purpose of philosophy, and philosophy acts as an escort for men through life.[130]

Marcus Aurelius has a much wider perception of the world and man. He sees man as part of the whole, not only as part of a society, but also as part of the cosmos.[131] He frequently reflects on death, offering several views of what follows it. He clearly does not believe in reincarnation, asserting that men have one life only, and in his varying views on the process after death he clearly envisages an absorption of some form into the Universal Nature.[132] For Marcus Aurelius everything constantly changes from one thing into another, and the idea of something ceasing to exist completely (or indeed deriving its existence from nothing) is totally alien.

Marcus Aurelius does mention the creation of the world, but does not describe the process; he merely says that the Universal Nature 'felt an impulse to create a world'.[133] Elsewhere he also seems to refer to the Stoic theory of periodic conflagration, but he does not draw the usual conclusion of cycles of repeated existence.[134] If Marcus Aurelius did in fact believe in periodic conflagration, then this would tally perfectly with his view of material and spiritual change, and existence itself would be a repeated re-absorption into Universal Nature.

A theme that Marcus Aurelius returns to repeatedly, and which is clearly very important to him, is the theme of providence. In his deterministic view of the world, men's fates are threads spun from the beginning.[135] Like Epictetus, he incorporates the concept of free will by claiming that man can choose to lead 'the higher life', governed by his reason.[136]

Epicureanism

Epicurus (c.341–270 BCE) founded the Epicurean school in 306 BCE. He based his philosophy on the atomic theory of Democritus, and developed a related system of ethics. What particularly characterizes Epicureans is their almost atheistic approach to religion; they placed the gods beyond the reach of man, thus removing divine activity from the world and denying the significance of the gods.

Epicureanism was present in the second century CE, although we have no extant material relevant to this study from this period. However, unlike the other movements we have considered so far, Epicureans remained remarkably faithful to the teachings of their founder. Thus we will obtain a reasonable picture of what second century Epicureanism was like if we turn to Lucretius, even though he lived two centuries before our period.

Lucretius (c.95–52 BCE) was a Roman poet, and his work *On the Nature of Things* gives us a very rounded picture of Epicureanism, which is incredibly close to the philosophy of Epicurus. Lucretius' philosophy is dominated by his atomic understanding of the universe. For Lucretius the universe consisted only of matter and void, matter being the atoms themselves, and the void the space in which those atoms move.[137] He postulates that the universe and space and matter are without limit, and conceives of an infinite number of worlds.[138]

Worlds are created through the motion of the atoms, the 'first-beginnings', as Lucretius terms them. He envisages an endless stream of atoms that are constantly moving, and it is through the erratic swerving of atoms that worlds are created. The purpose of such erratic motion is to allow free will within the Epicurean system, although Lucretius does claim that without the swerve, the atoms would not have touched and nothing would have been created.[139] Epicureans react quite strongly against theories of fate and providence, perhaps fuelled by the divine immanence implied in such theories.

By suggesting that it is atomic motion that produces worlds, the Epicureans are also denying divine involvement in the process of creation.[140] Lucretius does admit the existence of the gods, but places them at such a distance from mankind that contact between man and the divine is unthinkable; the gods live in tranquillity, undisturbed by human concerns.[141]

Meanwhile man, according to Lucretius, is composed of body, mind (which is part of a man like the feet or eyes), spirit (which lies within the body), and a second spirit, a 'spirit of the spirit', which is obviously intended as a controlling element.[142] All of these elements, including the mind and spirits, are corporeal and particulate, each a mass of fine atoms, the mind being seated in the breast, the first spirit penetrating the entire body, and the second spirit interpenetrating the first.[143] Lucretius considers the entire atomic structure that makes up a man to be mortal; thus when the body dies, mind and spirit also die and the atoms disperse.[144] Thus Lucretius denies an afterlife for man, and claims that death is therefore nothing.[145]

Scepticism

Scepticism, as a tradition, began with Pyrrho of Elis (*c*.365–270 BCE), and was essentially a reaction against the dogmatism of the Stoics and the Epicureans. Pyrrho presented an agnostic approach to philosophy, claiming that it was impossible to attain any knowledge whatsoever.

In the third century BCE the Platonist Academy moved towards a Sceptical stance, but this was a different kind of Scepticism, which worked on an intellectual level and was extremely analytical in its approach, denying all claims to knowledge. The Academy was essentially destroyed with the fall of Athens in 88 BCE, and when the more dogmatic position of the Middle Platonists took hold, representing a separate stream within Platonism, Scepticism disappeared from the Platonist movement. However, the Pyrrhonist branch of Scepticism was still very much alive in the second century CE. The most prominent Sceptic of this time was Sextus Empiricus (*c*.200 CE). The key phrase of his philosophy was 'suspension of judgement', and he gives us a neat and concise definition of Scepticism in his work *Outlines of Pyrrhonism*:

> Scepticism is an ability, or mental attitude, which opposes appearances and judgements in any way whatsoever, with the result that, owing to the equipollence of the objects and reason thus applied, we are brought firstly to a state of mental suspense and next to a state of 'unperturbedness' or quietude.[146]

The Pyrrhonist branch of Scepticism thus offered more than just a method of knocking down the arguments of one's opponent, and believed that freeing the philosopher from futile attempts at gaining knowledge led to a state of tranquillity.

In view of the Sceptical stance, it should come as no surprise that Sextus is unable to make any positive statements about the issues we come across in Tatian. Sextus does speak about issues like the nature of the divine, but does not reach any conclusions.[147]

Conclusion: hellenistic philosophy in the second century

In the second century, Platonism was rapidly becoming the dominant philosophy of the time. This is evidenced not least by the fact that there are five Middle Platonists – six if you include Numenius –

who are relevant to this study.[148] Moreover, philosophies like Aristotelianism and Stoicism are clearly on the wane. At the beginning of the third century Neoplatonism appears, a philosophy that was to have a great impact on pagan and Christian thinking. Indeed, many scholars only consider Middle Platonism and the other philosophies of this period in terms of their influence upon the development of Neoplatonism.[149]

The second century was also a time when eclecticism was rife, although one should be cautious in using this term. Middle Platonism was influenced to a certain extent by both Stoicism and Peripateticism, whilst Pythagoreanism became so great an influence to philosophers like Numenius that they termed themselves Pythagoreans. Meanwhile amongst the Peripatetics we find a tendency to reconcile Aristotle and Plato, and, in *On the Cosmos*, a significant Stoic influence. Amongst second century Stoics we find a tendency towards Platonism, although this was more marked in their predecessors Panaetius and Posidonius.

Most of these philosophers would have operated primarily within the Graeco-Roman education system and the various philosophical schools that existed in the second century.[150] Indeed, as we have seen, Atticus may have held the first Chair of Platonic philosophy set up in Athens by Marcus Aurelius in 176 CE, whilst Alexander of Aphrodisias probably held the Peripatetic Chair at the end of the second century. Ideas were presented in the form of public lectures, which frequently became diatribe. Rivalries between schools were often intense.[151]

This, then, is the hellenistic philosophy with which Tatian would have been confronted. He may not have been familiar with the individual philosophers I have outlined, but, given his knowledge of philosophy (most notably Platonism and Stoicism), it seems likely that he would have been aware of some of the ideas and trends current within the various philosophical schools. It is now time to consider how he interacted with this mix of philosophies.

Tatian's relationship with hellenistic philosophy

Tatian's apparent hostility towards hellenistic philosophy

Tatian's external attitude towards hellenistic philosophy is extremely hostile. Although Tatian mentions none of the contemporary philosophers we have met in this chapter, he repeatedly attacks philosophers from earlier periods, and often uses myths current about them in his day in order to do this. An exploration of these attacks will provide us with an insight into the negative side of his interaction with hellenistic philosophy.

The first area of Tatian's hostility that I shall consider is his criticism of philosophical doctrines. Tatian aims his criticism at two pre-Socratic philosophers and at four of the hellenistic schools mentioned above, attacking both general doctrines of those schools and the doctrines of individual adherents.

The atomic philosopher Democritus (c.460–371 BCE), who so influenced Epicurus, comes under attack from Tatian for the doctrine of sympathies and antipathies.[152] This doctrine was attributed to Democritus by the third century BCE,[153] and so by the time of Tatian the atomist was probably firmly established as the originator of this theory. Tatian's attack on Democritus essentially consists of an insult to Democritus' home town of Abdera, and a threat of destruction on judgement day.[154]

The other pre-Socratic philosopher whose doctrines Tatian ridicules is Anaxagoras (c.500–428 BCE), although he does not mention the philosopher by name. Tatian mocks Anaxagoras' theory of the composition of the sun and moon by claiming that they are competition entries for storytelling.[155]

Tatian's attack on Platonism is limited to a vague criticism of two key Platonist doctrines.[156] The first is the concept of the immortality of the soul, which he initially attacks in *Or* 3, where he dismisses Pherecydes' 'old wives' tales' and Pythagoras' and Plato's use of them.[157] As Whittaker points out,[158] what Tatian is referring to here is in fact the doctrine of the immortality of the soul. Tatian's rejection of this theory is emphasized again in Chapter 13, where he opens his section on anthropological theory with the words: 'The soul, men of Greece, is not in itself immortal but mortal.'[159] This is clearly a refutation in favour of Tatian's own belief in the inherent mortality of the soul.

The second Platonic concept that Tatian attacks is the idea that demons are the disembodied souls of men. Tatian rejects this idea because he believes demons to be independent, fallen beings.[160]

Tatian's criticisms of the Aristotelian doctrines are, for the most part, more direct than his criticisms of Platonism. His chief complaint centres on the question of providence. As we discovered above when we considered the Aristotelian treatise *On the Cosmos*,

Aristotelians placed the divine in the highest place in the cosmos beyond the stars, and divine power trickled down through the planets to earth, decreasing in potency the further an object was from God. It should therefore come as no surprise that Tatian accuses the Aristotelians of limiting providence, and of excluding it from 'sublunary affairs'.[161]

Tatian also attacks Aristotle for his definition of happiness.[162] Aristotle's definition of happiness was difficult to achieve; it involved fulfilment of all human potentialities, and required a combination of beauty, wealth, strength, good birth, and health.

Tatian's attack on Stoic doctrines begins with his rejection of the Stoic concept of cycles of existence.[163] Tatian's main criticism of this theory is simply that, if everyone merely repeats the events of previous existences, there would be no purpose in life.[164] Another criticism that Tatian makes is against the Stoic doctrine of divine immanence within matter. He objects to it because it would involve the entanglement of his transcendent God with evil.[165]

The Epicureans also come under attack for their doctrines. Tatian criticizes Metrodorus of Lampsacus, a close associate of Epicurus, for his metaphorical method of reading Greek writers. His method of attack is mockery.[166]

Going beyond the content of philosophical doctrines, Tatian also condemns philosophers for their behaviour. The standard against which he measures the philosophers is set down in the latter part of his *Oration*, and is clearly the lifestyle expected from Tatian's Christian philosophers. Tatian presents them as being non-exclusive, not driven by a need for profit or personal glory, appealing to a higher authority above man, and concerned with maintaining high moral standards.[167] Against this standard Tatian measures hellenistic philosophers, and in contrast accuses them of self-display, hypocrisy, vanity, and greed.[168]

Tatian also singles out individual philosophers whom he condemns for their behaviour. He heavily criticizes the pre-Socratic philosopher Heraclitus (fl *c.*504–501 BCE) on several levels. Heraclitus was known as 'the obscure'. In fact his obscurity was deliberate, since he believed his philosophy to exceed the limits of ordinary language. Tatian mocks Heraclitus for this, by claiming that Euripides easily revealed Heraclitus' obscurities from memory. Tatian also denounces Heraclitus for his arrogance in claiming that he taught himself, although in fact this is a misquotation of a statement found in the extant remains of Heraclitus' work.[169] Furthermore, Tatian accuses him of attempting to achieve publication mysteriously by hiding his work in the temple of Artemis, and claims that his death, the result of a cure for oedema, only pointed up his ignorance.[170]

Empedocles (c.484–424 BCE) is also attacked by Tatian. According to one of the stories of his death, Empedocles leapt into the crater of Mount Etna. Tatian claims that he did this in an attempt to make people believe he was a god, but that his deception was proved when a volcanic eruption spewed up his shoe.[171]

Tatian makes only one reference to the behaviour of a Platonist, and that is to Plato himself. However, the attack is not directed against Plato but against Dionysius I, the tyrant ruler of Sicily, who sold Plato into slavery.[172]

Tatian criticizes the behaviour of Aristotelians in a stream of stories connected with Alexander the Great.[173] Tatian begins by accusing Aristotle of being obsessed with Alexander, of 'fawning' on him.[174] He then refers to the historian Callisthenes, whom Alexander imprisoned,[175] and finally, Tatian denounces Alexander's murder of his friend Clitus.[176]

Tatian also attacks the hedonist Aristippus of Cyrene (c.435–356 BCE). Aristippus was a pupil of Socrates, and in a sense is the predecessor of Epicurus, seeing pleasure as the only absolute good in life. Tatian's attack on Aristippus is based on his espousal of hedonism; Tatian accuses him of 'abandoning himself to luxury under a cloak of respectability'.[177]

The Cynic Diogenes of Sinope (c.412–323 BCE) was famed for his practice of living in an earthenware tub, and Tatian criticizes this activity as demonstrating Diogenes' pride. Tatian also claims that Diogenes' death, of an internal blockage after eating raw octopus, demonstrated his intemperance.[178] As we saw earlier, the word 'Cynic' derives from the Greek κύων, meaning 'dog'. Tatian mocks Crates, the teacher of Zeno, for his marriage to a fellow Cynic, Hipparchia, calling it a 'dog-marriage'.[179]

Finally, Tatian also attacks Crescens, a Cynic who was active in the time of Justin and Tatian.[180] Both apologists accuse him of plotting their deaths, but Tatian also accuses him of hypocrisy; although, Tatian says, Crescens preached contempt of death, he himself feared it, and therefore plotted to have Justin and Tatian put to death.[181]

A further criticism that Tatian levels at hellenistic philosophers is that they do not agree amongst themselves. It is true that the different schools disagreed on many issues, and that the polemical tracts that ensued, such as Atticus' anti-Peripatetic work, often became heated and accusations were flung wildly. In criticism of this trend, Tatian writes:

> Do not be swept away by the august crowds of those who love noise rather than wisdom. They express views that contradict one another, and each says whatever comes into his head. And there are many causes of friction between them, for each one hates his fellow and they hold different views, each taking up an exaggerated position out of self-importance.[182]

However, it is not just the manner in which the philosophers express their disagreement that Tatian condemns; he also rebukes them for the fact that disagreement even exists within their philosophy:

> If you follow the doctrines of Plato then the Epicurean sophist is in total opposition to you; suppose on the other hand you want to support Aristotle, and you will incur abuse from some follower of Democritus. Pythagoras claims to have been Euphorbus and to be heir to the teaching of Pherecydes, but Aristotle disparages the immortality of the soul. Because you have inherited contradictory teachings you quarrel with one another, but oppose those who agree among themselves.[183]

Tatian is concerned with discovering 'the truth', and this he believes to be a unified and consistent system. From this supposition alone he discounts much of hellenistic philosophy, and the lack of agreement among hellenistic philosophers is thus a cause for derision in Tatian's eyes. Indeed, this criticism of discord amongst Greek philosophers also extends to mockery of arguments over the correct form of the Greek language,[184] the contradictory stories told of the gods,[185] the use of different codes of law, and inconsistencies in Greek historical texts.[186]

The desire for internal consistency was central to Tatian's form of Christianity. This is reflected not only in his criticism of the inconsistencies of Greek traditions and practices, but also in his praise of the ordered and harmonious structure of the body and the world,[187] and especially in his presentation of Christianity as 'the truth'. Tatian's principle of internal consistency may also have been a significant factor in his composition of the *Diatessaron*.[188]

Tatian's understanding of Christianity as a 'philosophy'

It is surprising in view of Tatian's apparent hostility towards all things Greek that he should present Christianity as a 'philosophy'. Yet in the *Oration* Tatian clearly speaks of Christianity as 'our philosophy', and refers to the activity of Christians 'philosophizing'.[189] In the final chapter of the *Oration*, he even calls himself a philosopher.[190] The problem that faces us is why Tatian should claim the term 'philosophy' for Christianity, and yet criticize hellenistic philosophy to the extent he does. The solution to this problem lies partly in the charge of plagiarism that he levels against the Greek philosophers and partly in the superior status that he demands for Christian philosophy, over and against that of the Greeks.[191]

Tatian's line of argument in asserting the superiority of Christian philosophy springs from his understanding of Judaism as the Christian heritage. During his conversion account, Tatian tells us that he was converted to Christianity through reading some 'barbarian writings'.[192] The 'barbarians' to whom he is referring are ultimately the Jews, and the writings are those contained within the Hebrew Scriptures, although he probably encountered them in the Septuagint version. Tatian clearly appropriates the Hebrew Scriptures and identifies Christianity with Jewish history, claiming it for his own. Thus Tatian appeals to the antiquity of the Jewish race and, in defence of Christianity, presents his Graeco-Roman audience with a detailed chronological account, intended to prove the greater age (and therefore priority) of Moses, over against that of Homer and other great Greek writers.[193]

Having argued his case very persuasively, Tatian goes on to claim that the Greek philosophers, living after Moses, plagiarized the barbarian wisdom laid down by the Jewish Patriarchs:

> So it is clear from the preceding arguments that Moses is older than heroes, cities, demons. We should believe one who has priority in time [i.e. Moses] in preference to Greeks who learned his doctrines at second hand. For with much labour their sophists tried to counterfeit all they knew from Moses' teaching and from those who philosophized like him, first in order to gain a reputation for originality, and secondly in order that by concealing their ignorance in a cloak of bogus verbiage they might distort the truth as mythology.[194]

Tatian's chronological argument clearly belongs to a tradition of interpreting the history of culture, which we find most importantly in Justin, but that also has its roots in Judaism and in nationalistic histories, such as Hecataeus' history of Egypt.[195] As Droge rightly points out, the importance of this interpretation of the history of culture to Tatian's apologetic argument should not be over-looked.[196] Nonetheless, for my purposes here in considering Tatian's relationship with hellenistic philosophy it is adequate merely to acknowledge the importance of this tradition to Tatian's *Oration*.[197]

If Tatian claims that the Greek philosophers are dependent upon Moses and other Biblical figures for their doctrines, it therefore follows that Tatian would feel justified in incorporating ideas from hellenistic philosophy into his own work, although he does not explicitly state such a position. In Tatian's eyes, such an assimilation would surely be a reclamation of doctrines pilfered from the Hebrew Scriptures. A detailed study of Tatian's thought reveals that he does in fact make use of ideas from hellenistic philosophy.

Tatian's use of hellenistic philosophy

If we look back to consider Tatian's treatment of the various philo-sophical schools outlined earlier, we find that one school in particu-lar comes off rather lightly amidst the barrage of attacks that Tatian showers upon Greek philosophy. That school is Platonism. With its transcendent divine principle, Middle Platonism is, in fact, the closest of these hellenistic philosophies to Christianity, and, as we have seen, Tatian's master Justin Martyr was himself influenced by this branch of philosophy. It should therefore come as no surprise that traces of Platonism can be found within Tatian's philosophy.

Tatian was not brought up a Christian; as *Or* 29 makes clear, he converted to Christianity later in life, driven by a quest for 'the truth'. Furthermore, as a reasonably well-born young man Tatian clearly received the conventional Greek education, which would have included training in rhetoric, as well as a smattering of philo-sophy.[198] Thus hellenistic philosophy would have been part of the intellectual framework to which Tatian was exposed.

In the *Oration* Tatian is essentially grappling with the problem of how to reconcile his hellenistic background with his new Christian faith, whether on a conscious or a subconscious level. The end result is a theology that incorporates those elements of Greek philosophy closest to Christianity with developing Christian doctrines.

Tatian's understanding of God is quite clearly based upon the

Judeo-Christian concept of a monotheistic God but, as we have seen, there is a certain amount of overlap between the Middle Platonic view of the divine and that of Christianity. Thus, although in describing God Tatian uses the same kind of negative terminology that we have already encountered amongst our second century Middle Platonists,[199] such terminology is not in itself particularly significant as it was also used in Judeo-Christian traditions. What is significant, however, is Tatian's reference to two specifically Platonist concepts: 'Being' and 'the Good'.

In Chapter 15 Tatian struggles to describe the divine nature, and in doing so designates it as 'Being'.[200] However, Tatian's use of the term is very vague, and in any case he concludes that he cannot describe the divine nature, since he would only be able to present something similar, and not the nature itself.

However, when we turn to consider Tatian's reference to 'the Good' we find that it is presented in rather less vague terms; Tatian speaks of 'the good which is God's alone'.[201] This would certainly seem to be a reflection of the Platonic concept of 'the Good', and, significantly, this concept is also present in both Philo and Justin.

As we have seen repeatedly, a necessary consequence of the assertion of a transcendent God is that some way must be found of expressing divine immanence. The Middle Platonists whom we have met deal with this problem in several different ways: Plutarch introduces daemons to mediate between man and the divine principle, and uses the Stoic Logos, represented by Osiris, to express his cosmogony; Atticus, meanwhile, utilizes a Stoicized form of the world soul to order matter during the process of creation, preserving his transcendent God from contamination; Alcinous, however, does bring his divine principle into more direct contact with the created world, claiming that God himself brought order to matter, but nevertheless assigns the creation of man and other creatures to the 'created gods' or 'daemons'; similarly, Apuleius introduces a third class of gods who perform intermediary functions; and finally Numenius, whom I shall class as a Middle Platonist, subdivides his second god, the Demiurge, to produce a third god, through whom the Demiurge performs the creation process.

Since he too espouses a transcendent God, Tatian is faced with the same problem as these Middle Platonists. His response to the issue of God's immanence is to incorporate the concept of the Logos into his system. This was originally a Stoic idea, but was appropriated, as we have seen, by Plutarch amongst others.

For Tatian, it is the Word who is responsible for fabricating matter and bringing order to it,[202] and for creating angels and men,[203] although the Word is so intimately connected with God that God can himself be called 'the sole creator of all that is'.[204] Thus Tatian's understanding of the relationship between the Word and God would seem to correspond with the Stoic notion of ἐνδιάθετος λόγος (the conception or thought in the mind of God) and προφορικὸς λόγος (the expression of that thought). Tatian's Word does not act autonomously during creation; the Word is a part of the being of God and, as the προφορικὸς λόγος, becomes the instrument through which God creates.[205]

However, although Tatian's use of the concept of the Logos may have its origins within Greek philosophy, it is far more likely to have reached him indirectly through elements in Judeo-Christian traditions. The Logos was already appropriated by the author of the *Fourth Gospel* in his Prologue, and if we turn to Justin we find a fully-fledged and developing Logos doctrine. It would therefore be unwise to conclude any direct link between Tatian and the Logos of Middle Platonists like Plutarch.

The world soul was a popular concept amongst Platonists, and there is some evidence in the *Oration* that Tatian incorporated this concept into his thought, although there is no trace of Plutarch's disorderly world soul. In Chapter 4, we read of 'material spirits' and 'the spirit that pervades matter'.[206] Then, in Chapter 12, Tatian elaborates on this material spirit. Essentially it would seem that he envisages a common origin for all material things, a raw matter that God orders.[207] For Tatian this raw matter would also seem to contain an inherent spiritual material,[208] which is distributed amongst the created things according to their function. Tatian envisages differing amounts of the material spirit in luminaries, angels, plants, waters, men (the soul), and animals, although it is still one and the same substance.[209]

Tatian's understanding of the process of creation also has much in common with that of the second century Platonists we have met. In Plutarch, Osiris, as the Demiurge, imposes order and form upon Isis, the Receptacle; for both Atticus and Alcinous, creation involves the ordering of disorderly pre-existent matter; for Apuleius, creation is the shaping and organizing of matter by 'God the craftsman'; for Maximus, creation is an ordering of pre-existent matter by a 'good Craftsman'; and finally, for Numenius, creation is also perceived as the ordering of disorderly matter, although in his case the process would seem to be on-going. Thus for all our relevant second century Platonists, creation, be it temporal or otherwise, is the ordering of a chaotic, pre-existent matter.

As we shall see, Tatian does not accept the Platonic presupposition that matter is pre-existent; he is anxious to claim that nothing is beyond the power and scope of God. Thus we find him stating that the Word fabricated matter, and that matter was produced by God.[210] However, the matter that is generated is not produced in its final, ordered form; the original matter, which God uses to create the universe, is 'raw and formless' and has yet to become 'organized and orderly'.[211] The process by which this happens is the same as the process our Platonists envisaged. Tatian uses the metaphors of speech and fire to illustrate how the Word performed the act of creation.[212] Thus for Tatian, it is through ordering the 'raw and formless' matter that the creation process takes place. As a Christian, Tatian is also forced to believe that creation was temporal (i.e. that it was not just a myth, but a reality). As we have seen, Plutarch and Atticus also espouse a temporal creation.

Tatian's anthropology may also show some affinities with the psychology of some Middle Platonists, and in particular with that of Plutarch. Plato himself proposed two alternative divisions of a man's soul; a bipartite division of rational and irrational, and a tripartite division of rational and two irrational parts. It is therefore no surprise that our second century Platonists also differed on this point. Three of them, Alcinous, Apuleius and Numenius, followed Plato's model of a tripartite division of the soul, whilst Atticus, although apparently contradicting himself, espoused the bipartite division, as too did Plutarch and Maximus.

Tatian envisages a bipartite division of the soul; man, in his original state, possessed two kinds of spirit.[213] Admittedly in his current, fallen state man no longer possesses this second spirit in full, but the union of human soul and divine spirit is clearly intended as man's natural state and the state towards which men strive during the process of salvation.[214]

However, it is the current state of man that offers a loose parallel with Plutarch. As we recall, Plutarch perceived the rational soul to be only partially resident within the body, even describing it as 'external', and he used the metaphor of a buoy floating to express this concept. In Tatian, the divine spirit is separated from man too, this time by the fall. However, Tatian clearly goes beyond the concept of Plutarch in his understanding of a total separation, where only a 'spark' of the spirit's power is left with man.[215]

The issue of how free will and providence, or fate, interact is one that every philosopher whom we have considered has been concerned with, whether their agendas were deterministic or non-deterministic. This problem was clearly very important in the second century. Tatian categorically denies the existence of fate, claiming that it is just the invention of demons to make themselves seem powerful.[216] Free will, however, becomes central to Tatian's system, not only because it allows for moral choice, but also because it provides an explanation for the existence of evil within a world created by his transcendent God, who is both perfect and absolutely good.

Conclusion: Tatian's relationship with hellenistic philosophy

Tatian's relationship with hellenistic philosophy is certainly complex – more complex, perhaps, than that of his master Justin. On the surface Tatian appears to be very hostile towards hellenistic culture generally, yet clearly he has also been influenced by aspects of hellenistic philosophy. It is likely that some of this influence operated on a subconscious level, but we have also seen how Tatian justifies his use of hellenistic philosophy through his claim that what is best in Greek philosophy was plagiarized from Moses.

However, there may be a further explanation for the paradox of Tatian's use of Middle Platonism in the face of his extraordinary hostility towards all things Greek; I believe that most of the parallels between Tatian and Middle Platonism can be identified already within the New Testament or in Tatian's master Justin and Philo of Alexandria. If Tatian encountered philosophical ideas within an already existing Judeo-Christian tradition, he may in fact have been genuinely unaware of the debt that his Christian philosophy owed to Platonism. If this is the case, then Tatian is drawing on more than just an education in philosophy belonging to his pre-conversion period.

Of course the apologists were not the only Christians of the second century to be influenced by hellenistic philosophy. There is evidence to suggest that less mainstream writers like Valentinus and Basilides were influenced by philosophy,[217] and some of the texts found within the Nag Hammadi Library likewise reveal Platonic leanings. Indeed, the corpus even includes a translation of Plato's *Republic* 588A–589B.

This should not surprise us, since, as we have seen, hellenistic philosophy permeated the intellectual atmosphere of the second century, fuelled by a renewed interest in all things Greek. It is therefore perfectly natural that hellenistic concepts should be incorporated into Christian belief systems. What distinguishes Justin and Tatian in their use of philosophy is that they present Christianity as a philosophy to rival the traditional Graeco-Roman systems.

5

TATIAN AND THE DEVELOPMENT OF A CHRISTIAN PHILOSOPHY

The roots of the Christian philosophical tradition can be traced back to the Jewish Middle Platonist, Philo of Alexandria (*c*.25 BCE–50 CE).[1] Philo was the first extant Jewish writer to unite hellenistic philosophy with Judaism,[2] reconciling the impersonal divine principle of Platonism with the personal God of the Hebrew Scriptures. Nearly a century later, Tatian's teacher, Justin Martyr, presented a Christian philosophy that also drew on the Middle Platonic tradition. If, as has been suggested,[3] some sort of relationship exists between the Platonism of Justin and that of Philo, then it may be that in Tatian we encounter a developing Christian philosophical tradition, inherited from his master. What I intend to do in this chapter is to explore the roots of Tatian's philosophical tradition in both Philo and Justin, and to examine Tatian's presentation of that tradition in his *Oration*.

Philo: precursor of Christian philosophy

Philo of Alexandria was primarily an exegete. In his many extant works,[4] Philo's concern is to explain and interpret Scriptural passages, and he frequently uses philosophical terms and concepts to do so.[5] Philo's precise relationship with hellenistic philosophy has been the subject of much debate; Wolfson, for instance, suggested that Philo's approach to hellenistic philosophy was primarily eclectic,[6] whilst more recently Dillon has argued convincingly that Philo draws his philosophy from Alexandrian Platonism, which was already influenced by both Stoic and Pythagorean concepts.[7]

In relation to this study, it is also important to note that Philo's relationship with gnosticism has been the cause of much debate.[8] The strongest statement of Philo's involvement with gnosticism was made by Jonas, who took the position that Philo was essentially gnostic.[9] However, following the Messina conference in 1966, where, as we have seen, important differentiations were made between the second century gnostic systems and earlier gnostic streams, a general scholarly consensus seems to have emerged that defines Philo as 'pre-gnostic', and some have even suggested that it was Philo who influenced second century gnostics.[10]

Before I embark on this brief study, I must justify my restricted use of Philo; given the limited scope of this chapter, my focus in this section will be exclusively concerned with Philo's contribution to the philosophical tradition that we find in Tatian. Thus in presenting Philo's philosophy, I will inevitably omit much that is significant in his thought.

Philo's God is a combination of the supreme divine principle of Platonism and the God of the Hebrew Scriptures, and where the God portrayed within the Hebrew Scriptures contradicts the divine attributes within Platonism, Philo uses allegory to smooth over differences.[11] What we are essentially faced with is conventional Platonic notions about divinity, which are applied to the personal God of the Jews.

Philo describes his God as the Good,[12] One or Monad, and even as beyond the Monad;[13] he also claims that God is immutable,[14] infinite, self-sufficient, and incomprehensible,[15] although a distinction is made concerning the incomprehensibility of God when Philo claims that the human mind can perceive God,[16] but that man is incapable of actually understanding God or his nature.[17] A further epithet that Philo uses to describe God is that of namelessness,[18] but this is clearly grounded within the Jewish tradition. Three further elements of Philo's doctrine of God can also be found within the Middle Platonic tradition; Philo incorporates the Platonic theory of Ideas into his system, as we shall see, and may consider the Ideas to be God's thoughts.[19] Philo also uses Pythagorean number theology, springing from God as the One,[20] and seems to make use of the Aristotelian notion of the 'unmoved mover', which was also appropriated by some Middle Platonists.[21]

Philo's cosmology is likewise a melding of the Platonic creation myth and the Biblical account of creation. In his treatise *On the Account of the World's Creation Given by Moses*, Philo interprets the creation stories of Genesis using Platonic concepts and terminology. Here, Philo states his belief that a model of the created world, the Platonic intelligibles (i.e. Ideas or Forms), existed before the physical creation of the world, and seems to equate the creation of this model with the first creation story in *Gen* 1.[22] He describes the creation process as an imprinting of matter with the pattern of the model, which seems to involve an ordering of pre-existent matter.[23]

The question of whether Philo perceives God to create the world out of pre-existent matter or whether he shifts towards the creation out of nothing theory is very interesting. Following the work of Gerhard May and others, it is probable that Philo belongs to a period before the theory of creation out of nothing was formulated within Jewish thought;[24] although there is evidence that suggests that Philo was struggling with this issue,[25] he does not appear to go so far as to suggest a creation out of nothing.[26] It would therefore seem reasonable to conclude that Philo was still restricted by the common philosophical axiom that nothing can come from nothing.

The Logos also has an important part to play within Philo's process of creation. In his treatise *On the Creation* Philo locates the intelligible model within the Divine Logos, and elsewhere he speaks of God 'stamping' the universe with the Word.[27] The relationship between the created world, the Logos, and God is a complex one in Philo, and I shall shortly return to consider the Logos' position within creation.

We turn now to consider how Philo envisaged the nature of the created world. Philo regards our world as unique, claiming that all matter that exists was used by God in forming the world.[28] He considers the created world to have reached its maximum potential and to be as perfect as it is capable of being, and he understands the Logos to have a key role in binding the created world together.[29] Philo does not consider the world to be eternal, but argues that, through God's providence, it is made imperishable.[30]

Philo's Logos essentially permits the immanence of his God to be expressed during creation and through mediation with man. Philo's understanding of the relationship between God and the Logos is quite complex, and a certain amount of fluidity exists when Philo speaks of God's involvement in creation. However, this can partly be explained by his claim that the Logos is understood by some people to be God, whilst the initiated know that the Logos is actually only the image of God.[31]

In expressing the Logos' interaction with the created world, the Logos splits, much as we saw with Numenius' Demiurge, to produce two powers: the creative power (through which God creates) and the royal power (through which God rules).[32] Philo clearly does not envisage this process of divine fragmentation to diminish God in any way, and indeed uses the same kind of metaphors to express the divine outpourings as we find in Justin and Tatian.[33] Thus the creative and royal powers must be considered aspects of the Logos, just as the Logos is considered an aspect of God.

Since the Logos contains the realm of Ideas, the Logos is referred to as 'the original principle behind all principles', after which God shaped the world,[34] and the Logos itself becomes the pattern of creation, and the archetype of human reason.[35] Interestingly, Philo also calls the Logos 'the Beginning'.[36] This almost certainly refers to the opening words of Genesis, and it is an appellation that we find again in Tatian,[37] and was probably further strengthened in Tatian by the Prologue to the *Fourth Gospel*.

Philo's Logos also acts as mediator between man and God, pleading for man, and acting as ambassador for God.[38] In this vein Philo also calls the Logos God's viceroy, High Priest, Archangel, and Manna.[39]

In view of the absolute transcendence of Philo's God, it should come as no surprise that Philo considers a gulf to exist between God and man.[40] However, Philo seems to offer two conflicting explanations for why this gulf is present, although both are based on the existence of evil; in some places, he considers man to be fallen because he is a created being, and relieves God from the responsibility of having created evil by delegating the creation of the inferior part of man (i.e. everything but the rational soul) to the subordinate powers;[41] whilst in other places, it would seem that man, created with free will, is himself responsible for his fall through choosing to turn to evil, and through this loses his immortality.[42]

Philo seems to suggest a bipartite division to man of body and soul and, in *On the Creation*, considers the soul of the first man to be imparted by God breathing upon him in *Gen* 2:7.[43] Yet in his treatise *On Giants*, Philo offers a more Platonic description of the descent of human souls from the divine,[44] and of how those souls can re-ascend to God:

> But the others descending into the body as though into a stream have sometimes been caught in the swirl of its rushing torrent and swallowed up thereby, at other times have been able to stem the current, have risen to the surface and then soared upwards back to the place from whence they came. These last, then, are the souls of those who have given themselves to genuine philosophy, who from first to last study to die to the life in the body, that a

higher existence immortal and incorporeal, in the presence
of Him who is Himself immortal and uncreated, may be
their portion.[45]

This passage throws up some interesting ideas and parallels, which
is why I have cited it in full. Here Philo expresses a salvation,
dependent on the study of 'genuine philosophy' and an ascetic
lifestyle, which offers man immortality and closeness to God. Parallels
with Tatian should become obvious by the end of this chapter.

Philo also has some interesting things to say about man's knowledge
of God. As we saw above, Philo claims that whilst the
existence of God is knowable, God's nature is incomprehensible to
man. Philo considers some knowledge of God possible through
intuition,[46] but he also allows further knowledge of God to be available
to man through divine revelation.

For Philo, prophecy is necessary to reveal what the human mind
is incapable of achieving alone.[47] Prophecy and revelation of truth
would also seem to offer an element of the divinity to man, since in
the treatise *Who is the Heir of Divine Things?* prophecy and revelation
of truth are in fact the divine inheritance.[48]

Philo's understanding of prophecy and its relationship with hellenistic
culture is very interesting indeed. It has been argued that
Philo substitutes the term 'prophecy' for the Platonic term 'recollection'.[49]
If this is the case, then Philo is interpreting traditional
Jewish views of prophecy in terms of a philosophical quest for
divine knowledge.[50] It has further been argued that Philo considers
himself to be a prophet.[51]

Philo perceives some prophetic experiences to be ecstatic, the
prophet being subject to total divine possession and unaware of
what he or she speaks.[52] Whilst there is some evidence of ecstatic
prophecy within the Old Testament,[53] an ecstatic interpretation of
Old Testament prophecy was beginning to become particularly
popular amongst Philo's Jewish contemporaries, and there are clear
roots within the Graeco-Roman oracular tradition.[54] In describing
the ecstatic state, Philo speaks of the Divine Spirit as a 'visitor and
tenant' to the 'citadel' of the soul of man:

> For no pronouncement of a prophet is ever his own; he is an
> interpreter prompted by Another in all his utterances,
> when knowing not what he does he is filled with inspiration,
> as the reason withdraws and surrenders the citadel of
> the soul to a new visitor and tenant, the Divine Spirit

which plays upon the vocal organism and dictates words which clearly express its prophetic message.[55]

Once again I have quoted this passage in full because of parallels with Tatian; the idea of the divine spirit dwelling within the prophet's purified body is also found in the *Oration*.[56]

Philo also has a very strong asceticism, which at times seems to be world denying. He gives a rather negative appraisal of the body, calling it a tomb and a corpse.[57] Yet Philo does not hold the body and the world to be entirely negative, as we have seen that the Valentinians did. He understands intercourse for the purposes of procreation to be a good thing, a participation in God's creativity, although he is nonetheless scathing of associated physical pleasures.[58] In some places, he also seems to consider the goods of man to include the external and the physical as well as the spiritual.[59]

Philo also disapproves of maltreating the body, believing it to affect the soul as well as the body, and does not advise those with wealth to throw it away.[60] His personal ideal would seem to be to live frugally with adequate but not excessive sustenance, and to balance a life of solitude and reflection with a public life.[61]

Philo's views on matters of intercourse are outlined most thoroughly in Book Three of *On the Special Laws*. He denounces adultery and incest, condemns pederasty, bestiality and prostitution, and censures rape and intercourse with widows or unmarried girls. For Philo, the whole purpose of sex would seem to be to procreate. Otherwise, he advocates continence within marriage, and discourages intercourse at other times, such as when a woman is barren, and during menstruation.[62]

Asceticism clearly played an important part in Philo's thought, perhaps even more so than in Justin. Interestingly, Ugo Bianchi has even suggested that Philo's metaphysical anthropology forms the basis of Encratism.[63]

Even from this briefest of sketches, it is obvious that Philo's philosophy bears some resemblance to that of Tatian. Beyond the commonalities of Platonism and the Judeo-Christian tradition, of which there are many, Philo's emphasis on the importance of prophecy in revealing knowledge of God, and his understanding of salvation in *On Giants* 13–14, seem particularly interesting. I suspect that a more detailed analysis of the precise relationship between Tatian and Philo might throw up some fascinating parallels, although such a study goes well beyond the scope of this book. Having given this thumbnail sketch of the relevant factors in

Philo's thought, it is now time to consider Justin's relationship with Philo.

Justin: the beginnings of Christian philosophy

There is some evidence of the incorporation of hellenistic philosophy into Christianity within the New Testament and the Apostolic Fathers,[64] but Justin Martyr is the first extant Christian writer to display signs of real dialogue with philosophy. As we have seen, Justin's relationship with philosophy is fairly complex, and is more than just an eclectic collation of philosophical elements; as Norris points out,[65] Justin uses philosophy as a framework within which his Christian teaching can be expressed, and so is presenting his theology in the logical terms of philosophy.

Following the work of Andresen, the influence of Middle Platonism upon Justin can hardly be denied;[66] clearly Platonism was a significant force in the forming of Justin's thought. However, the question of how that influence exerted itself is a little less certain. Some scholars, who accept the historicity of his conversion account in the opening chapters of the *Dialogue*, assert that Justin carried this Platonic influence with him from the period of his life prior to his conversion. However, other scholars have noted that a precedent for the incorporation of Platonic ideas is found in Philo.[67] Did Philo's Middle Platonism have any influence over Justin, and if so, how was that Philonic influence expressed?

The principal proponent of the school of thought that perceives Philonic influence in Justin is Goodenough. In his monograph on Justin, Goodenough outlined several important similarities between Justin and Philo.[68] Besides significant correlations in exegetical approach and philosophic outlook, Goodenough points to usage of Philonic terminology in Justin's concept of God and indicates several parallels in Justin's understanding of the Logos – including the metaphor for the generation of the Logos, a spiritualized understanding of the spermatic logos, and a list of titles for the Logos common to both Justin and Philo.[69]

Several scholars have concurred with Goodenough's basic theory, the most notable being Trakatellis, who, whilst exploring the concept of the pre-existence of Christ in Justin Martyr, convincingly argues that much of the Stoic and Platonic language in Justin is due to Philonic influence.[70] He also points out that some of the similarities between Justin and Philo are not only terminological and conceptual, but also contextual and functional.[71]

However, other scholars have disagreed quite strongly with Goodenough's hypothesis. Barnard has presented the most negative response in his own monograph on Justin, although even he is forced to agree a general influence of hellenistic Judaism.[72]

The current state of the debate is summed up fairly accurately by Runia, who points out that because Philo is no longer considered representative of hellenistic Judaism, the relationship between Justin and Philo has been questioned. Runia proposes three possible hypotheses to explain the available evidence:

1 Justin knew Philo, but used him so freely that it is difficult to identify precise debts.

2 Justin became familiar with Philo during the earlier part of his life but later lost track of his works, obscuring similarities between the two in Justin's extant works.

3 Justin knew themes within hellenistic Judaism, but knew them through other sources and not through Philo.[73]

Runia points out that the general consensus of scholarship has moved from hypothesis one to hypothesis three, and then wrongly asserts that there is no correlation between Philo and Tatian and that, therefore, the possibility of any connection between Justin and Philo is further weakened.[74]

Yet despite his negative evaluation at the end of this section on Justin, elsewhere Runia still seems to suggest that Justin was in fact influenced by Philo. Earlier in his survey, Runia suggests that the Neopythagorean Numenius, whom we met in Chapter 4, knew Philo, and that copies of his works were in circulation in second century Syria.[75] He therefore argues that contact between Justin and Philo, before his move to Rome, is not impossible. He also tentatively suggests that the unavailability of Philo's writings at Rome may account for the imprecision of the similarities between Justin and Philo, although he readily admits that there is no real evidence to support this hypothesis.[76] However, the possibility of this turn of events seems to be what leads him to propose hypothesis two above.

The danger with adhering to trends in modern patristic scholarship is that in accepting and using a new trend, the old trend is often rejected entirely. Thus although I think it is important to be aware that Philo represents only a small stream of hellenistic Judaism, which was based in Alexandria and cannot be considered as representative of hellenistic Judaism as a whole, I do not think that we should discount the possibility of his influence on Justin.

This is very much the approach adopted more recently by Edwards in an article that examines the links between Justin's Logos and the Word of God in Jewish thought; whilst Edwards considers the influence of other forms of Judaism on Justin's thought, he still includes a study of the influence of Philo.[77]

Perhaps what we are looking at is not in fact a direct influence of Philo upon Justin, but the influence of a Philonic stream within Judeo-Christianity, which preserves some of the themes and ideas of Philo. This would certainly help to explain the vagueness of the similarities between Justin and Philo. With this in mind I shall now turn to consider the parallels between Justin and Philo briefly, with a view to identifying the key characteristics of the philosophical tradition that I believe Justin handed on to Tatian.

The most obvious expression of the philosophical tradition that I believe can be traced in Philo and Justin is the incorporation of Middle Platonic terminology and ideas. The first concept where this becomes apparent is in their understanding of the nature of God; both writers use conventional Platonic notions about divinity and combine them with the personal God of Judaism and Christianity. Thus we find that they use Middle Platonic concepts like 'the Good', 'Being', 'unchanging' and 'unbegotten' to describe God, and still perceive a personal creator, intimately involved in the world through his Logos.

Goodenough has also identified more specific parallels between Philo's doctrine of God and that of Justin. These include the argument put forward by both for the existence of God beyond space, the paradox of combining a Jewish notion of a location for God with the Greek denial of spatiality to God, and the way in which they use the notions of the namelessness and unutterableness of God.[78]

However, the key area where this philosophical tradition is expressed is in their Logos theology. Goodenough has pointed up several significant parallels between Philo's doctrine of the Logos and that of Justin. Both Philo and Justin interpret the God of the Old Testament theophanies to be the Logos, basing their arguments primarily on the transcendence of God, and both also have lists of titles that they apply to the Logos.[79] However, the most important parallels for this study, since they are also found in Tatian, are the metaphors used by Philo and Justin to describe the generation of the Logos and the developing concept of the spermatic logos.

We noted in Chapter 3 the use made by Justin and Tatian of parallel metaphors to describe the generation of the Logos, and we

were unable to reach any firm conclusions about the relationship
between them due to the existence of similar metaphors in other
writers. However, a further study of these metaphors in the light of
the hypothesis that they belong to a philosophical tradition passed
on from Philo (or a Philonic stream) to Justin and then to Tatian
proves to be very interesting indeed.

There are several passages in Philo where the metaphors of fire
being kindled from fire, rays of light being produced by the sun,
and streams flowing from a spring are used. In *On Giants*, Philo uses
the metaphor of fire to describe how the passing on of knowledge
does not diminish the giver:

> But think not that this taking of the spirit comes to pass as
> when men cut away a piece and sever it. Rather it is, as
> when they take fire from fire, for though the fire should
> kindle a thousand torches, it is still as it was and is dimin-
> ished not a whit. Of such a sort also is the nature of know-
> ledge.[80]

What is particularly interesting, in view of Grant's claim that
Tatian's rhetorical background provides the distinction that the
Logos came into being by partition (κατὰ μερισμόν) and not by
section (κατὰ ἀποκοπήν),[81] is that we find a similar distinction
here in Philo (who uses the word ἀποκοπήν), which is again present
in Justin (who uses the word ἀποτομήν). At the most, then, Tatian
embellished an existing argument with his knowledge of grammar.

Meanwhile, in *Questions on Exodus* Philo uses the metaphor of
streams flowing from a spring to describe the splitting of the Logos
into two powers:

> And from the divine Logos, as from a spring, there divide
> and break forth two powers.[82]

Clearly these metaphors of projection are used by Philo in two
separate contexts; one to describe the transmission of knowledge
(albeit an esoteric interpretation of knowledge as the spirit of
prophecy) and the other to describe the emanation of powers from
the Logos.

As we noted in Chapter 4, the Neopythagorean philosopher
Numenius also uses the metaphor of a torch being lit from another
torch without diminishing it to describe how knowledge is passed
on:

This beautiful process occurs with knowledge by which the Receiver profits, as well as the Giver. This can be seen when one candle receives light from another by mere touch; the fire was not taken away from the other, but its component Matter was kindled by the fire of the other. Similar is the process with knowledge, which by both giving and taking remains with the Giver, while passing over to the Receiver.[83]

Numenius' use of this metaphor in the above passage is clearly very close to that of Philo. This would easily be explained by Runia's hypothesis that Numenius knew the works of Philo.[84]

However, Justin uses the fire metaphor and argument of *On Giants* 25 to describe the kind of projection of the Logos that we find in *Questions on Exodus* II.68:

We can observe a similar example in nature when one fire kindles another, without losing anything, but remaining the same, yet the enkindled fire seems to exist of itself and to shine without lessening the brilliancy of the first fire.[85]

As we have seen, Tatian follows his master in his use of this metaphor. Indeed, the metaphors are far closer in Justin and Tatian than they are to Philo and Numenius, which suggests a closer relationship between Justin and Tatian's use of fire and speech metaphors than we were able to postulate in Chapter 3.

Metaphors of projection are also used by Tertullian to describe the generation of the Logos in his treatise *Against Praxeas*:

For God brought forth the Word, as the Paraclete also teaches, as the root brings forth a tree and a fountain a stream, and the sun a ray. For these spectacles too are processions of those substances from which they proceed.[86]

Tertullian's usage of these metaphors is similar to that of Justin and Tatian in that he applies them to the generation of the Logos, although the metaphors themselves are different.

So, what conclusions can we draw about the use of projection metaphors in these five writers? I would see a fairly close relationship between the metaphors of Philo in *On Giants* 25 and Numenius, and perhaps even one of dependence, although it is difficult to make any firm conclusions without comparing other aspects of their thought. The metaphors of Tertullian, however, seem quite separate from those of Philo, and may well represent a separate tradition that uses the same concept.

However, in relation to Philo the metaphors of Justin and Tatian appear to stand somewhere in between these two possibilities. They are certainly not close enough to argue for dependence upon Philo, and yet their transposition of the fire metaphor and emanation argument in *On Giants* 25 to the projection of the Logos in *Questions on Exodus* II.68 may indicate a development of Philo's usage, reflecting the kind of philosophical tradition that I am proposing.

There is a further parallel between Philo and Justin in Justin's metaphor of speech, which he also uses to describe the generation of the Logos:

> When we utter a word, it can be said that we beget the word, but not by cutting off, in that the sense that our power of uttering words would thereby be diminished.[87]

Here Justin seems to be expressing the distinction that the Stoics made between λόγος ἐνδιάθετος (as a thought in the mind) and λόγος προφορικός (as the expression of that thought), although he does not state the theory explicitly. Goodenough discovers the same tendency in Philo, and suggests that this reflects Justin's dependence on a Philonic tradition.[88]

Parallels between Justin's spermatic logos theory and the spermatic logos of Philo have also been set forward by Holte[89] and supported by Trakatellis,[90] although clearly Justin has developed the concept considerably.

We recall that Runia rejected any evidence of Philonic influence in Tatian, and considered this a final weakness in the case for Philonic influence upon Justin, despite his earlier optimism.[91] I suspect that Runia makes this assessment of Tatian because he assumes that Tatian was influenced by gnosticism. However, as Runia himself points out, Martín has identified several passages in the *Oration* that parallel Philonic thought, including the torch metaphor and passages relating to the nature of the soul and the relationship between the spirit and matter.[92] In Philo we find a concept of salvation that is far closer to Tatian than the Valentinians, or even Justin. The emphasis on asceticism as prerequisite for prophecy and the stress that he places on prophecy in revealing a philosophized knowledge of God are very close indeed to Tatian.

These factors, combined with the proximity of the general

thought worlds of Philo and Tatian, offer a persuasive case for Philonic influence on Tatian. I would therefore conclude that a philosophical tradition existed that began with Philo, was passed on by Philonic streams within Judaism and/or Christianity to Justin, and was then inherited by Tatian. This, I believe, is the 'Christian Philosophy' to which Tatian was introduced.

Tatian's philosophy

It is now time to consider Tatian's presentation of his Christian philosophy. In so doing, I shall attempt to point out those elements in his thought that I believe reflect the philosophical tradition received from Justin.

As we saw in Chapter 4, Tatian presents Christianity as a philosophy. If we stand back and view the Christian teaching that Tatian sets down in his *Oration*, we realize that the notion of presenting Christianity as a philosophy is far more than an apologetic device; Tatian incorporates elements of hellenistic philosophy into his system, and the questions with which he is concerned are the same as those that contemporary Middle Platonists were themselves grappling with. I believe that Tatian's Christian teaching can easily be understood as a philosophical system, and I would suggest that Tatian has gone one step further than his master Justin in this; for Justin, Christian philosophy was one facet of his Christianity, but for Tatian, philosophy has a much higher priority. In my opinion, Tatian should be considered primarily as a Christian philosopher.

Martin Elze comes to much the same conclusion about Tatian as a philosopher, although he arrives at it from a very different direction. Elze understands the basic concept in Tatian's thought to be a search for the truth, and takes this as his principle of interpretation.[93] He argues that Tatian was familiar with Middle Platonism prior to his conversion to Christianity, and that despite Tatian's protests to the contrary Tatian retains elements of the philosophy from his pre-Christian phase – especially the concept of the search for truth.[94]

There is much in Elze's work with which I agree, but there are also some fairly significant points that I would question. First, I would agree that an important driving force behind Tatian's philosophy is a search for the truth,[95] and the consistency of truth is clearly important in his criticisms of philosophers and, I suspect, in his motivation for compiling the *Diatessaron*.[96] For Tatian, Christianity is the consistent truth for which he was searching.[97]

However, in support of his argument that the truth is the key concept in Tatian's thought, Elze places a heavy emphasis on Tatian's position as 'the Herald of Truth'.[98] I find this emphasis far too strong. Although Tatian does seem to call himself 'the herald of truth' in *Or* 17:1, it is important to consider the context of this apparent self-designation:

> Therefore, O Greeks, listen to me when I issue my platform call, and do not in mockery transfer your own irrationality to the herald of truth.[99]

There are several points to be made here. First, Tatian does not explicitly state that he considers himself to be the herald of truth, and although it is possible to infer this meaning, its ambiguity necessarily weakens Elze's argument. Second, the phrase appears to have specific and intended overtones of hellenistic philosophy, since it was common practice for philosophers to debate in public. This could be interpreted purely as an apologetic device, which therefore may not reflect Tatian's orientation particularly accurately. Third, the phrase appears within the wider context of Tatian's criticism of Greek medicine and magic, which makes the sentence something of an aside, and further implies that even if 'the herald of truth' is a self-designation, Tatian's use of it is of relatively little importance. Moreover, Tatian seems to perceive only the prophets to be capable of revealing the truth to man,[100] and Tatian nowhere claims to be a prophet himself. It strikes me that Elze has over-stressed this one passage without taking other, more fundamental elements in Tatian's thought into consideration.

Elze places Tatian as a philosopher within the Middle Platonic tradition, and argues that at some points Tatian is particularly close to several individual Middle Platonist philosophers.[101] Elze suggests that Tatian's dualism and his view of transcendence bear a close resemblance to the ideas of Albinus (i.e. Alcinous) and Gaius, but the principle Middle Platonist to whom he appeals is Atticus; Elze claims that both Tatian and Atticus argue against the Aristotelian doctrine of providence, the ethical issue of external goods, and against self-teaching and the autonomy of human thought. He also points to a parallel claim in Tatian and Atticus that 'only like perceives like', and highlights the fact that both speak of two levels of knowledge.[102]

I think that Elze is right in saying that Tatian uses Platonic arguments and terminology, but I would be rather more cautious

in drawing such parallels between Tatian and individual philosophers.[103] Tatian's thought world is certainly very close to the
Middle Platonist tradition, and he is concerned with answering the
same kind of questions as we find amongst Middle Platonists.
However, there is another avenue through which Tatian may have
come across Middle Platonic ideas, and this is the developing tradition of Christian philosophy, which is significantly present in
Tatian's own teacher.

It seems to me that Elze has also overemphasized Tatian's life
prior to his conversion, and that he has relied too heavily on this
pre-Christian phase. The fact is that we know practically nothing
about the early period, or indeed the later period, of Tatian's life.
We know that he was born in Assyria,[104] that his parents were
pagans, and that Tatian was probably given a conventional Greek
education, which may have included philosophy. Tatian may also
have been exposed to the popularized philosophy that permeated
the intellectual atmosphere of his day.[105]

Tatian may have been aware of Platonist doctrines prior to his
conversion, but we know from Philo and Justin that Middle Platonic ideas were already present in the Judeo-Christian tradition. If
Tatian did inherit a philosophical tradition influenced by Platonism
it is also possible that Tatian was not even aware of the full debt
that his Christian philosophy owed to Platonism, and this would
certainly explain the paradox of Tatian's use of Platonism in the face
of his extreme hostility towards the Greek world. If this was the
case, Tatian's philosophical education must have been fairly rudi-
mentary; perhaps sufficient to be conversant with the characteristic
doctrines of individual schools. The charge of plagiarism that he
levels at philosophers would have explained similarities between his
own Christian philosophy and the other hellenistic philosophies,
and most especially the strong parallels with Platonism. After all, as
far as Tatian was concerned his Christian philosophy was handed
down from the 'barbarians' (i.e. the Jews) and, as my study has
shown, Jewish philosophers like Philo had already united the
Hebrew Scriptures with Middle Platonism.

I would suggest, then, that although Tatian may have had some
sort of basic introduction to hellenistic philosophy during his
youth, when he converted to Christianity he inherited a Christian
philosophy that had already absorbed a great deal of Middle Platonic doctrine. I strongly suspect that he was unaware of the incorporation of Platonism into Christian philosophy, and that he
thoroughly believed any similarities between Greek philosophy and

his own Christianity to be due to plagiarism. This would therefore mean that his pronounced hostility and rejection of all things Greek is genuine. The implication that follows from this, of course, is that in presenting his Christianity to the Graeco-Roman world Tatian is not consciously reconciling his hellenistic background with his Christian faith, as Justin seems to. For Tatian the assimilation had already occurred, and it seemed perfectly natural that his Christianity should take the hellenized, philosophical form it did.

God

Tatian's understanding of God, as we have seen, owes something of its essence to Middle Platonism. It is true that, in their portrayal of the divine, Platonism and Christianity have much in common, but Tatian's inclusion of the particularly Platonic concepts of 'Being' and 'the Good' in describing his God does suggest some Platonic influence. The question is; how did Tatian come upon these ideas?

Tatian's understanding of divinity is monotheistic,[106] he portrays his monadic God as a transcendent being, using negative terminology to describe him,[107] and considers his God to be the creator of the cosmos.[108] These three ideas are common to both Middle Platonism and Judeo-Christian traditions. However, if we turn to consider what Tatian says about God as the creator, we find that there are some elements that may seem to display more of a Platonic flavour.

In describing how God creates the world, Tatian introduces the Logos as the instrument through which God works; the Logos 'springs forth' from God and in turn begets creation.[109] Thus Tatian is distancing his transcendent God from direct contact with matter. We saw much the same thing happening within Middle Platonism where, in describing divine involvement in creation, philosophers also used divine agents to perform the work of creation. Plutarch, for instance, uses the concept of the Logos in the figure of Osiris, whilst Atticus involves the Platonic World Soul in the creation process. Meanwhile, Numenius presents us with two gods from the start, a supreme God and a Demiurge, and suggests that the process of creation actually fragments the divine further, producing a third God, divided from the second, which becomes a lower aspect of the Demiurge.

However, as we have seen, the concept of the Logos 'springing forth' is also found in Justin, accompanied by the same projection metaphors that Tatian uses, and can also be traced back to Philo. It therefore seems likely that Tatian acquired this concept through his master rather than through the direct influence of Middle Platonism. Moreover, as we shall see when we consider the Logos in more detail, Tatian bases much of the passage about God creating through the Logos on the opening chapter of the *Gospel of John*, and it is also possible that he was influenced by Jewish traditions about the 'Word'. There is also a more specifically Christian flavour to Tatian's understanding of God as creator. In claiming that God's relationship with the world through his function as creator enables man to take his first faltering steps towards knowing God, Tatian actually cites a passage from the Pauline Epistles.[110]

If we turn to consider further aspects of Tatian's God, we find that distinctions between philosophic and Judeo-Christian influence remain blurred; Tatian describes his God as judge,[111] ruler,[112] and father.[113] 'Father' is a common term for God in the New Testament, but it is also used by Middle Platonists, and the idea of judgement was also familiar within philosophy. What Tatian says about the nature of God also remains ambiguous; he says that God is a spirit, apparently citing from *John* 4:24. However, he goes on to say that this divine spirit does not pervade matter, but constructs and forms it.[114] Here, Tatian is clearly writing against the Stoic perception of divinity.

To return to the question of how the specifically Platonic concepts of 'Being' and 'the Good' fit within Tatian's thought, we find that both of these concepts are present in Justin and Philo.[115] I would therefore suggest that Tatian's Platonic understanding of God is not dependent upon his knowledge of Platonic doctrines prior to his conversion, but rather originates from a Christian philosophical tradition.

Logos and other powers

In common with other Christian and Middle Platonic writers who stress divine transcendence, Tatian finds it necessary to introduce other powers that enable divine contact with the created world. The most important such power in Tatian is the Logos.

Tatian introduces the Logos using language that comes from the Prologue to the *Fourth Gospel*:

> God 'was in the beginning' and we have received the tradition that the beginning was the power of the Word. The Lord of all things who was himself the foundation of the

whole was alone in relation to the creation which had not yet come into being. In so far as all power over things visible and invisible was with him, he with himself and the Word which was in him established all things through the power of the Word. By his mere will the Word sprang forth and did not come in vain, but became the 'firstborn' work of the Father. Him we know as the beginning of the universe.[116]

In fact, it seems as though Tatian is trying to clarify the relationship between God and the Logos as set out in *John* 1:1–3. Thus Tatian stresses God's priority over the Logos, stating that it is God himself, acting through the Logos, that performs the work of creation. He also distinguishes between God and the Logos by using the opening phrase of the *Fourth Gospel* to indicate a temporal difference; whilst God 'was in the beginning' (i.e. was pre-existent), the projection of the Word marks the beginning of the universe itself. As the 'firstborn' work of God, the Word is the beginning of the universe.[117]

However, Tatian is also anxious to emphasize that the Logos is not a separate entity, but rather part of the divine; the Logos 'springs forth' from God, a projection of the divine. This is most clear in the fire and speech metaphors that Tatian uses to express the generation of the Logos:

He [i.e. the Word] came into being by partition, not by section, for what is severed is separated from its origin, but what has been partitioned takes on a distinctive function and does not diminish the source from which it has been taken. Just as many fires may be kindled from one torch, but the light of the first torch is not diminished because of the kindling of the many, so also the Word coming forth from the power of the Father does not deprive the begetter of the power of rational speech.[118]

These metaphors, as we have seen, are also present in Justin and Philo. In view of the fact that Tatian uses the Logos theology at the beginning of *John* as the starting point for his exploration of the Word, and then goes on to use metaphors already existent within the Christian philosophical tradition, it is again unlikely that Tatian is relying directly on hellenistic philosophy here. The Logos is clearly a philosophical concept for Tatian, but its source seems to be Christian philosophy. Moreover, Tatian's treatment of the Logos seems to place him in dialogue with the *Fourth Gospel* and interpretations of its Logos theology; his explanation of the Logos bears all the features of a refinement enforced by controversy.

If we turn to consider the rest of Tatian's philosophy about the Logos, we find nothing that really contradicts this impression, although there are a couple of peculiarities. First of all we must examine the Word's function as God's instrument of creation, which is in fact the main role of the Logos in the *Oration*. In Tatian the Word is not an autonomous instigator; whilst distinct from God, the Word is still part of the divine, and does not act without God's will guiding it.[119] Thus although the Logos is directly responsible for creating the cosmos, Tatian can still talk of God as the sole creator of everything.[120]

As we have already seen, Tatian describes the Word as the beginning of the universe, which suggests that the generation of the Word marks the start of the whole creation process. This is supported by the fact that a little later, in Chapter 5, Tatian links the begetting of the Word with the begetting of the created world.[121] It would seem, therefore, that for Tatian the whole purpose of the generation of the Word was to enable God to create the world.

Tatian speaks of the creation process as an ordering of confused matter, but he also speaks more directly of the Word's involvement in creation when he describes the creation of men and angels:

> The celestial Word, made spirit from the Spirit and Word
> from the power of the Word, in the likeness of the Father
> who begot him made man an image of immortality.[122]

There are a couple of problems with this text; first, the phrase 'made spirit from the Spirit' may originally have been 'made spirit from the Father',[123] and second, the way in which Whittaker has worded her translation of this sentence seems to imply that the 'celestial Word' is a separate entity from the Word. In fact, it is likely that this opening phrase refers back to the discussion in Chapter 5, and that the 'celestial' Logos of *Or* 7:1 is the same entity as the Logos of *Or* 5. Thus it would seem that the next phrase, 'made spirit from the Spirit (or Father) and Word from the power of the Word' is merely an insert that is intended to clarify something of the nature of the Logos (i.e. that the Logos is both spirit and reason).

Other than the involvement of the Word in creation, the Logos is not much discussed in Tatian; in *Or* 7, Tatian tells us that prior to the fall the Word was involved in maintaining the order of the created world by issuing predictions and prohibitions, and that it was the Word that banished angels and men at the fall.[124] From this point on, the Word appears to vanish from view.

As we shall see shortly when we consider Tatian's anthropological theory, prior to the fall man possessed a material spirit (his soul) but also a divine spirit, which was 'the image and likeness of God'.[125] A consequence of the fall was man's loss of this divine spirit.[126] After the fall, the divine spirit takes up the role of mediator between fallen man and the divine by revealing knowledge of God through prophecy.[127]

What seems to be happening in the *Oration* is that before the fall mankind and God lived in harmony; man possessing the divine spirit, and the Word ordering life. At the fall, direct contact between man and God was severed; man lost the guidance of the divine spirit, and the Word's task of maintaining creation was terminated. The whole relationship between God and man seems to have moved down a notch, and within the divine hierarchy only the spirit, which was after all originally permitted contact with man, could reach down to touch only the best of humanity.[128]

Although this separation of the Word and the divine spirit into function and hierarchy may seem to present two distinct identities, I doubt that this is really what Tatian intended; he goes to great lengths to describe the Word's generation as by partition and not by abscission.[129] I believe that we should understand the spirit's generation in much the same way.

Tatian also alludes to Christ, although he does not actually use the term 'Christ' anywhere in his *Oration*.[130] The first of these allusions seems to refer to the Incarnation:

> We are not fools, men of Greece, nor are we talking non-sense when we declare that God has been born in the form of man.[131]

This passage must surely refer to the Incarnation, since Tatian goes on to present Greek myths of a similar nature. The second reference to Christ is rather more oblique:

> Those which were disobedient [to wisdom] and rejected the servant of the suffering God were clearly shown to be enemies of God rather than his worshippers.[132]

This seems to be a reference to Christ, and if this is the case, Tatian's use of the participle πεπονθότος (from πάσχω, to suffer)[133] displays a non-docetic view of Christ. One can't help wondering whether those who were 'disobedient and rejected the servant of the suffering God' and who were his 'enemies' rather than his 'worshippers' is a veiled and anti-Semitic reference to those Jews who rejected Jesus' messiahship.

Of course, Tatian's allusions to Christ raise the interesting question of what Tatian has chosen not to include in the *Oration*. Given Justin's strong identification of Christ with the Logos, it may be that Tatian assumes the Incarnation of the Logos, and that the Logos' activity does not end following the fall. It would be interesting indeed to learn how Tatian would have envisaged the generation of Christ.

Cosmology

Tatian is not overly concerned with cosmology, despite the fact that he cites the creation account in the Hebrew Scriptures as one of the reasons for his conversion.[134] However, what Tatian does have to say about creation holds some interesting parallels with Platonism, and proves to be very helpful in placing Tatian within the Christian philosophical tradition.

The process of creation is outlined in detail in *Or* 12:

> It is possible to see that the whole construction and creation of the world has derived from matter, and that matter has itself been produced by God in such a way that we are to think of it partly as raw and formless before its separation, partly as organized and orderly after its division. And so by division the heavens are derived from matter, and also the stars therein; and the earth and all that is engendered from it has the same constitution, so that everything has a common origin.[135]

Here Tatian is clearly outlining the Platonic concept that creation involved the organization of pre-existent, disorderly matter, and in his inclusion of this particular Platonic concept, we find precedents in both Philo and Justin.[136] However, in Chapter 5 Tatian also claims that God creates matter prior to its ordering, apparently stating a theory of creation out of nothing.

Before the appearance of Gerhard May's book, *Schöpfung aus dem*

Nichts,[137] scholars generally assumed that Christians had inherited from Judaism the notion that God created the world 'out of nothing'. However, May quite rightly distinguishes between the strict doctrine of creation out of nothing and the earlier, far vaguer notion that God created the cosmos out of the non-being (i.e. formlessness) of pre-existent matter.[138] Thus whilst the formula ἐκ μὴ ὄντος was used in both cases, how 'out of nothing' was conceived was very different, and it becomes necessary to consider the arguments behind the use of this formula.

Both Philo and Justin understood ἐκ μὴ ὄντος to be the creation of the world out of the 'nothingness' of matter, although, as we have seen, Philo may have been struggling towards the concept of creation out of nothing. As May points out, a natural consequence of Judeo-Christian insistence on the omnipotence of God is the implication that nothing should be beyond the scope of God, and it therefore becomes necessary to conceive of matter as being created by God. As with Philo, this concept was probably latent in the early church, but was not directly confronted. It is a notable fact that doctrines are often only formulated in full in the face of controversy, and May identifies two forces that drove Christian theologians to address the issue of creation in the late second century; the cosmology of gnosticism, and dialogue with Greek philosophy.[139]

The first figure whom May identifies as proposing the idea of true creation out of nothing is Basilides (mid-second century).[140] In Hippolytus' account, Basilides apparently attributes the creation to the supreme God, and not the Demiurge.[141] May argues that it was from this understanding of a transcendent creator that Basilides rejected the anthropomorphic image of God working as a craftsman with the matter before him, and arrived at the notion of creating matter out of nothing.

However, there are several problems with May's thesis, not least the fact that Irenaeus offers a conflicting picture of Basilides.[142] As Young has pointed out, there are also some ambiguities about exactly how Basilides uses the term 'non-existent'; Basilides talks of a non-existent world being produced from non-existence by a non-existent God, revealing a negative outlook on the reality of the physical world.[143]

The next figures whom May identifies as proposing creation out of nothing are the contemporaries Theophilus of Antioch (late second century) and Tatian, both about a generation later than Basilides.[144] Theophilus arrives at the concept of creation out of nothing whilst in debate with Platonism; he criticizes the Platonic

concept of pre-existent matter because he believes that it under-
mines God's role within creation and his divine sovereignty, and
that it erroneously attributes a god-like status to matter. He also
seems to attack the Platonic image of the craftsman for its anthro-
pomorphism.[145]

Tatian, like Theophilus, also arrives at the concept of a creation
out of nothing through the concern that the notion of pre-existent
matter compromises divine omnipotence. In *Or* 5 he writes:

> For matter is not without beginning like God, nor because
> of having beginning is it also of equal power with God; it
> was originated and brought into being by none other, pro-
> jected by the sole creator of all that is.[146]

Thus Tatian's process of creation is somewhat innovative, as it
involves the ordering of unformed matter 'originated' by God.
However, there are some important distinctions to be made concerning Tatian's theory of creation out of nothing. As May points
out, Tatian does not actually use the term ἐκ μὴ ὄντος.[147] This
may be due to the Platonic use of this language to describe formlessness, since, in Chapter 6, Tatian uses this kind of language to
describe the state of man prior to birth and after death.[148] Perhaps
Tatian has chosen not to use ἐκ μὴ ὄντος because he has not rede-
fined this formula as Theophilus seems to have done.

A further difference between Tatian's creation out of nothing and
that of Theophilus is in their motivations; although both argue
against pre-existent matter because of the consequences for divine
omnipotence, they are pushed to this conclusion from quite different directions. Whilst Theophilus' hand seems to have been forced
by second century Platonists, such as Hermogenes, I suspect that it
is Tatian's principle of internal consistency that leads him to reject
the concept of pre-existent matter. It is true that if the passive principle of matter were to coexist with God prior to creation, Tatian's
monotheism would be compromised, but I believe that it is only
Tatian's demand for consistency that forced the issue.

In his analysis of Tatian's theory of creation out of nothing, May
offers an interesting perspective on Tatian's relationship with gnosticism. May perceives some sort of contact with Valentinianism in
Tatian's cosmology, and especially in his use of the term
προβάλλεσθαι (to project). Although I have argued for caution in
analysing parallel terms in Tatian and individual gnostics, May's
suggestion that this contact is due to the development of Tatian's

cosmology in opposition to that of gnostic rivals is certainly interesting.[149]

In his cosmology, Tatian also gives us some indication of the nature of the created world. Perhaps influenced by Stoicism, Tatian describes how a material spirit permeates matter, producing a spirit within all kinds of things from angels and men to animals and plants. He also explains how material things, such as the body and the world itself, were constructed with a purpose, and contain differing amounts of material spirit.[150]

Because Tatian understands his God to be ultimately responsible for creation, the created world offers men a unique insight into the transcendent God; he claims that some knowledge of God can be attained through his creation, and even through men as created beings.[151] Since Tatian cites *Rom* 1:20, the basis for this notion is probably Biblical and not philosophical.

Demons and angels

Tatian's demonology is central to his understanding of the world; when reading Tatian, one tends to feel as though demons are hovering at the edge of his awareness. Of course this was not uncommon in Tatian's day; as we have seen, Justin's perception of demons was also quite keen, and there was a strong demonology tradition within Semitic cultures as well as within hellenistic philosophy.

So how does Tatian perceive of his demons? First of all, in describing the creation of angels and their involvement in the fall he seems to equate the demons with fallen angels; Tatian tells us that the Word created angels before he created men, and that both were given free will. Because the angels had free will, they were able to choose to follow the arch-rebel and thus play their part in the fall, being consequently banished as demons.[152] Thus prior to the fall these beings would seem to be designated as 'angels', and afterwards as fallen angels they become 'demons'.

However, we do encounter a potential problem with this interpretation of Chapter 7, since in her translation of a passage in Chapter 20 Whittaker seems to differentiate between the demons and 'those created first' (i.e. the angels):

> The demons had to move house, and those created first were banished, the former were cast down from heaven, the latter not from this earth, but one better ordered than here.[153]

The actual Greek text reads:

μετῳκίσθησαν <γὰρ> οἱ δαίμονες, ἐξωρίσθησαν
δὲ οἱ πρωτόπλαστοι· καὶ οἱ μὲν ἀπ' οὐρανοῦ
κατεβλήθησαν, οἱ δὲ ἀπὸ γῆς μὲν ἀλλ' οὐκ ἐκ ταύτης,
κρείττονος δὲ τῆς ἐνταυθοῖ διακοσμήσεως.[154]

There are several problems with this text. Where Whittaker trans-
lates '*and* those created first were banished', we find the conjunction
δὲ, which has in any case been emended by Schwartz from γὰρ in
manuscripts M and V, which would therefore read, '*for* those created
first. . .' Where Whittaker chooses to use the words 'the former' and
'the latter', the construction οἱ μὲν ... οἱ δὲ is used by Tatian.
Whilst ambiguous, this construction would usually be used to
denote 'some ... others'. I would therefore emend Whittaker's
translation as follows:

> The demons had to move house, for those who were created
> first have been banished; some have been cast down from
> heaven, whilst others [have been cast down] not from this
> earth, but from [one] better ordered than here.

If this text and translation is correct then we do not need to differentiate between demons and angels, and Tatian would seem to be
suggesting two different levels of fall for these beings.

However, I suspect that understanding demons simply as fallen
angels overlooks a subtlety in Tatian. Much of how one interprets
Tatian's demonology is coloured by one's perception of the word
'demon'. As we have seen, in the hellenistic world demons were not
considered inherently evil; δαίμων was the word used to denote
supernatural beings (sometimes including the gods), some of whom
were bad but some of whom were good. The prevalent Judeo-
Christian understanding of 'demon', meanwhile, was coming to have
a purely negative meaning. This was partly in opposition to polythe-
ism, and was a definition that gathered speed as Christianity differentiated itself more and more from hellenistic culture and beliefs.

In Tatian, I believe we find a tension between the hellenistic and
developing Judeo-Christian definitions of δαίμων. Throughout the
Oration we find references to the demons' wicked intentions, in
particular with reference to their use of matter to enslave men;
Tatian argues that the demons deliberately cause disease in men's
bodies, and then create the cure through potions.[155] The ultimate

goal of demons would seem to be to prevent men from regaining the union with the spirit, and thereby immortality.[156] In *Or* 15, Tatian even claims that the demons are 'reflections of matter and evil', and that there is no possibility for them to repent.[157]

All of this paints a very black picture of demons, yet in *Or* 12 we read:

> The demons too, as you call them ... became profligate and greedy, some of them turning to what is purer, others to what is inferior to matter and behaving like it.[158]

Here, Tatian seems to be saying that he does not consider all demons evil; some 'turn to what is purer'.[159] Notice that Tatian also qualifies these demons with 'as you call them', which may suggest that Tatian does not necessarily use the same terminology.

So what is actually going on here? I suspect that partly Tatian is working from the hellenistic position that δαίμων is a term used to refer to spiritual beings, which would explain his equating demons and angels. Meanwhile, Tatian is also part of a Judeo-Christian process of negativizing demons. Thus the conflict in Tatian's thought may be due to the developing state of this particular concept.

During the tale of the fall, Tatian introduces us to an intriguing figure; an 'arch-rebel' who incites and is ultimately responsible for the fall:

> Then came one who was cleverer than the rest because he was first-born, and men and angels followed along with him and proclaimed as god the traitor to God's law, and so the power of the Word banished the arch-rebel and his followers from life with him.[160]

The reason that the fall occurs at all, according to Tatian, is that the arch-rebel covets divine status, and is 'proclaimed god' by men and the other angels.[161] This charge of desiring divine status is levelled at the demons repeatedly,[162] and is perhaps expressed in Tatian's claim that the demons are the pagan gods. Tatian also obliquely accuses mankind of being involved in this divinization of demons.[163]

Tatian also gives us some fairly detailed information about the nature of demons. He asserts that they are not the souls of men,[164] and that they are not composed of flesh, and are therefore to a certain extent immortal. Tatian understands demons to be spiritual beings, 'compacted from matter' (although of the more 'spiritual' matter like fire and air) and possessing a material spirit.[165]

Tatian claims that demons can be perceived by men; those 'guarded by the spirit of God' can see them easily, and that demons can also show themselves to 'psychics' (i.e. to those without the spirit) to fulfil their own devious ends. However, ultimately Tatian considers the demons to be powerless. God tolerates their activity and allows them to continue, but their ability to create mischief is limited.[166]

A favourite accusation that Tatian hurls at the demons is that they are responsible for human diseases and, paradoxically, for man's dependence on drugs.[167] Tatian also accuses demons of inventing fate, and considers the demons partly responsible for leading man to his present state of mortality.[168] In describing the activities of demons Tatian uses the metaphor of banditry; in reference to manipulating matter through disease and cure, and to deceiving men.[169]

Despite the more positive outlook that Tatian seems to suggest in Chapter 12, the ultimate destiny Tatian envisages for the demons is somewhat grim. From what Tatian says in Chapter 15,[170] it would seem that the demons are incapable of turning towards good, and therefore punishment inevitably awaits them at the end of the world.[171]

Man

Tatian's exploration of man's nature and his position within the created world is one of the key themes in the *Oration*. Tatian's anthropological theory begins with man's creation, deals with the fall and its consequences, and runs through until a future day of judgement. His main concern within this anthropological theory seems to be to explain why man finds himself in his current state, and to offer hope of a reunion with the divine.

Tatian's understanding of the creation of man is clearly influenced by *Genesis*, since he states that the Word made man 'in the likeness of the Father'.[172] However, Tatian's interpretation of the likeness of God seems to be more philosophical. In Chapter 15, we read:

> But the important question now is what is meant by the divine image and likeness. That which is not susceptible of

comparison is Being itself; what is susceptible of any comparison is nothing other than that which is similar. Now the perfect God is fleshless, but man is flesh. The bond of the flesh is soul, but it is the flesh which contains the soul. If such a structure is like a shrine, 'God' is willing to 'dwell' in it through the 'spirit', his representative.[173]

Here Tatian is stressing the absolute transcendence of God, and in so doing is rejecting any anthropomorphic interpretation of God's likeness. Instead, he suggests that it is man's connection with the divine spirit that makes him become 'the image of God'. This impression is confirmed by a passage in Chapter 12, where Tatian states that the divine spirit is the 'image and likeness of God'.[174] It would also seem that man's possession of the divine spirit before the fall endowed him with the divine quality of immortality.[175] As we have seen, this notion of kinship with God through a divine element within man, such as the Intellect, is common within Middle Platonism. Tatian envisages man's existence before the fall to be simultaneously material and incorporeal.[176]

The key to understanding man's involvement at the fall is Tatian's insistence on free will. He believes that man was created from the first with free will. Whilst the fall was incited by the arch-rebel, man still had the free will to reject him. Man chose to follow the arch-rebel, and was therefore banished along with the arch-rebel and the angels.[177]

Man's state following the fall would seem to be pretty hopeless; as a consequence of his banishment, man lost his union with the divine spirit and thereby became mortal.[178] This separation blinds man to God, and apparently leaves him in a downward spiral, since without the spirit man is naturally attracted towards matter.[179]

From this position, there would seem to be no return. Yet the picture is not entirely bleak; Tatian repeatedly hints at a reversal of the fall. This reversal is apparently made possible by man's free will.[180] Thus Tatian tells us that we should strive to achieve reunion with the divine spirit,[181] and in Chapter 13 we learn that this reunion is achieved by gaining knowledge of God or the truth.[182] So for Tatian the search for the reunion becomes a search for the truth encapsulated within Christian philosophy.

Given Tatian's fairly negative estimation of man's present condition, the practical question arises of how man becomes aware of his current state and thereby begins the search for truth. It is true that in Chapter 13 Tatian tells us that the soul retained a spark of the spirit after the fall, implying a direct link between God and man.[183] However, as I demonstrated in Chapter 3, Tatian does not explicitly use this connection, and man's spark may be a throwback to Justin's spermatic logos. As we shall see, Tatian turns instead to prophetic revelation; he clearly understands prophecy to be the method through which the history of the fall and the possibility of salvation are communicated to man.[184]

To balance the fall, Tatian envisages a future day of judgement when men will have to answer for their actions. He clearly states his belief in a physical resurrection, and even counters the practical question of how the bodies of the dead can rise if they are torched, drowned, or consumed by animals.[185] Tatian also believes that there will be a conflagration to mark the end of the world.[186] On the day of judgement, two possible fates await man; immortality with pleasure or immortality with pain.[187] The difference between these two destinies hinges upon whether the individual has attained knowledge of God or the truth,[188] and the reward for gaining this knowledge would seem to be reunion with the divine spirit, and thereby restoration to man's state prior to the fall.

In an interesting passage in Chapter 20, Tatian hints at a divine realm that he envisages beyond our universe. Here he takes the same stance of incomprehensibility that we saw when he was speaking of the concept of 'Being'; he argues that man alone is incapable of perceiving this divine place, but implies that it has been revealed by the prophets.[189]

To sum up, then, Tatian's anthropological theory is intended to explain man's current level of existence, and offers a coherent account of mankind's history. Man's current state belongs only within the parameters of the fall and the day of judgement, which may explain Tatian's view of time; arguing against the Stoic doctrine, Tatian rejects the division of time into past, present and future, and instead envisages one ongoing 'age'.[190]

As we have seen, the most important element in Tatian's understanding of man is free will. Since free will was also a live issue within Middle Platonism at this time, we must turn to consider how Tatian copes with the philosophical paradox of reconciling man's free will with God's divine providence.

First of all, Tatian clearly denies the existence of fate and attributes its invention to the demons.[191] He also attacks the Aristotelians for their rejection of providence, which would therefore suggest that Tatian himself accepts the concept.[192] However, first and foremost

Tatian is anxious to emphasize man's free will; he stresses man's responsibility for his own actions to the full.[193]

Many early Christians saw the working of providence in divine foreknowledge of the results of human choice, and we may come across this in Tatian too. Although he does not directly mention the notion of providence, a passage about the Logos in Chapter 7 may hint at how providence works within his system:

> The power of the Word having in itself foreknowledge of the future, not according to fate but through the free decision of the choosers, used to foretell the outcome of future events, prevent wickedness by prohibitions, and commend those who remained steadfast in well-doing.[194]

The Logos would seem to provide the element of divine providence before the fall, and performs this task by direct intervention through prohibition and commendation. Tatian does not elaborate on how, or even whether, divine providence works after the fall; perhaps the spirit takes over this function. However, given that Tatian seems to perceive the time between fall and judgement as a temporary phase of man's existence, perhaps he did not consider it important.

Tatian also tells us something about the nature of man's body and soul. They are indissolubly linked, constructed from a plan, and since the fall, body and soul in themselves do not make man a rational being. Without the spirit, 'man is superior to the beasts only in his articulate speech'.[195]

Prophecy

There are three instances in the *Oration* where Tatian seems to refer to prophecy. In Chapter 20, Tatian mentions the prophets explicitly:

> But we have learned through the prophets what we did not know, who being convinced that the spirit in conjunction with the soul would obtain the heavenly garment of mortality – immortality – used to foretell all that the rest of the souls did not know.[196]

From the details given in this passage, I believe we should infer that Tatian is also speaking of the prophets in Chapter 13:

> God's spirit is not given to all, but dwelling among some
> who behaved justly and being intimately connected with
> the soul it revealed by predictions to other souls what had
> been hidden.[197]

The link between these two passages, then, is the revealing of previously unknown, hidden knowledge, and it seems fairly safe to assume that those indwelt by the spirit in the second passage are also the prophets of the first passage.

Our third reference to prophecy, in Chapter 15, is slightly more problematic:

> Now the perfect God is fleshless, but man is flesh. The
> bond of the flesh is soul, but it is the flesh which contains
> the soul. If such a structure is like a shrine, 'God' is willing
> to 'dwell' in it through the 'spirit', his representative.[198]

Since we came across the indwelling of God's spirit as an apparent means of prophetic inspiration in the second passage cited above, it seems likely that Tatian is also referring to prophetic inspiration here. However, in view of the more general context in Chapter 15, where Tatian urges the reader to search for the divinely ordained union between Holy Spirit and human soul,[199] we must inevitably question whether this third passage might not simply refer to Christians in general.

Tatian's understanding of prophetic inspiration in the *Oration* is complicated by his anthropological theory; as we have seen, Tatian believes that originally man was created with a share of the divine spirit, that this was lost at the fall, and that man's hope of salvation depends upon being able to regain the union between the soul and the divine spirit. Given that Tatian also envisages man's original state to be material as well as spiritual,[200] it becomes very difficult indeed to differentiate between Tatian's soteriology and his understanding of prophetic inspiration through the indwelling of the Spirit.

However, if we turn to consider the context in which prophetic passages are found in the *Oration*, we discover that prophetic activity is inextricably interwoven with the salvation process. This comes across most strongly in Chapter 13. Here, Tatian writes at length about how it is possible for the mortal soul to achieve immortality. He stresses that by itself (i.e. without divine aid) the soul is doomed to sink down towards matter and destruction, but that if the soul gains knowledge of God (or the 'truth') then it can be saved.[201] The method by which such knowledge is imparted to the soul is through divine revelation, and the passage that explains this is the second of our three passages above; God's spirit reveals (through the prophets) the knowledge necessary for salvation. I can find no other means in the *Oration* by which such knowledge is imparted, and the redemptive process made possible.

The context of our first prophetic passage, in Chapter 20, also displays close connections with the salvation process. Here Tatian is describing the fall, the end of the world, and how various geographers have described heaven. He dismisses the conjectures of the geographers by saying that the truth about heaven (and other things) has been revealed through the prophets. Tatian's use of the words 'we have learned . . . what we did not know' strongly reflects Chapter 13 and his claim that the soul can attain immortality, providing that it gains knowledge of God, and his linking statement that we must 'yearn for our ancient condition' (i.e. union with the spirit)[202] is further proof that our first prophetic passage should be understood within a soteriological context; the prophets are revealing the truth about man's past, and in so doing provide knowledge of God, and thereby the means to achieve salvation.

Clearly, prophetic activity is closely linked with the revelation of the salvation process. If we turn to Chapter 15, we discover that the context of our third prophetic passage is also soteriological.[203] When Tatian speaks of how man can become the image and likeness of God he is elaborating on the salvation process, since elsewhere he tells us that the 'image and likeness of God' is the divine spirit itself;[204] gaining such a likeness would therefore involve reuniting soul and spirit, and result in a redemptive state.

However, the crucial question here is this; in Chapter 15, is Tatian referring to the prophets as he does in Chapters 13 and 20? To tackle this problem, we need to look at the issue of hierarchy in Tatian's thought. If we are to understand the prophets to be a spiritual elite, indwelt by the divine spirit so that they can reveal knowledge of God, there must be at least one lower order in Tatian's thought. This we find in Chapter 15, when Tatian mentions 'psychic' Christians and contrasts them with 'those guarded by the spirit of God'.[205] Those without the spirit of God, then, would seem to represent an ordinary class of Christians whom Tatian designates as 'psychics'.

Is it then possible that the prophets, as men indwelt by – and therefore reunited with – the Holy Spirit, are in a sense providing a model of the union that Tatian believes all men should strive for? I suspect that this is in fact the case; for Tatian, prophetic activity seems to be the basis for salvation. The prophets form a spiritual elite who disclose, through revelation and possibly by example, the redemptive process.

If Chapter 15 is a reference to the indwelling of the spirit in prophets, as I suspect it is, then a further point needs to be raised here about prophetic behaviour; in Chapter 15, only those whose body and soul are like a shrine receive God's spirit and become the divine likeness. The body as a temple has strong links with Pauline material, and suggests an ascetic base for Tatian's understanding of prophecy. This is backed up by a phrase that Tatian uses in our second prophetic passage; in Chapter 13, Tatian states that God's spirit only dwells 'among some who behaved justly'.[206] Given Tatian's ascetic interests, it seems likely that Tatian considered asceticism a prerequisite for prophecy.

Inevitably Tatian's concept of prophecy has its roots in Judeo-Christianity, and particularly in the Old Testament – his 'barbarian writings'.[207] However, we must still ask whether Tatian's use of prophecy reveals anything of the Judeo-Christian philosophical tradition that I am postulating.

As we have seen, for Justin Old Testament prophecy plays a key role in his thought, and his argument from prophecy is central to his justification of the Christian faith. However, whilst prophecy is evidence of divine activity amongst men and proves the truth of Christian claims, it is not key to his understanding of salvation. Instead this function is taken over by his spermatic logos theory.

If we turn to Philo, however, we find some interesting parallels. We have seen that for Philo, prophecy becomes necessary to reveal what the human mind is incapable of achieving alone,[208] and that in describing the ecstatic state Philo speaks of the Divine Spirit as a 'visitor and tenant' to the 'citadel' of the soul of man.[209] Philo may also draw on the Platonic concept of recollection to present prophecy as a philosophical quest for divine knowledge.[210]

Conclusion: Tatian and the development of a Christian philosophy

From this survey of Tatian's theology it has become apparent that, as Elze has argued, Tatian was indeed influenced by Middle Platonism, but that this Middle Platonic influence was mediated through a Christian philosophical tradition that was passed on by Justin.

Almost all Platonic concepts within Tatian's thought can be found in Justin and/or Philo, and this neatly explains his extreme hostility towards Graeco-Roman culture and his conviction, which I consider to be genuine, that the Greek philosophers plagiarized from Moses. In placing Tatian within second century Christianity, I therefore believe that we should see him as a philosopher and apologist, presenting his inherited Christian philosophical tradition to the Graeco-Roman world.

6

TATIAN AND SYRIAC
CHRISTIANITY

To complete the picture of where Tatian belongs within the second century, we must return to the charges of the heresiologists mentioned in Chapter 2. I have, I hope, refuted the charge of Valentinianism laid against Tatian, but what of the charge of Encratism? Did Tatian found a sect called the Encratites on his return to the East, and what influence did he exert on his homeland? In this chapter we therefore turn to consider Tatian within the context of Syriac Christianity.

Tatian's ties with Syriac Christianity

It is clear that before he began the travels that led him to Rome, Tatian came from Syria. There is plenty of patristic evidence that assumes his Syriac provenance, and in the *Oration* Tatian himself tells us that he was born in Assyria.[1] However, his Syriac parents were not Christians, and it was not until some point during his travels, either before his arrival in Rome or during his stay there, that Tatian was converted to Christianity.[2] Thus it seems highly unlikely that Tatian came into contact with Syriac Christianity during his youth.

After his master Justin's death Tatian returned to the East, and, as we have seen, evidence from Epiphanius places the date of Tatian's return to about 172 CE.[3] Epiphanius also claims that Tatian established his own school in Mesopotamia, and although Epiphanius cannot always be considered reliable, the notion of a Tatianic school is certainly not impossible.[4]

Burkitt has made a further connection between Tatian and Syriac Christianity. During his survey of Syriac Christianity, Burkitt makes the surprising suggestion that the apostle Addai of the legend of the *Doctrine of Addai*, who supposedly converted Edessa, should be equated with Tatian himself; Burkitt suggests that 'Addai' was the Syriac version of Tatian's name, and the name by which he was known in the East.[5]

First, there is a linguistic problem with this hypothesis; one would expect a consonant (a 't' or 'd') at the start of 'Addai'.[6] It is also highly probable that Christianity had arrived in eastern Syria long before Tatian's return in the last quarter of the second century.[7] Moreover, the work of Drijvers on the question of the historical origin of the *Doctrine of Addai* further questions the validity of Burkitt's hypothesis; Drijvers argues most convincingly that the Addai legend is a Christian appropriation of a tradition within Manicheism.[8] So I must conclude that Burkitt's claim that Addai and Tatian were one and the same person is pure conjecture, and cannot be supported by the evidence.

Tatian and Encratism

We recall from Chapter 2 that, as well as charging Tatian with Valentinianism, the heresiologists also accused him of adherence to Encratism. Irenaeus introduces Tatian as an Encratite, and claims that he considered marriage 'corruption' and 'fornication';[9] Eusebius cites Irenaeus and then adds that Tatian was the leader of the Encratite sect;[10] meanwhile, Epiphanius asserts that the Encratites are Tatian's successors.[11]

Encratism (from the Greek ἐγκράτεια, meaning 'self-control' or 'continence') was the term given by western heresiologists to an eastern sect that practised extreme asceticism. Although I have my reservations about how this term can be applied to Tatian in the context of primitive eastern Christianity,[12] in evaluating Tatian's relationship with Syriac Christianity it is clearly important to consider Tatian's involvement with Encratism.

'Encratite' glosses in the Diatessaron

Tatian's *Diatessaron*, or the *Euangellion da-Meḥalleṭe* (*Gospel of the Mixed*) as it was known in the East, was a gospel harmony, uniting the texts of our four New Testament Gospels and possibly one or more Judaic-Christian gospel(s). The *Diatessaron* was the first text of the New Testament to be introduced to the East, where it became the standard gospel text.[13] The *Diatessaron* was also the form of the gospels used by eastern missionaries, and thus it became the text to which new converts were introduced in countries as far afield as China.[14]

Unfortunately no extant copy of Tatian's *Diatessaron* survives, since it was removed from widespread circulation in the fifth century and replaced by the four canonical Gospels.[15] However, due to its immense success, some of the *Diatessaron* can be pieced together from secondary sources that made use of, or quoted from, Tatian's gospel harmony. The process of extracting variants from Diatessaronic witnesses is quite laborious, often unprofitable, and of varied reliability. It is thus with caution that I proceed to consider the 'Encratite' variants found among the witnesses by Diatessaronic scholars.

Five variants referring to marriage and intercourse have been identified.

1 *Matthew* 1:19:

> And her husband Joseph (ὁ ἀνὴρ αὐτῆς), being a just man (δίκαιος) and unwilling to put her to shame, resolved to divorce her quietly.

In at least three Diatessaronic witnesses (the Middle Dutch Liège Harmony, the Middle Italian Venetian Harmony, and the Curetonian Syriac), the definite article (except of course in the Syriac) and possessive pronoun are omitted, thus relating ἀνὴρ to δίκαιος. This renders a more general interpretation of ἀνὴρ as 'man' possible, and avoids referring to Joseph as the 'husband' of Mary.[16] However, if Tatian did make this variant, one can not help wondering how he would have explained Joseph's decision to divorce Mary a little later in the same verse.

2 *Matthew* 1:24:

> When Joseph woke from sleep, he did as the angel of the Lord commanded him; he took his wife (παρέλαβεν τὴν γυναῖκα αὐτοῦ).

In the Armenian version of Ephrem's *Commentary on the Diatessaron* and in the Persian Harmony, the sense of the last clause is changed to mean that Joseph 'guarded' Mary, again avoiding the suggestion of marriage.[17]

3 *Matthew* 19:4–5:

> He answered, 'Have you not read that he who made them from the beginning made them male and female,

and said, "For this reason a man shall leave his father and mother and be joined to his wife, and the two shall become one flesh"?'

In the Liège Harmony, the word 'Adam' is added to the beginning of verse 5, thus reading 'And Adam said', placing the physical union advocated in *Genesis* 2:24 into the mouth of Adam, and indicating that such a union was never intended by God.[18]

4   *Luke* 2:36:

> And there was a prophetess, Anna, the daughter of Phanuel, of the tribe of Asher; she was of great age, having lived with her husband seven years from her virginity.

Several witnesses (the Persian, Stuttgart and German Zürich Harmonies) replace the preposition ἀπὸ (from) with 'in' or 'with'. This changes the sense of the verse to mean that Anna lived with her husband for seven years 'in her virginity'. In addition to this the Persian Harmony renders ζήσασα as 'she remained', thus emphasizing Anna's continued state of virginity.[19]

Two other witnesses (the Sinaitic Syriac and Ephrem's *Hymn on Abraham* 10.17) substitute 'days' for 'years', reducing the amount of time Anna shared the marital life with her husband. The Sinaitic even adds 'only' at this point, so that the text reads 'seven days *only* was she with a husband after her virginity'.[20]

5   Vööbus identified a final variant in the Liège version of *Luke* 20:27–40. The alteration occurs during a dialogue between the Jews and Jesus about seven brothers and a woman whom they were successively obliged to marry when she was widowed. Jesus' reply, that in the age to come none are married,[21] is taken by the Liège Harmony to refer to the situation of Christians in the present day, and not in the age to come. Thus the modification reads:

> The people of this world take a wife and make marriages; but they who shall be worthy of the life of that other world and of the resurrection of the blessed, will neither take wives nor make wedding feasts.[22]

There are also five suggested variants concerning references to alcohol in the *Diatessaron*.

1   *Matthew* 11:19:

> The Son of man came eating and drinking, and they say, 'Behold, a glutton and a drunkard!'

In Ephrem's *Hymn on the Resurrection of Christ*, however, Jesus is presented merely as someone who 'drinks', rather than as a 'wine-drinker'.[23]

2   *Matthew* 26:29:

> I tell you I shall not drink again of this fruit of the vine until that day when I drink it new with you in my Father's kingdom.

In the Armenian version of Ephrem's *Commentary on the Diatessaron*, this verse is shortened considerably to suppress the idea that wine will be drunk in the kingdom. Instead, in this work the verse reads:

> From now on I shall not drink from this generation of the vine until the Kingdom of my father.[24]

3   *Matthew* 27:34:

> They offered him wine to drink, mingled with gall.

In the Armenian version of Ephrem's *Commentary*, the wording is changed so that Jesus is offered 'vinegar' and gall rather than 'wine' and gall.[25]

4   The remark 'when men have drunk freely' during the account of the marriage at Cana in *John* 2:10 is also omitted in the Armenian version of Ephrem's *Commentary*.[26]

5   *John* 15:1:

> I am the true vine, and my Father is the vinedresser.

In the Persian Harmony, this verse is altered to read 'I am the tree of the fruit of truth', thus avoiding the vine imagery.[27]

It is interesting indeed to note that apart from the last variant, which is found in the Persian Harmony, all of these Diatessaronic variants relating to alcohol are found in works composed by Ephrem. This necessarily raises the question of whether Tatian was responsible for these alterations, or whether they are due to Ephrem's own ascetic inclinations, or are the work of the editor of the Syriac version of the *Diatessaron* that Ephrem used.

There are three further variants which are left to be considered.

1   *Matthew* 13:52:

> And he said to them, 'Therefore every scribe who has been trained for the kingdom of heaven is like a householder who brings out of his treasure what is new and what is old.'

In the Persian Harmony, this verse is subtly altered so that the man trained for the kingdom is not compared with a householder who possesses treasure. It is thus changed to:

> He said to them: Thus every scribe who has been made a disciple and attracted into the Kingdom of heaven, is like a householder who brings out from all that he has in his house, old and new.[28]

2   *Mark* 10:30:

> Who will not receive a hundredfold now in this time, houses and brothers and sisters and mothers and children and lands, with persecutions, and in the age to come eternal life.

The Persian Harmony adds the words 'all is affliction and anxiety' following 'persecutions'. In the context, this implies that the life of possessions is one of suffering.[29]

3   *Luke* 14:26:

> If anyone comes to me and does not hate his own father and mother and wife and children and brothers and sisters, yes, and even his own life, he cannot be my disciple.

In the Persian Harmony, the Sinaitic Syriac and the Curetonian Syriac, the verb 'to hate' is replaced by the alternative 'to abandon'. Clearly, this reflects the ascetic demand to renounce one's former life.[30]

So what can be gathered from these suggested variants? Some variants, in particular the variants concerning Anna the prophetess in *Luke* 2:36, display overwhelming evidence of alterations of an ascetic flavour, which may indeed go back to the original text of the *Diatessaron*. Where several reliable Diatessaronic witnesses contain the same variant, and especially if these include witnesses from both East and West, as in *Luke* 2:36, we seem to be on firm ground. Elsewhere, and particularly in the alterations concerning alcohol that are found in Ephrem, the claim to a variant within the original *Diatessaron* is rather more dubious. Thus the suggested variants are of varied reliability, and it is difficult to reach any firm conclusions about them.

There is also a further problem, which I have been hinting at, and this is the circular methodology used by Diatessaronic scholars. Since western heresiologists, from the time of Irenaeus, condemned Tatian as an 'Encratite', scholars of the *Diatessaron* have been working their way through the Diatessaronic witnesses searching for 'Encratite' variants. What they have in fact found are variants of an ascetic nature, which may be due to Tatianic influence.

The question I wish to ask is this; what makes these variants specifically 'Encratite' rather than generally ascetic? All three classes of variants display ascetic ideals that were also common within mainstream Christianity,[31] and if one were to argue that an 'orthodox' Christian would not have altered the text of the Gospels, we must remember that at the time when Tatian composed the *Diatessaron* the Gospels were not firmly fixed and did not command the kind of status that they did in the West a generation later. Surely the only reason that these variants are labelled 'Encratite' is due to the accusations of the heresiologists, who, as we have seen, were not entirely infallible, and in the case of Tatian's relationship with Valentinianism were misinformed. So I proceed with caution, and must ask whether we have firm proof, apart from the heresiological claims, that Tatian leant towards asceticism. I shall now turn to consider the ascetic hints in Tatian's *Oration*.

Ascetic references in the Oration

There are few explicit references to asceticism in the *Oration*. This may be due to its genre and aim, since the *Oration* is primarily an apologetic work, attacking Greek culture. However, we should also bear in mind the possibility that the heresiologists were correct in their claim that Tatian's asceticism became more pronounced after his master's death.

The most significant reference to asceticism in the *Oration* occurs in Chapter 11, where Tatian is arguing against the control of fate:

> Why if everything is fated, are you often racked with desire, and often die? 'Die to the world' by rejecting its madness; 'live to God' by comprehending him and rejecting the old birth.[32]

As we have seen, Tatian's command to 'die to the world' and 'live to God' seems to have its roots in Pauline terminology.[33] This terminology is frequently used as a call to asceticism, and Tatian's reference to being 'racked with desire' seems to confirm his ascetic understanding of these Pauline passages. This is reinforced by the wider context of Chapter 11, where Tatian renounces power, wealth and ambition.[34] Clearly Tatian is advocating ascetic values here.

The demand to reject worldly things is one that is commonly made upon ascetics. Indeed, one might argue it is the key command. In Tatian this demand takes on a particularly significant role, since his call to the ascetic lifestyle is also a call to reverse the effects of the fall and achieve immortality.[35]

Another strong reference to asceticism is found in Chapter 8. Here Tatian is again disputing the reality of fate, and in so doing points up the mortal behaviour of the demons (i.e. the pagan gods) whom he believes to be responsible for introducing the concept of fate:

> Now do we not regard as mortal those who watch gladiators and take sides? Who marry, and seduce boys, and commit adultery? Who are subject to laughter and anger? Who run from the battlefield, and get wounded?[36]

It is significant indeed to note that here Tatian seems to place lawful marriage on a par with pederasty and adultery. The charge that those engaged in these activities should be regarded as mortal is considered trivial by Hawthorne, and admittedly, as he points out, in the direct context of Chapter 8, Tatian is arguing against the divinity of the pagan gods (i.e. the demons), and uses the involvement of Greek gods in sexual activity in order to do this.[37] However, in the wider context of the *Oration* the charge becomes rather more serious; Tatian states that men should be striving beyond their mortality, towards immortality through reunion with the divine spirit, and I suspect that ascetic principles are vital to this process.[38] Therefore the accusation that those who marry or are engaged in pederasty or adultery are mortal implies that they will not be saved on the day of judgement.

We now move on to consider less certain ascetic references. In Chapter 23, Tatian attacks gladiatorial shows and states:

> You sacrifice animals in order to eat meat and you buy men
> to provide human slaughter for the soul, feeding it with
> bloodshed of the most impious kind.[39]

Here Tatian seems to be implying that just as these men 'sacrifice' animals in order to fulfil a depraved physical desire, so they also slaughter human beings in order to fulfil a perverted desire of the soul. Whilst Tatian's use of the verb 'to offer sacrifice' may merely refer to the practice of the eating of meat offered to the pagan gods, Tatian's distaste for the eating of meat may actually reflect a rejection of any meat eating.

We find the same kind of ambiguity in Chapter 33, where Tatian is defending the inclusion of women in Christian meetings:

> For this reason, I want to prove from what you consider
> honourable that our behaviour is chaste, while yours
> borders on madness ... All our women are chaste, and our
> girls at their distaffs talk in godly terms to better effect
> than that girl of yours.[40]

The word 'chaste' (from σωφρονέω, meaning 'to practise self control') probably refers to the exemplary moral behaviour displayed by Christian women. Whilst perhaps not a direct reference to asceticism, it certainly reflects Tatian's view that Christian women should practice temperance.[41]

Although these passages containing ascetic references are so few, one should note the intrinsic level at which they occur. These passages are not dealing directly with ascetic issues; asceticism is mentioned as part of Tatian's argument about entirely different subjects. In the first passage Tatian is calling men to reject fate and other things of this world, whilst in the second he argues against the divinity of the pagan gods. The third passage is an aside inserted in Tatian's tirade against gladiatorial shows, and the fourth is used in justification of the inclusion of those whom Greek society might consider inappropriate into the Christian community.

One might argue that the fact that these ascetic references are merely mentioned in passing and do not form the main part of the argument indicates that for Tatian, asceticism is not an important part of his Christianity. However, I would suggest that, to the contrary, this proves that asceticism is a very basic and important part of Tatian's faith; these references are made at a subconscious level.

Having established that asceticism is expressed in the *Oration*, I shall now turn to two passages that I believe refer to prophecy. In Chapter 15, where Tatian is considering the indwelling of God's spirit, we read:

> The bond of the flesh is the soul, but it is the flesh which contains the soul. If such a structure is like a shrine, 'God' is willing to 'dwell' in it through the 'spirit', his representative.[42]

To place this passage in context, it occurs as an explanation of how man can become 'the image and likeness of God', and I would suggest that here Tatian intends to refer specifically to the prophetic experience in this life.[43] Given the existence of ascetic ideals in the *Oration*, I think it highly likely that maintaining body and soul as a 'shrine' implies the application of an ascetic lifestyle.

Our final passage is found in Chapter 13:

> God's spirit is not given to all, but dwelling among some who behaved justly and being intimately connected with the soul it revealed by predictions to the other souls what had been hidden.[44]

Once again, although the notion of behaving 'justly' is ambiguous, I believe that Tatian is referring specifically to ascetic behaviour. If this is indeed the case, it would seem that, for Tatian, asceticism is a prerequisite for prophecy.

Asceticism and On Perfection According to the Saviour

There is one further text we must consider, a text that confirms my understanding of the ascetic references in the *Oration*. This is a fragment of one of Tatian's works, *On Perfection According to the Saviour*, now lost. This fragment is preserved by Clement of Alexandria in his *Stromateis*, and is clearly ascetic in nature:

> He [i.e. the Syrian Tatian] writes in his work 'On Training Following the Saviour', and I quote, 'Agreement conduces to prayer. The common experience of corruption means an end to intercourse.' At any rate, his acceptance of it is so grudging that he is really saying No to it altogether. He agreed to their coming together again because of Satan and because of weakness of will, but he showed that anyone who is inclined to succumb is going to be serving two masters, God when there is agreement, and weakness of will, sexual immorality, and the devil when there is not.[45]

On reading this passage, one is immediately reminded of Irenaeus' third accusation against Tatian; that he declared marriage to be 'corruption and fornication'. At first glance this seems to be an accurate appraisal, yet on reflection we realise that for Tatian marriage itself is not the problem; it is rather any form of intercourse within marriage, which leaves room for exactly the kind of spiritual marriage we find among the sons and daughters of the covenant in Aphrahat's sixth *Demonstration*, where 'husband' and 'wife' live together as 'brother' and 'sister' in complete continence.[46] This inevitably raises some interesting questions about how Tatian's asceticism and the asceticism of Syriac Christianity are linked, and of course about the charge of Encratism laid against Tatian.

Conclusion: Tatian and Encratism

It is very difficult indeed to identify a heretical Encratite sect amidst the strong asceticism of early Syriac Christianity. Whilst it is true that several texts of Syriac provenance have been labelled 'Encratite', this seems to have been based entirely on their ascetic content.[47] The label 'Encratite' originates with the western heresiologists, and we should remember that the heresiologists had agendas of their own.[48] What seemed radical in the West as regards ascetic practices appears to have been the norm in the East, and whilst

Tatian is denounced as an arch-heretic in the West, in the East the 'heresy' of Tatian is passed over in silence – a silence that seems very significant in its acceptance of Tatian's views.

I believe that it is in fact misleading to consider 'Encratism' a heretical sect within early Syriac Christianity; an extreme asceticism appears to have been present within most streams of Syriac Christianity of the second and third century, and is also found in later 'orthodox' figures like Ephrem and Aphrahat. If we must insist on the use of the term 'Encratism', it seems more appropriate to speak of a 'spirit' of Encratism, which permeated the East at this time.

However, I believe that something of Tatian's legacy can be found within Syriac Christianity, although not within widespread ascetic trends. I believe that this legacy can be traced through the appropriation of Tatian's brand of 'Christian Philosophy', which we explored in the last chapter. I shall therefore now turn to examine the relationship between Tatian's philosophy and ideas within several Syriac texts.

Tatian and the Syriac texts

The Acts of Thomas

The *Acts of Thomas* were written in East Syria in the early third century and were probably composed in Syriac, although, due to the bilingual nature of the area, a Greek translation soon followed.[49] The original Syriac text has been lost, and although later Syriac versions may contain some of the original, preference is given to the extant Greek text. Part of the *Acts of Thomas*, the 'Hymn of the Pearl' (*Acts of Thomas* 108–113), has been labelled as 'gnostic'.[50] Whilst a gnostic-type interpretation is possible, it is not necessary or indeed particularly significant in understanding the hymn's relationship to the *Acts of Thomas*;[51] the 'Hymn of the Pearl' may have circulated separately within gnostic circles, yet it seems to be an integral part of the narrative thread of the *Acts of Thomas* since, as we shall see, it provides a poetical reflection on many of the central concepts in the *Acts*. Once again, more caution is required when attempting to identify gnostic terminology and concepts in this text.

Of the Syriac texts available for comparison, the *Acts of Thomas* is undoubtedly the closest to Tatian. The similarities between the two have led Klijn to conclude that the Greek influence in the *Acts of Thomas* is inherited from Tatian,[52] whilst Drijvers claims that both the *Acts of Thomas* and the *Odes of Solomon* reflect Tatian's ideas 'to such an extent that they can be considered a commentary on them'.[53] The parallels between the theology of the *Acts of Thomas* and that of Tatian are certainly striking. I shall now consider those parallels in detail.

The concept of union between human soul and divine spirit plays a key role in Tatian, and appears to be the only means by which the salvation process can occur. In the *Oration* Tatian says that this state of unity was present before the fall, and so the salvation process becomes a regaining of humanity's previous level of existence.[54] The means by which the union of soul and spirit occurs is through knowledge of God (or the truth), imparted to humanity through the prophets. Nor is this union reserved solely for a post-resurrection existence; the prophets are those souls in whom God's spirit already lives, and asceticism seems prerequisite for prophecy, purifying the prophet's body and preparing it to become a 'shrine' for the spirit to live in.[55] As we shall see, the *Acts of Thomas* do not reproduce these ideas exactly; they are developed and expressed in new ways, including the medium of poetry.

Twinning is a recurrent theme, running throughout the *Acts of Thomas*. Judas Thomas is repeatedly presented as the twin brother of Christ, and the likeness between the two is emphasized;[56] in two resurrection stories, those revived speak of seeing Jesus standing next to Judas Thomas, and comment on the likeness between the two.[57] The same remark is made by a demon during an exorcism performed by Judas Thomas,[58] although in all three cases it is not clear whether the likeness referred to is physical or spiritual.

The twinning of Jesus and Judas Thomas becomes most clear when Jesus is said to take on the appearance of the Apostle. In *Acts of Thomas* 11, we are told that the royal bridal couple converse with Jesus 'in the likeness of the apostle Judas Thomas',[59] and his message to them is identical to that of Judas Thomas elsewhere; complete continence is the only way to reach eternal life. The same thing happens in *Acts of Thomas* 151–153, where Jesus takes on the form of Judas Thomas and leads Tertia and Mygdonia to the prison where Judas Thomas is being held.

However during the account of Judas Thomas' martyrdom, the distinction between Judas Thomas and Jesus is made clear when Judas Thomas states that he is not Jesus, but rather his servant and minister.[60] Judas Thomas also seems to be expressing a desire to become like Jesus here, and this may mean that the twinning in the *Acts of Thomas* demonstrates Judas Thomas' desire to imitate

Christ.[61] This theme is also found in passages where Judas Thomas' actions mirror those of Jesus recounted in the Gospels.[62]

Curiously, Judas Thomas and Jesus seem to be linked in the same sort of way that the soul of the prophet and God's spirit are linked in Tatian. Admittedly there is no mention of Jesus 'indwelling' Judas Thomas in any way, but there is certainly a strong spiritual link.[63] When we consider the function that Judas Thomas performs in the *Acts of Thomas* and compare it with Tatian's prophets, the parallel is obvious; both are revealing the knowledge of God to other souls, as Tatian would put it. The missionary activity of the apostle is not that different from prophetic activity in this respect. Moreover, for Tatian asceticism seems to have been a precondition for such a spiritual link to occur, and when we look at Judas Thomas we find that he too followed an ascetic lifestyle.[64]

The union of human soul with the divine is also expressed in terms of marriage; Judas Thomas preaches that in place of a human, carnal marriage, God offers a spiritual marriage in heaven.[65] This spiritual marriage can take precedence over earthly marriage before or after it has taken place.

In the opening scenes of the *Acts of Thomas*, Jesus (appearing in the form of Judas Thomas) prevents a royal marriage from being consummated. He commands the young couple to reject intercourse and introduces them to the 'incorruptible and true marriage', by which is clearly meant a spiritual union.[66] It is particularly interesting to note that in this passage we find the same temple imagery that Tatian uses to describe the necessary conditions for the indwelling of the divine spirit in Chapter 15 of the *Oration*. The couple are persuaded by Jesus to abandon their recent marriage, and commit themselves to the heavenly union. The bride tells her parents that the heavenly marriage far surpasses the earthly marriage that she has rejected.[67]

The second marriage that is dissolved in the *Acts of Thomas* is again a royal marriage, this time between Charisius, a kinsman of King Misdaeus, and his wife Mygdonia. This marriage has been consummated, and is nearly one year old. The latter part of the *Acts of Thomas* is concerned with the chaos that follows its dissolution in favour of a spiritual marriage. Once again, spiritual marriage is presented as being far more desirable than Mygdonia's union with Charisius.[68]

The figure of Vazan, the son of King Misdaeus, presents us with an example of chaste marriage in the *Acts of Thomas*. Forced to marry by his father, Vazan has nonetheless kept his virginity and lived for seven years in complete chastity with his wife.[69] Yet clearly, from the tone of the narrative, although such behaviour is commended, Vazan's chaste marriage is a poor substitute for the heavenly marriage that Judas Thomas offers.

The bridal hymn in *Acts of Thomas* 6–7 is essentially a celebration of the heavenly marriage that Judas Thomas advocates. Somewhat esoteric in expression, it is placed in opposition to the earthly marriage that the celebrants are feasting.[70]

Presented with this concept of the heavenly marriage preached in the *Acts of Thomas*, with its imagery of Jesus as the Bridegroom, one might be tempted to associate it with traditional Western ideas of the church as the Bride of Christ. Such terminology clearly has its basis in the New Testament, and whilst the concept of the church as the Bride of Christ may be implied, there is no collective understanding of salvation present in this document; the soteriology, like Tatian's, is entirely individualistic. Thus the emphasis of the bridal imagery in the *Acts of Thomas* is on the union of the individual Christian with the divine.[71] Moreover, when we come to consider the fact that in the *Acts of Thomas* the individual's heavenly union is a return to an immortal state existent prior to the fall, we are again encountering ideas more akin to those of Tatian.

This concept, similar to Tatian's, is touched on only briefly in the *Acts of Thomas*, and does not form a major part in its soteriology. There are only two passages that refer directly to the notion that the spiritual union is a return to man's immortal state prior to the fall.

For the first passage we must return to the royal bridegroom in the opening scenes of the *Acts of Thomas*. As we have seen, the bride's response is to speak of the spiritual union in terms of a heavenly marriage. However, the bridegroom speaks of this union in terms of self discovery and reunion; he says he is redeemed from the fall through the revelation of his current condition, and is taught to seek himself so that he may regain his previous condition.[72] The same idea is repeated later in the *Acts of Thomas* by a woman troubled by a demon. The woman asks to be returned to her original nature, and to receive the gift given to her kindred.[73]

These are not explicit, expansive references to the kind of concept we find in Tatian.[74] Yet, if we turn to the 'Hymn of the Pearl' in *Acts of Thomas* 108–113, we can see that its subject is in part a poetical elaboration of the concept of the soul returning to its immortal state.

Sent into Egypt by his parents, the prince is ensnared by the Egyptians, forgets the purpose for which he left his homeland, and even forgets his identity. His perceptions are reawakened by a letter from his parents, and the prince charms the serpent, guardian of the pearl, and returns home to be rewarded by the return of his 'splendid robe' and toga, which had been stripped from him before he began his journey.[75] This robe seems to represent a re-clothing with immortality for the prince.[76] When the prince returns with the pearl and regains his robes, the robes become the mirror image of the prince.[77] In this we find echoes of the twinning between Judas Thomas and Jesus, but also an echo of Tatian's union between soul and spirit and the heavenly garment of immortality.[78] The robe is also described as displaying a likeness of the king of kings, which again brings us back to the twinning of Judas Thomas and Jesus, and may contain echoes of *Genesis* and the creation of man in God's image.[79]

There are also further instances in the *Acts of Thomas* where clothing imagery is used. In another hymn, which celebrates the spiritual marriage, we read that the celebrants shall put on royal robes.[80] Likewise, in the lead up to Judas Thomas' death the apostle uses clothing metaphors twice to describe how his martyrdom will result in the gaining of immortality,[81] and in *Acts of Thomas* 135 Mygdonia tells Tertia, prior to her conversion, that she stands 'clothed in robes that grow old'.[82]

Although we should be cautious in analysing the relationship between the clothing imagery in the *Acts of Thomas* and *Or* 20, since such metaphors were frequently used by Syriac authors,[83] it is nonetheless significant that such imagery is used in the *Acts of Thomas*, and especially in the 'Hymn of the Pearl', to describe the very Tatianic concept of regaining immortality through spiritual union with the divine.

From our investigation into the concept of spiritual union, it has become apparent that several striking parallels exist between the salvation process envisaged by Tatian and that expressed in the *Acts of Thomas*. However, as I have hinted, there are also some important distinctions to be made, and the emphasis shifts quite radically in the *Acts of Thomas* to include the sacraments.

There seem to be three main stages in the salvation process of the *Acts of Thomas*, and we find a clear progression from continence to baptism to the eucharist.[84] The call to continence is one that Judas Thomas preaches repeatedly throughout the *Acts of Thomas*, and the message that whoever joins in the 'impure union' has no part in the Christian life is imprinted firmly in the minds of Judas Thomas' followers.[85] It later develops into a more general asceticism, yet the call to chastity is the first demand that Judas Thomas makes, and without the fulfilment of this demand for chastity would-be Christians can advance no further.[86]

In the cases of Mygdonia and Tertia, Judas Thomas responds to their entreaties for inclusion in the Christian life by sending them home to their husbands, presumably to prove their commitment to the Christian faith by practising continence.[87] It is only after a period of sexual abstinence that Judas Thomas admits them to baptism. This connection between continence and admission to Christian baptism is again reflected in Acts of Thomas 131, where Siphor promises that he and his family will live in holiness, and then asks Judas Thomas to baptize them.[88]

The baptism outlined in the Acts of Thomas involves anointing with oil, baptizing in water, and then the sharing of a eucharistic meal. So the sacraments are intimately linked, and a eucharistic meal becomes part of the baptismal process. It is only after the sharing of bread and a mixture of water and wine that Judas Thomas turns to Mygdonia and tells her that she has received her 'seal' and gained eternal life.[89]

Before the baptism of Siphor and his family, Judas Thomas offers an interesting explanation of the sacrament. He sees baptism as a forgiveness of sins, which offers Christians the opportunity of rebirth and of union with a 'hidden power'.[90] There are parallels in this passage with ideas found in Tatian, and especially with Or 11:2. However, before we move on to compare the soteriology of Tatian with that of the Acts of Thomas, let us consider the role of Christ and the eucharist in the salvation process of the Acts of Thomas.

As we saw earlier when we considered the twinning of Judas Thomas and Jesus, imitation of Christ plays an important role in the theology of the Acts of Thomas. Drijvers claims that there is no doctrine of a Redeemer in the Acts of Thomas,[91] but I believe that there are occasional hints in this document of an intimate involvement of Christ in the salvation process. For example, Christ's physical presence in the eucharistic meal is stressed in Acts of Thomas 158, as too is the relevance of key elements of Christ's passion for the salvation of Christians; the gall and vinegar Christ is given to drink are presented as a removal of the gall of the devil and human weakness;[92] Christ's crown of thorns becomes a 'crown that does not fade away',[93] and Christ's grave and burial becomes a renewal of soul and body.[94] Clearly, Christ is presented as a Redeemer in the eucharistic theology of the Acts of Thomas.

As we discovered in Chapter 5, Tatian's soteriology is based on a

far more philosophical level than we find here in the *Acts of Thomas*;
it is through gaining knowledge of God (or 'the truth') that the soul
is saved.[95] Yet there are still some significant parallels between
aspects of Tatian's salvation and that of the *Acts of Thomas*.

The spiritual union which I outlined earlier is the first similarity.
Although the spiritual union in the *Acts of Thomas* is not identical
to that of Tatian, we can see elements that reflect back to Tatian –
especially in the robe imagery of the 'Hymn of the Pearl', the
significance of the likeness of God, and the regaining of lost immortality. We can also see a shift in emphasis in the *Acts of Thomas*
towards a sacramental salvation process, which may be hinted at in
Or 11:2, and the spiritual union, which is so central to Tatian's view
of redemption, becomes secondary in the *Acts of Thomas*.

In both Tatian and the *Acts of Thomas*, emphasis is laid on the salvation of the individual. In Tatian, individual souls are saved by knowledge of God, and likewise condemned through personal ignorance.[96]
In the *Acts of Thomas*, this emphasis is most clearly expressed in the
idea of spiritual marriage; spiritual marriage here is not a collective
experience, with the church as the Bride of Christ, but a personal
union between individual Christians and Christ.[97] However, as far as
the *Acts of Thomas* are concerned, it is possible to anticipate a more
collective consciousness of salvation that might develop from the
importance laid on the sacraments, and especially on the eucharist.

Treasure metaphors are also used to illustrate the soteriological
theories of both writers. In *Or* 30, Tatian uses the imagery of hidden
treasure:

> He held power over our property like a kind of 'hidden
> treasure': in digging it up we were covered with dust, but
> provided the occasion of guaranteeing its possession. For
> everyone who recovers his own property wins possession of
> the most precious wealth.[98]

In Chapter 2, I argued that the treasure metaphor in this passage
referred to the union with the divine spirit, and thereby immortality. As Drijvers points out, this metaphor is paralleled in the *Acts of
Thomas* by the pearl in the 'Hymn of the Pearl'.[99] Although it is not
quite clear what the pearl is intended to represent (the robe represents the divine spirit and therefore the prince's immortality), it is
possible in the context of the *Acts of Thomas* that the prince symbol-
izes Judas Thomas himself, and the pearl the treasure of those he
has saved.

There are other instances in the *Acts of Thomas* where treasure imagery is used, but the most significant example in the context of this study is found in *Acts of Thomas* 136, where Judas Thomas speaks of Jesus as his one precious possession.[100] In view of the special twinned relationship between Judas Thomas and Jesus, the possession of which the apostle speaks is surely the spiritual union, which offers immortality.

The final similarity between the soteriology of Tatian and that of the *Acts of Thomas* is the inclusion of free will. In Chapter 5, we saw how central the concept of free will is to the *Oration*. It is also present in the call to continence of the *Acts of Thomas*. For instance, the royal bridal couple in the opening scenes are offered a choice; married life with children and all the anxieties this brings, or continence and the promise of spiritual marriage without grief or anxiety.[101] Jesus does not bombard the couple with commands and prohibitions, and there is a clear choice that they are free to make.

Likewise, when Judas Thomas is forced by King Misdaeus to persuade Mygdonia to return to her husband, she is evidently free to make this decision, although Judas Thomas does comment that if Mygdonia has truly converted, nothing will divert her from the Christian path.[102] Clearly, free will has an important part to play in the soteriology of both Tatian and the *Acts of Thomas*.

We now move on to consider demonology in Tatian and the *Acts of Thomas*. As we saw in the last chapter, Tatian has a very strong demonology and a keen perception of the proximity of demons. In the *Acts of Thomas*, demons also play a prominent role, and Judas Thomas performs many exorcisms. Besides this general heightened awareness of the existence of demons, which is present in both documents, there is also a more direct point of contact; as Drijvers points out, the ability to perceive demons is restricted in the *Acts of Thomas* to the apostle and a few others.[103] This is very reminiscent of Tatian's claim that only the spiritual can easily see demons.[104]

The final concept common to Tatian and the *Acts of Thomas* is the notion that the body should be kept as a 'temple', a dwelling place for the Holy Spirit.[105] This Pauline idea is used by Tatian to describe how man can become the image of God:

> The bond of the flesh is the soul, but it is the flesh which contains the soul. If such a structure is like a shrine, 'God' is willing to 'dwell' in it through the 'spirit', his representative.[106]

This concept is repeatedly used in the *Acts of Thomas*, and is frequently connected with the call to continence, and thence with the salvation process and baptism.[107] There is even a reference to this concept in a passage that is highly reminiscent of the Beatitudes.[108] The notion of the body as a 'temple' for God, of purifying it so that the divine may dwell in it, is a very positive image of the corporeal. Yet in the *Acts of Thomas* there is a tension between this image and a more negative one, which we do not find in Tatian.

Clearly there are some very strong similarities between the *Acts of Thomas* and Tatian, particularly in the concept of the union between the soul and the divine. Indeed these parallels are so striking that some sort of link must be postulated to explain them. However, if we consider Tatian and the *Acts of Thomas* in isolation, it is impossible to arrive at any firm conclusion of their connection. It is only when we take into account other Syriac texts, and especially the *Odes of Solomon*, that we can trace the influence of a Tatianic tradition in Syriac Christianity.

Of course there are also many elements in the *Acts of Thomas* that differ from what we find in the *Oration*; the union of soul and spirit, which is so central to Tatian's soteriology, is present in the *Acts*, but is overshadowed in importance by the call to continence and the sacraments, and whilst the *Acts of Thomas* make use of the Pauline concept of the body as a temple, the *Acts* display a more negative appraisal of the body.

What becomes apparent, then, is that in the *Acts of Thomas* Tatianic concepts are being mingled with other influences and developed. We know that one such influence was the Thomas tradition, which is found in the *Gospel of Thomas* and the *Book of Thomas the Contender*, but there may well have been other traditions that the redactor drew upon. The *Acts of Thomas* represents a developing tradition.

The Odes of Solomon

The *Odes of Solomon* provide us with our second Syriac Christian text.[109] However, any evaluation of the testimony that the *Odes* offer is complicated by uncertainty about their place of origin and date, which means that issues of provenance and dating must first be clarified. Although this is by no means certain, since the *Odes* survive in both Greek and Syriac manuscripts,[110] it seems likely that they originated in Syria.[111] The question of dating the *Odes* is more problematic; scholars have suggested anything from the late first to the late second century,[112] and Drijvers has even suggested that they were written in the third century.[113] The problem is that the date assigned to the *Odes* is inevitably coloured by one's view of their contents.

There has been much debate about whether the *Odes* are gnostic or not.[114] The *Odes* contain several ideas that could be construed as gnostic,[115] yet the general tone of the *Odes* and several key concepts are not gnostic.[116] Like the *Oration*, the *Odes of Solomon* belong to a complex time within church history, when Christianity was still struggling to define itself. In determining where the *Odes* belong within the streams of early Christianity, use of the anachronistic label 'gnostic' does not offer clarification.[117]

This may sound surprisingly similar to my argument about the *Oration* in Chapter 2. In fact, as we shall see, there is much about the *Odes* that is similar to the *Oration*, and in view of these links it seems likely that the *Odes* are related to Tatian in some way. I suspect that the *Odes* were actually written in Syria shortly after Tatian's return to the East, and were influenced by his particular brand of Christian philosophy.[118] I would therefore follow Drijvers, and date the *Odes* between the very late second and early third centuries. Although the *Odes* are very different in form and tone from the *Oration*, they contain several concepts that are very similar to those found in Tatian. Some of these similarities have been outlined briefly by Hans Drijvers, who sees a very close link between Tatian and the *Odes*, and has even suggested that the *Odes* should be considered a commentary on Tatian's ideas.[119] Let us now turn to consider the parallels between Tatian and the *Odes*.

The concept of obtaining knowledge of the truth (or God) is central to Tatian's understanding of salvation; without such knowledge man is doomed, but with it man can regain union with the divine spirit and thereby achieve salvation.[120] As we have seen, Tatian's prophets play a key role in revealing this knowledge. Indeed, since Tatian's spark appears to be redundant, it would seem that the prophets are the only means by which knowledge of the truth can be imparted to man.

Knowledge and truth are also important concepts in the *Odes of Solomon*, and there are several factors that link the concepts of knowledge and truth in the *Odes* with the knowledge of the truth found in the *Oration*. First, we find that, as in Tatian, knowledge and truth are intimately connected with the salvation process in the *Odes*.[121] Like Tatian, the Odist also seems to perceive knowledge and truth to be revealed by the prophets; in *Ode* 8, the Odist exclaims: 'hear the word of truth, and receive the knowledge of the Most High.'[122] Although the Odist does not say that this is a prophetic statement,[123] it seems very much like a prophetic call to faith, and this is confirmed by the prophetic commandments that follow. We find a similar phenomenon in *Ode* 12.1–3, so clearly revelation of the knowledge and truth of God is part of the prophetic function in the *Odes*.

Where the *Odes of Solomon* differ from Tatian in their use of the concepts of knowledge and truth is that the Odist separates them; the Odist does not speak of 'knowledge of the truth', but rather distinguishes truth as an auditory revelation, and knowledge as an intellectual revelation received in the mind.[124] However, elsewhere the Odist speaks about the 'knowledge of the Lord', a phrase that is strikingly similar to Tatian's alternative (and more frequent) phrase, 'knowledge of God'.[125] I would therefore suggest that the Odist's separation of the concepts of knowledge and truth is part of his poetic mode of expression, and a development from Tatian.

As we have seen, Tatian's anthropological theory is dominated by his emphasis on the union between man's soul and the divine spirit. We also find evidence of this concept in the *Odes*. However, in the *Odes* the union is not restricted solely to the divine spirit and man; we also find more general references to 'the Lord', 'the Son', and 'the Perfect Virgin'.[126] The Odist also uses different images to describe the divine union. In *Ode* 1, the union between the Odist and God is described using the imagery of a living crown.[127] In *Ode* 3, the Odist compares his union with the Son to the reunion of a lover and his beloved, and also speaks of the union as a process of imitation.[128] This imitation is found again in *Ode* 13, and may in fact reflect a tradition of twinning, which we noted in the *Acts of Thomas*, and which seems to be a development of Tatian's concept of union with the divine.[129]

Given the prophetic nature of the *Odes*, it is likely that this union reflects the Odist's understanding of prophetic inspiration. However, like Tatian, this concept is also intimately linked with redemption, and distinctions between prophetic inspiration and the personal experience of salvation are likewise blurred.[130]

In speaking of prophetic inspiration, the Odist uses the metaphor of the prophet functioning as a dwelling place for the divine.[131] This is, of course, highly reminiscent of the passage in *Or* 15 where Tatian speaks of man being indwelt by the Spirit of God.

To conclude, the key area where we have found parallels between the *Odes of Solomon* and the *Oration* has been soteriological. Tatianic concepts such as knowledge of the truth, the significance of prophecy and the union between man and the divine were clearly present in the *Odes*. We found many of the same concepts within the *Acts of Thomas*, albeit expressed in a different form. In particular the Tatianic notion of spiritual union is explored and developed, and the author explicitly incorporates the sacraments into the salvation process. We move away from Tatian in the *Odes* in that the mode of expression and tone are different.

I suspect that what we are dealing with in these Syriac documents is a tradition, growing from Tatian, which uses and develops Tatianic philosophy, and in particular his soteriology. These documents favour more extreme ascetic practices, and whilst superficially they may seem to be influenced by gnostic streams because of their esoteric spirituality, they are most certainly not gnostic.

Bardaisan

Bardaisan (*c*.154–222 CE) was a courtier at the Edessene court of King Abgar IX. He wrote a large number of hymns with his son Harmonious, none of which have survived. The only extant work representing his ideas is *The Book of the Laws of Countries* or *Dialogue on Fate*, which was written by Bardaisan's pupil Philippus. Fragments of Bardaisan's teachings are also recorded by Ephrem, but are coloured by a marked hostility towards the courtier, which leads us to question Ephrem's reliability in these matters.

As with the *Odes of Solomon* and the *Acts of Thomas*, Bardaisan has been accused of being 'gnostic' and especially of being influenced by Valentinianism.[132] However, there is much in Bardaisan that is non-gnostic; he believes that God is One and is responsible for creation, his salvation is not based on revelation to an elite but is made possible by the free will of every man or woman, and he presents a positive world view.[133] In Bardaisan's *Book of the Laws of Countries* we are confronted by a synthesis of Christianity, hellenistic philosophy, Parthian–Iranian dualism, and astrology.[134] Tentative parallels with Tatian are present, especially in Bardaisan's presentation of free will.

As we have seen, knowledge of the truth or of God is a concept that is present in Tatian.[135] It is also found in Bardaisan,[136] although his use of the term 'knowledge of truth' is in the context of faith, and it is impossible to draw any conclusions on influence from this. The only significance here is his use of the concept.

In Chapter 5 we noted how important the existence of angels and demons was to Tatian's world-view. Men and angels were created with free will, and as a result some chose to follow the arch-rebel.[137] In Bardaisan we find that again both men and angels are created with free will, and he also teaches that the fall of the angels is due to their free will.[138] In Bardaisan we also meet 'the enemy'.[139] However, it is difficult to tell whether Bardaisan's 'enemy' relates to Tatian's 'arch-rebel', although the existence of such a figure within Bardaisan's thought is still worth noting. Of more significance is the involvement of free will in the angels' fall, and that man is made equal to the angels.

There are also parallels between Tatian and Bardaisan in their explanations for why man was created with free will. In *Or* 7, Tatian writes:

> Each of the two forms of creation [i.e. men and angels] has free will … This is in order that the bad man might be justly punished, since he had become depraved through his own fault, and the good man deservedly praised for his good works, since in the exercise of his free will he had not contravened God's purpose.[140]

We find a very similar argument indeed in the *Book of the Laws of Countries*:

> And it is also given him to lead his life according to his own free will, and to do all he is able to, if he will, or not to do it, if he will not, justifying himself or becoming guilty. For if he were so created that he could not do evil, so that he could not incur guilt, then in that way the good he did would not be his own either and he could not justify himself by it.[141]

Both writers also express an acceptance of the *status quo*. In Chapter 11 of the *Oration*, Tatian states his satisfaction with his current circumstances and says that whatever a person's position in life, there is one death for everybody.[142] The theme of accepting one's lot runs throughout the *Book of the Laws of Countries*. However, Bardaisan's acceptance is based on his understanding of the workings of nature and fate on man.[143] This is in stark contrast to Tatian, who writes of his satisfaction in Chapter 11 during a refutation of astrology.

Finally, Tatian and Bardaisan also speak of man as the image of God. In Tatian, man can become the image of God through the indwelling of God's spirit.[144] Meanwhile in Bardaisan, man is the image of God when, through his free will, he does what is good.[145] Of course the concept of man's creation 'in the image of God' stems from the creation story in Genesis. It is therefore impossible to draw any conclusions from Bardaisan's use of the term.

Parallels between Tatian and Bardaisan are very tenuous indeed, and, given Bardaisan's fondness for astrology and its association with fate, I would have to conclude that there is no direct influence of Tatian on Bardaisan. If we are to think in terms of a Tatianic stream of tradition within Syriac Christianity, we must admit that in Bardaisan any such tradition again moves further from Tatian's original philosophy.

However, Tatian's legacy does not peter out with Bardaisan; evidence of Tatianic influence can be traced within more 'orthodox' eastern Christian streams, in the writings of the fourth century Syriac writers Ephrem and Aphrahat.

Ephrem

Ephrem (c.310–373 CE) spent most of his life in Nisibis, and his final ten years in Edessa. He is probably most famous for his poetry, although he also wrote prose and, importantly for this study, commentaries on biblical books, including the Commentary on Tatian's *Diatessaron* mentioned earlier. There are in fact a surprising number of parallels between Ephrem and Tatian.

Like Tatian, Ephrem conceives of a transcendent God whose divine nature cannot be understood by human beings. He envisages a chasm between God and his creation, which emphasizes the absolute transcendence of God.[146] Ephrem believes that something of divine reality can be seen in the types and symbols that are present in creation and scripture.[147] The notion that God can be perceived through his creation is also found in Chapter 4 of Tatian's *Oration*, where he alludes to *Rom* 1:20.[148] However, here our two writers diverge, since for Tatian the main method in which God reveals himself to man is through prophecy,[149] whilst Ephrem understands the fullest self-revelation to be the Incarnation.[150]

As we have seen, through his belief in the physical reality of the Incarnation, a bodily resurrection, and the notion that the spirit can dwell within the body, Tatian offers a positive view of the human body. A positive evaluation of the body is also presented by Ephrem, whose attitude springs from the idea that since the body is part of God's creation, it should not be despised.[151] Ephrem also appeals to the temple imagery of 1 *Cor* 6:19, and speaks of the body as the bridal chamber where the bride, the soul, meets the heavenly bridegroom.[152]

This positive estimation of the body is important in exploring the motivation behind ascetic practices, and is particularly significant in distinguishing Tatian and Ephrem from gnostic-type groups.

In Chapter 5 we saw how Tatian's exploration of man's nature and his position within the created world spans the history of humanity from creation, through the fall and its consequences, to a future day of judgement. Ephrem offers a similarly expansive view of human history, and, like Tatian, places a very strong emphasis on the role of man's free will.[153] According to Ephrem, God created Adam in an intermediate state, which was neither mortal or immortal, in the hope that through the exercise of his free will Adam would chose to keep God's commands and thereby earn immortality.[154] It is likewise because of free will that humanity can return, through faith and love, to the eschatological Paradise, and receive the gift of divinity originally intended for Adam and Eve from the Tree of Life.

Once more, we find traces of Tatian's philosophy in Ephrem's salvation process. Ephrem's understanding of salvation is based on God's attempts to restore mankind to Paradise by reversing the fall process, whilst respecting the free will with which men are endowed. In describing this process of restoration, Ephrem uses the same kind of clothing and bridal imagery that we encountered in the *Acts of Thomas*.

Ephrem presents the salvation process as a regaining of the primordial robe of glory with which Adam and Eve were clothed.[155] Perhaps more significantly, Ephrem also describes this robe of glory as the divine spirit bestowed at baptism.[156] However, Ephrem envisages a more active role for Christ in man's regaining of the robe of glory; through Christ's baptism, the divine spirit mingles with the baptismal waters and is thus imparted to Christians at baptism.[157]

In his use of the metaphor of the robe of glory Ephrem is clearly drawing on a widespread Syriac tradition with strong biblical roots,[158] but in his use of this metaphor to describe the union between the spirit and the baptized Christian, Ephrem may be utilizing the Tatianic tradition present in the *Acts of Thomas*.[159]

In the *Acts of Thomas*, bridal imagery was used to describe the union between man and the divine, and Christian baptism became a betrothal to Christ. This idea is repeated in Ephrem, where, whilst he includes the concept of individual union, he also expresses a more collective understanding.[160]

Although the parallels between Tatian and Ephrem are not as close as those between Tatian, the *Acts of Thomas* and the *Odes of Solomon*, they are still present. Most striking is Ephrem's understanding of the relationship between God and man, whilst elements of his soteriology seem to echo the Tatianic concept of the union between the soul and the divine spirit. There are, of course, also some significant differences, such as Ephrem's emphasis on Christology, and his greater collective awareness of the salvation process when he calls the church the Bride of Christ. Indeed these differences may themselves help to explain Ephrem's separation from Tatian, since some of the functions expressed in Tatian's soteriology, such as the position of the prophets, are taken over by Christ in the thought of Ephrem.

Aphrahat

Aphrahat, sometimes known as 'the Persian Sage', lived during the early fourth century. According to legend, he was head of the monastery of Mar Mattai. Of his writings, 23 essays are extant. These are known as *Demonstrations*, and were written between 337 and 345 CE in Syriac. Most of them are available in English translation, and it is these *Demonstrations* that I shall focus on.[161]

As we have seen, Tatian believed that God was responsible for creating the world, and that he formed matter with a plan so that some material things were better than others.[162] When Aphrahat is talking of marriage in *Demonstration* 18, we find something similar:

> Far be it from us that we should attribute anything shameful to marriage which God has placed in the world, for thus it is written, 'God saw all that he had made, and it was very good' (*Gen* 1:31). But there are some things which are better than others. God created heaven and earth, and they are very good, but the heaven is better than the earth ... He created marriage, worldly procreation, and it is very good; but virginity is more excellent than it.[163]

Of course, tied in with Aphrahat's notion that marriage cannot be shameful since God created it is the concept that God is not responsible for creating anything evil. This is echoed in Tatian's assertion that God is the good, and is not responsible for creating evil.[164]

The concept that virginity is preferable to marriage is also echoed in the fragment of Tatian's *On Perfection According to the Saviour* preserved in Clement of Alexandria's *Stromateis*, which we encountered at the beginning of this chapter.

In describing how God produced the Logos to perform the act of creation, Tatian used the following metaphor, which we noted was also present in Philo, Justin Martyr and the Neopythagorean Numenius:

> Just as many fires may be kindled from one torch, but the light of the first torch is not diminished because of the kindling of the many, so also the Word coming forth from the power of the Father does not deprive the begetter of the power of rational speech.[165]

Aphrahat uses this metaphor a number of times in his *Demonstrations*. In *Demonstration* 5, he uses it in relation to the undiminishable nature of God and his Word:

> For the riches of God can not be computed or limited ... And if thou kindle fire from a burning, it will not a whit be lessened. And if thou receive of the Spirit of Christ, Christ will not a whit be diminished ... And all these things that I have enumerated for thee were created by the word of God. Therefore know thou, that as concerning the word of God no man has reached or will reach its end.[166]

In *Demonstration* 6, Aphrahat uses the metaphor of fire to assert the unity and undiminished nature of God and Christ:

> Also when thou kindlest fire from fire in many places, the place from whence thou takest it, when thou kindlest it, lacks not, and the fire is called by one name. And because thou dividest it into many places, it does not on that account become possessed of many names ... Thus also God and his Christ, though they are One, yet dwell in men who are many. And they are in heaven in person and are diminished in nothing when they dwell in many.[167]

Finally, in *Demonstration* 10, we come across the fire metaphor once more when Aphrahat is talking of men receiving knowledge of God:

> So is the knowledge of God. Though all men should receive of it, yet there would come no lack in it, nor can it be limited by the sons of flesh. He that takes from it can not take away all; and when he gives, he lacks nothing. When thou takest fire with a candle from a flame, though thou kindle many candles at it, yet the flame does not diminish when thou takest from it, nor does the candle fail, when it kindles many.[168]

In all three examples the metaphor of a fire is used to explain the undiminished nature of the divine, and in our first example the metaphor is even used to describe the Word, which is also linked with creation in this passage. Furthermore, in our last two passages the Tatianic concepts of divine indwelling and knowledge of God are present, and it is to these concepts that we now turn.

As we recall, knowledge of God, revealed through the indwelling of God's spirit in the prophets, is vital to Tatian's soteriology.[169] Aphrahat mentioned the knowledge of God in our third example of the fire metaphor cited above. Here it is presented as a gift that is not diminished by the giving. The phrase is used again in *Demonstration* 17. As I have stressed throughout, parallel terminology without consideration for individual contexts should not be used to argue for direct influence. However, in Aphrahat the fire metaphor used of man's reception of the knowledge of God, and which essentially demonstrates the divine nature of God, is also used to describe the indwelling of Christ, and elsewhere, Aphrahat states that the indwelling of the Spirit of Christ produces prophecy.[170] As we have seen, these ideas are also closely linked in Tatian.

Another Tatianic concept that we encountered in Aphrahat's use of the fire metaphor was the divine dwelling within men. In Tatian, divine indwelling is dependent on the condition that the body is kept 'like a shrine', and he states that if it is not, man is superior to the beasts only in his speech.[171]

In his *Demonstration On Faith*, Aphrahat writes at great length about God dwelling within man. He presents a long list of conditions that prepare man for divine habitation; he states that fasting, virginity, holiness and purity are necessary to prepare oneself for Christ.[172] In *Demonstration* 17, Aphrahat states that unless man is a temple, he is considered to be the same as the animals.[173] Moreover, in *Demonstration* 6, he also equates the indwelling of the Spirit with prophecy:

> For the Prophets received of the Spirit of Christ, each one of them as he was able to bear. And of the Spirit of Christ again there is poured forth today upon all flesh, and the sons and the daughters prophesy, the old men and the youths, the men-servants and the handmaids ... Therefore, my beloved, we also have received of the Spirit of Christ, and Christ 'dwelleth' in us ... Therefore let us prepare our temples for the Spirit of Christ.[174]

Whilst imagery of the Body as a Temple has its roots within the Pauline Epistles, where Tatian and Aphrahat draw closer is in their assertion that men are considered animals if their bodies are not temples, and they have no knowledge of God. The need for ascetic preparation of the body for divine indwelling is also present in both, although it is stronger in Aphrahat.

We now turn to consider the figure of the arch-rebel. In his demonology, Tatian introduces the figure of the arch-rebel, who essentially instigates the fall. The arch-rebel and the angels who fall with him become demons, and Tatian states that only the spiritual can easily see the demons.[175]

Aphrahat presents us with an 'adversary', seen by the spiritual, who moves against men,[176] but it is difficult to tell how Aphrahat's 'adversary' relates to Tatian's 'arch-rebel', since Aphrahat does not tell us anything of his adversary's involvement in the fall. However, he does use the Tatianic concept that the spiritual are able to see demons, and the notion that the spiritual can fly from the adversary may reflect a passage in Tatian that describes the spirit as the soul's wings.[177]

There are also similarities in Tatian's and Aphrahat's view of the salvation process. As you will remember, Tatian speaks very clearly of a physical resurrection, in which the matter making up the body is restored.[178] Aphrahat makes a similar argument when he says that the dead, who have wasted away and are now nothing, shall become something according to their former nature, and rise.[179]

Similarly, whilst Tatian's salvation revolves entirely around man's reunion with the spirit,[180] the same is true of Aphrahat. In *Demonstration* 6, he says that the Holy Spirit will request to be rejoined to the body that kept Him in purity.[181] The main difference in Aphrahat's presentation of this reunion is that whilst Tatian views the spirit as something endowed on all men at creation and then lost at the fall, for Aphrahat the spirit is received at baptism.[182]

Finally, we turn to consider the ascetic interests of Tatian and Aphrahat. As we noted, Tatian's references to asceticism in the *Oration* are sparse, yet there is evidence in the Diatessaronic witnesses, the fragment of Tatian's *On Perfection According to the Saviour* in Clement of Alexandria, and heresiological claims that Tatian espoused ascetic values. From what can be gleaned of Tatian's asceticism in the *Oration*, his belief that asceticism is a prerequisite for prophecy is particularly significant with reference to Aphrahat.

Aphrahat displays a marked asceticism, and the 'solitary ones' in his sixth *Demonstration* have been the subject of much debate.[183] In *Demonstration* 6, Aphrahat makes much use of wedding imagery, which is reminiscent of the *Acts of Thomas*, and he even makes use of the metaphor of the pearl.[184]

In this *Demonstration*, Aphrahat also talks about prophecy. As we have seen, he believed that the divine spirit joined man at baptism, and there is a question over whether only ascetics were baptized. If only fully committed 'solitary ones' attained full admission to the church, via baptism and the receiving of the spirit, and only those indwelt by the spirit could prophesy, there is a parallel with Tatian's expectation of asceticism as a prerequisite for prophecy.

There are several considerable parallels between Tatian and Aphrahat, the most striking being Aphrahat's use of fire metaphors to describe the undiminishable nature of God. In several places Aphrahat also echoes Tatian's arguments. This is apparent when he says that men are like beasts if they have no knowledge of God and are not temples, as well as his claim that 'the spiritual' are able to see the adversary, and his method of asserting a physical resurrection. In Aphrahat we encounter the Tatianic concepts of the knowledge of God, and the reunion with the divine spirit, as well as the link with asceticism as a prerequisite for prophecy. Aphrahat's 'solitary ones' also presents us with the kind of continent, spiritual marriage that Tatian appears to approve in Clement's fragment, and is also present in the *Acts of Thomas*.

Given this long catalogue of parallels and the fact that the general thought worlds of both writers converge in places, I would argue that there is strong evidence of Tatianic influence on Aphrahat. This may in part have been transmitted via the stream of Syriac Christianity that produced the *Acts of Thomas*, as there are several parallels with this earlier text.[185] However, it is also possible that Aphrahat's use of several Tatianic arguments may indicate a closer relationship between Aphrahat and the *Oration*, although it is difficult to prove direct dependence conclusively.

Conclusion: Tatian's legacy

We have seen that Tatian's legacy to Syriac Christianity does not consist solely of the *Diatessaron*, although his gospel harmony did prove to be hugely successful. Evidence of Tatianic influence can also be found in several Syriac texts, the closest of which are the *Acts of Thomas* and the *Demonstrations* of Aphrahat. Thus I would conclude that Tatian's philosophy, and especially some of his soteriological theories, became part of a developing Syriac tradition.

In Chapter 1, we noted that Roman Christianity of the second century was fractionalized into house churches and that these contained school communities. Given this grounding in Christian modes of operation (indeed Tatian may have been introduced to Christianity in this form), I suspect that on his return to the East Tatian did found a school, as Epiphanius claims. I would therefore suggest that Tatian's ideas were not passed down through the *Oration*,[186] but were propagated through the tradition of oral teaching that he had learnt from Justin Martyr. If this was the case, Tatian's ideas would have been incorporated into Syriac traditions, and the identity of the originator of the concepts forgotten.

CONCLUSION

Tatian and second century Christianity

The aim of this book has been to attempt to locate Tatian within the divergent streams of early Christianity, and in so doing to shed some light on the nature of second century Christianity. In Chapter 2, I argued against Grant's claim to Valentinian influence on Tatian, and proved decisively that Tatian should not be considered a Valentinian on the basis of his *Oration to the Greeks*. I also argued that it was highly unlikely, in the light of the thought world expressed within the *Oration* and the significance of Tatian's principle of consistency, that Tatian later turned to Valentinianism. Moreover, my study of Tatian's use of Pauline material pushed him closer to the stream of Christianity that was to become dominant, and their battle for the appropriation of Paul.

In Chapter 3, I explored Tatian's relationship with his master Justin Martyr, and found the thought worlds and attitudes of the two to be very close. This study also revealed the influence of hellenistic philosophy on both writers, and so I devoted Chapters 4 and 5 to examining Tatian's relationship with philosophy, presenting his theology as a philosophical system at the end of Chapter 5. I concluded that although Tatian's education may have included a grounding in basic philosophical principles, the Christian philosophy that he presents in his *Oration* was part of a tradition passed on from Philo to Justin through a Philonic stream within Judeo-Christianity, and thence to Tatian. This means that Tatian was not consciously reconciling his hellenistic background with his Christian faith, since the assimilation had already occurred, and that he was genuinely unaware of the debt that his Christian philosophy owed to Platonism.

In Chapter 6, I went on to consider Tatian's relationship with Syriac Christianity. I rejected the notion of Tatian's involvement with an Encratite 'sect', pointing to the extreme form of asceticism that characterizes early Syriac Christianity, although I acknowledged Tatian's own ascetic interests. However, I did find other evidence of Tatianic influence within Syriac Christianity; close links exist between Tatian and the *Acts of Thomas*, and Aphrahat's *Demonstrations*, and in the light of corresponding parallels in the *Odes of Solomon* and more vague similarities with Ephrem, I concluded that a Tatianic tradition can be traced within Syriac Christianity. I accounted for this tradition by suggesting that on his return to the East Tatian founded a school, modelled on those found within Roman house churches, and passed on his philosophy through oral teaching.

I would therefore place Tatian as a Christian philosopher and apologist, in direct descent from Justin Martyr. In his *Oration to the Greeks*, Tatian defends Christianity against the accusations and persecutions of the Graeco-Roman world, and in so doing cites aspects of his Christian philosophy as proof that Christianity is not the nonsense that many pagans of his day assumed it to be.

I consider Tatian's *Oration* to be a true representation of his theology, and whilst I acknowledge that a person's religious convictions rarely remain stagnant, I find nothing in the *Oration* to indicate that after Justin's death Tatian became an arch-heretic. Moreover, there is much within the *Oration* that points away from Valentinianism, and since Tatian's principle of consistency is so central to his understanding of Christianity I cannot conceive of him embracing Valentinian values at a later stage in his life.

I believe that in Irenaeus' charge of Valentinianism and Encratism, we are faced with political propaganda rather than a true representation of Tatian's views. At the end of the second century some fairly major changes were happening within western Christianity; the stream that was to become known as 'orthodoxy' was beginning to achieve dominance, and the consolidation of that power involved an increasing intolerance towards more extreme Christian groups and a formalization of the content of mainstream Christian teaching. It may well have been Tatian's disillusionment with the direction that the mainstream church was taking that led him to leave Rome. At any rate, Irenaeus' claim of apostasy seems a convenient way to discredit Tatian whilst retaining the teaching of Justin for orthodoxy.

As we have seen, Syriac Christianity at the turn of the third century was primarily composed of 'gnostic' streams, and the Christianity of the East during this period was characterized in both 'orthodox' and 'heretical' circles by a strong ascetic bent.[1] It may be that Tatian offered a convenient means for developing western orthodoxy to reject this ascetic current within eastern Christianity.

The charge of Valentinianism, meanwhile, was probably part of Irenaeus' theory of the genealogy of heresy, and was needed to link 'Encratism' with existing heresies. Whether Irenaeus had extracted the tenets of Valentinianism from a misunderstanding of ideas like those presented in the *Oration* or whether they were a malicious invention designed to further the cause of the mainstream western church is not clear.

The Tatian of the heresiological literature thus became a tool to discredit the extreme asceticism of the East, in much the same way that the legendary Paul of *Acts* and the Pastoral Epistles became a tool to reclaim the historical Paul. Tatian, who was not present to defend himself, has therefore been remembered as the conceited and mutinous pupil of Justin Martyr, who followed the teachings of orthodoxy whilst his master was alive but was drawn towards heresy after Justin's death, and in his arrogance returned to his homeland to set up his own school.

Clearly, this understanding of Tatian has some significant implications for our understanding of the heresiologists. We need to be more cautious in assessing the information they present, and not merely accept their version of history at face value. We need to be aware that the heresiologists are not presenting an impartial report; they are part of history, and in some cases may be rewriting history to favour the cause of orthodoxy. We may therefore need to re-evaluate the position of the heresiologists in dealing with other second century figures.

This book has also called into question the methodology of Grant and other scholars in using only rough parallels to identify second and third century writers with the gnostic-type movements. We saw the inadequacy of this approach most clearly in Chapter 2, where I confronted Grant's claim to Valentinian influence on Tatian, but we also questioned its validity with reference to the *Acts of Thomas* and the *Odes of Solomon* in Chapter 6. The use of parallel terminology and concepts does not necessarily indicate close links between writers; such parallels need to be placed in context, and the forces and influences acting upon writers need to be taken into consideration. This calls for a refinement of approach and a greater knowledge and awareness of background issues.

APPENDIX

Tatian and Clement's accusation in *Stromateis* III.82.2

In *Stromateis* III.82.2, Clement of Alexandria accuses Tatian of rejecting the Old Testament because he considered it to have been produced by another god:

> Tatian makes a distinction between the old humanity and the new, but it is not ours. We agree with him in that we too say that the old humanity is the Law, the new is the gospel. But we do not agree with his desire to abolish the Law as being the work of a different god.[1]

As we noted in Chapter 2, this accusation clearly has Marcionite overtones, since Marcionites, along with some other gnostic-type groups, rejected the Old Testament as being the work of the Demiurge. However, there is evidence within the *Oration* that calls into question Clement's claim about Tatian's attitude to the Hebrew Scriptures.

In his conversion account, Tatian claims to have been converted to Christianity through reading some 'barbarian writings'.[2] From the chronological argument that follows it is clear that these 'barbarian writings' are in fact the Hebrew Scriptures, and Tatian is far from damning of them; he claims that the Hebrew Scriptures are older and more divine than Greek writings, and produces a list of positive reasons why they appealed to him.

These are hardly the words of someone disaffected by the Hebrew Scriptures. Moreover, in his chronological argument Tatian goes on to base his justification for the truth of Christian philosophy upon the antiquity of Moses; Tatian is clearly appealing to Hebrew Scripture as the basis upon which Christian truth is formed.[3]

The notion that the Hebrew Scriptures are the work of a different God is also totally alien to Tatian's thought as expressed in the

Oration. His understanding of the divine is strictly monotheistic,[4] and he goes to great pains to describe how the one transcendent God was himself able to create the universe.[5] There is no second god in Tatian's *Oration*.

If one maintains an early date for the *Oration*, it would be possible to argue that the *Oration* reflects only an early period in Tatian's thought, and that it was only later that Tatian's ideas took on a 'heretical' bias like those described by Clement. However, Tatian's acceptance and approval of the 'barbarian writings' in the *Oration* is so central to his justification of the truth of Christian philosophy that to deny the validity of the Hebrew Scriptures would have been to deny the validity of Christianity itself. It therefore seems unlikely that such a shift in Tatian's thought could have occurred.

NOTES

INTRODUCTION

1 In *Or* 42, Tatian claims to have been born 'in the land of the Assyrians', by which he probably means the region of Mesopotamia, east of the Euphrates.

2 *Or* 29:1. When Tatian speaks of 'barbarian writings' he is referring to the Hebrew Scriptures, although he probably encountered them in their Septuagint version.

3 Eusebius, *Ecclesiastical History* V.13.1, 8.

4 Irenaeus, *Against the Heresies* I.28.1. Whether Tatian formally rejected Roman Christianity or whether his return to the East was merely interpreted as such is a question to which I shall return.

5 Epiphanius, *Panarion* 46.1.6. Antoninus Pius was Emperor from 138–161 CE, but we know that Justin's martyrdom took place about four years after this. So, it has been suggested that Epiphanius meant to refer to Antoninus Pius' successor, Marcus Aurelius, who was Emperor from 161–180 CE (W.L. Petersen 1994: 71).

6 Theodoret of Cyrrhus, *History of Heresies* I.20; Rabulla, *Canon* 43.

7 *Stromateis* III.81. Harris claims to have found this lost work in a treatise attributed to Ephrem (Harris 1924: 15–51). Although the tract does express a marked emphasis on asceticism and picks up some of the issues hinted at in the *Oration* (e.g. the position of prophets, and the child and treasure terminology of *Or* 30), I do not believe that it can legitimately be attributed to Tatian without further proof. However, this tract does seem to originate from the East, and may have been influenced by Tatian.

8 *Or* 15:2.

9 Eusebius, *Ecclesiastical History* V.13.8.

10 *Or* 40:2.

11 *Or* 31–41. Tatian's chronological argument lays claim to Jewish history and asserts that Moses (and therefore Christianity) is older than Homer and the Greek writers (cf. Origen, *Against Celsus* 1.16).

12 M = Codex Mutinensis III D7, C12 (eleventh century); M[bis] = end of *Oration* added to M at an early date (eleventh century); P = Codex Parsinus 174, C12 (twelfth century); V = Codex Marcianus 343, C11 (mid-eleventh century); cf. Marcovich 1995: 3.

13 M. Whittaker 1982.

14 Marcovich 1995.

15 Grant 1953: 99–101.

16 Grant suggests early 177 or late 178 (Grant 1953: 100). Grant's thesis for this very late date essentially hinges on a comment which Tatian makes in *Or* 19:1 about philosophers who receive 600 aurei a year from the Roman emperor. Grant believes that this refers to Marcus Aurelius' establishment of four chairs of philosophy in Athens in 176 CE, despite the discrepancy in the salary (the salary of the chairs was 10,000 drachmae, or 400 aurei). Grant concludes that the *Oration* must therefore have been written after this date. As Clarke points out (G.W. Clarke 1967: 123–126), there are several problems with this thesis, not least the fact that imperial patronage had become somewhat commonplace in the second century. Likewise, the other arguments that Grant proposes in support of this date (e.g. persecutions) do not prove a firm date for the *Oration*. Grant's dating of the *Oration*, whilst not inconceivable, is certainly not compelling.

17 Harnack (1882: 286–289) and Zahn (1891: 279) date the *Oration* to the same period that they date Justin's first *Apology* (i.e. 150–155 CE) (cited in Barnard, 1968a: 2).

18 Puech (1912: 151, cited in Barnard 1968a: 1) suggests 172, whilst Grant (1953: 100) suggests late 177 or early 178.

19 *Or* 19:1; 'Crescens ... who advised contempt of death was himself so afraid of death that he set about involving Justin – as he did me too – in the death penalty, as if it were an evil.' (M. Whittaker 1982: 39, reprinted by permission of Oxford University Press).

20 2 *Apol* 3: 'I therefore am expecting to be plotted against and fixed to a rack by some of those named, or perhaps by Crescens, that lover of bravado and boasting.' (Barnard 1997: 75).

21 Eusebius, *Ecclesiastical History* IV.16.

22 Barnard 1968a: 2–3.

23 This view appears to have originated with Irenaeus, who claims that after Justin's martyrdom, Tatian apostatized from the church (*Against the Heresies* I.28.1).

24 I am aware of the problems with this assumption, but because of Tatian's driving principle of internal consistency (expressed in his criticism of contemporary philosophy, and in his composition of the *Diatessaron* – cf. p. 98 f), I suspect that although his theology certainly would not have remained the same throughout his life, the *Oration* probably formed the foundation from which further ideas would have blossomed. One can even explain Irenaeus' misrepresentation of Tatian as a Valentinian using the *Oration* as a starting point; as Grant has proved, there are elements in the *Oration* that, although not actually Valentinian, might be interpreted as such. One could easily assume that such elements were an embryonic form of Tatian's later heresy.

25 In comparing Tatian's *Oration* with these texts, I have concentrated mainly on primary material, going back to the original wherever possible, and as a consequence I have only referred to that secondary material which is of particular significance. My bibliography attests to a wider, but not exhaustive, reading of secondary material.

1 CHRISTIANITY IN THE SECOND CENTURY

1 Christianity (the 'Nazarenes' as they were known in Jewish circles) was just one of many such sects within Judaism at this time (e.g. Pharisees, Sadducees, Essenes and Zealots). For a survey of this early period, see J.T. Sanders 1993.

2 See Simon 1986: xii.

3 i.e. Male circumcision, immersion, acceptance of the Torah, and Sacrifice.

4 See E.P. Sanders 1981: 226–244.

5 Schiffman in E.P. Sanders 1981: 150.

6 cf. *John* 9:22; 12:42; 16:2.

7 See E.P. Sanders 1981: 155.

8 *Against the Heresies* I.22. NB: 'Ebionite' is probably derived from the Hebrew for 'poor'.

9 See Ruether 1974: 117–181.

10 *Dial* 1; Falls 1977: 147–148.

11 *Dial* 9; Falls 1977: 162.

12 cf. *Dial* 1.

13 *Dial* 11–12.

14 *Dial* 45; Falls 1977: 215.

15 *Dial* 47; Falls 1977: 218–219. NB: In this chapter, Justin makes it clear that not all Christians share his tolerance.

16 Justin repeatedly blames the Jews for Christ's death, and in *Dial* 17 claims that the Jews sent messengers to spread lies about the Christians.

17 *Dial* 47.

18 Justin's acceptance of the possibility of Jewish salvation prior to the appearance of Christ is probably due to his spermatic logos theory.

19 *Dial* 142.

20 E.P. Sanders 1980: 100–125.

21 See Frend 1965.

22 2 *Apol* 2. Pagels has put forward the interesting suggestion that the concept of the fall of the angels in Justin and other apologists is actually a veiled attack on Imperial divinity and authority, and is a response to this kind of persecution (Pagels 1985: 301–325).

23 Beiträge zur historischen Theologie Vol 10, Tübingen: J.C.B. Mohr (Paul Siebeck).

24 The difficult, technical style in which *Rechtgläubigkeit und Ketzerei im ältesten Christentum* was written may also have affected its initial reception, as too did the political tensions prior to and during the Second World War.

25 Robinson and Koester 1971.

26 Dunn 1977; Pagels 1979.

27 Turner 1954.

28 Flora 1972 (cited in Harrington 1980: 295).

29 For a review of the responses to Bauer, see Harrington 1980: 289–298; Desjardins 1991: 65–82.

30 Bauer 1972: 113–114.

31 Bauer 1972: 128.

32 La Piana 1925: 201–277.

33 *Prescription Against Heretics* 30.

34 Lampe 1987; cf. Jeffers 1991.
35 Brent 1995: 368–457.
36 1 *Apol* 26; 58.
37 *Dial* 80.
38 The earliest form of this story is found in Eusebius, *Ecclesiastical History* I.13, and a developed Syriac form of the document appears to have been in circulation in Edessa from the early fifth century.
39 Supposedly Abgar V who ruled from 9–46 CE, although it has been suggested that it was Abgar IX (179–214 CE) who converted to Christianity (Bauer 1972: 4).
40 In Eusebius, the name of this disciple is Thaddaeus.
41 Vööbus 1958: 6 f. NB: The *Doctrine of Addai* states that Addai stayed with a Jew named Tobias during his stay in Edessa.
42 Bauer 1972: 36.
43 Bauer 1972: 20.
44 *Hymns Against Heresies* 22.
45 Bauer 1972: 22.
46 Bauer 1972: 24.
47 Robinson and Koester 1971: 114–157.
48 Robinson and Koester 1971: 129. NB: Koester considers the *Gospel of Thomas* to reflect a genuine apostolic tradition which is separate to Q and the other gospel sources, although he suggests that it was used by Q (Robinson and Koester 1971: 135–136). He admits that the *Gospel of Thomas* contains a 'seed of Gnosticism', due to its dualistic anthropology, but argues that it is not 'typically Gnostic', and prefers to describe it as 'a typical example of Hellenistic syncretism' (Robinson and Koester 1971: 140–141).
49 Brock 1979b: 212–232; cf. Barnard 1968b: 161–175.
50 Burkitt 1939: 492–496.
51 Drijvers comments: 'Marcion and Tatian were the most influential personalities in the shaping of that typical Syriac theology which gave rise to so many speculations and fantasies. Its whole development can be explained as due to their influence, to reactions to, polemics against and a further, sometimes poetical, elaboration of their ideas.' (Drijvers 1984: I.3).
52 e.g. In his *Dialogue with Trypho*, Justin appeals to prophecies within the Hebrew Scriptures as proof that his claims about Christ are true. On Christian reception and appropriation of the Hebrew Scriptures, see Young 1997: 9–28.
53 *Galatians*, 1 and 2 *Corinthians* (which he counted as one letter), *Romans*, 1 and 2 *Thessalonians* (which he again counted as one letter), *Ephesians* (*Laodiceans* according to Marcion), *Colossians* and *Philemon* (which he also grouped together due to the similarities in the list of greetings), and *Philippians*.
54 cf. von Campenhausen 1972: 147–165. NB: Adolf Ritter has claimed that Marcion was merely the catalyst in the church's development of the canon (Ritter 1987: 93–99), whilst Kenneth Carroll has put forward the theory that the principal factor in the development of the canon was the explosion of pseudepigraphal and apocryphal writings in the second century (Carroll 1961–62: 327–349).

55 Von Campenhausen 1972: 210–268.
56 *Against the Heresies* III.11.
57 The principle of inner consistency runs throughout Tatian's *Oration*, and is a major element in his thought. I shall discuss this in greater depth in Chapter 4.
58 cf. W.L. Petersen 1990: 512–534.
59 Pagels 1992.
60 Von Campenhausen 1972: 178.
61 Skarsaune 1987.
62 Von Campenhausen 1972: 181; Barrett 1974: 229–245; cf. Babcock 1990.
63 The most comprehensive modern study of the gnostic phenomenon is probably that of Kurt Rudolph (1987), although he ignores the distinctions between the terms 'pre-gnostic', 'proto-gnostic' and 'gnostic' as defined by the Messina Conference.
64 The issue of whether Marcion can be considered a gnostic is debatable.
65 e.g. The existence of beings (often 'aeons') between the divine and the created world; the perception of creation as the result of a fall away from the divine; understanding matter as evil; equating knowledge with salvation; and a tendency to elitism and traditions of secret revelations.
66 Irenaeus seems to have coined this phrase from 1 *Tim* 6:20: 'Avoid the godless chatter and contradictions of what is falsely called knowledge.'
67 Especially Grant 1954: 62–68 (discussed further in Chapter 2).
68 It has been suggested that the Nag Hammadi Library may have been collected and hidden by Pachomian monks following Athanasius' Easter letter of 367 CE (see J.M. Robinson 1996: 17–20).
69 NB: Such a background is disputed by some scholars.
70 Van den Broek 1983: 56–61. NB: Grant has suggested that the rise of gnosticism may have been due to failed Jewish apocalyptic hopes following the fall of Jerusalem (Grant 1959).
71 Yamauchi 1973; Pétrement 1991.
72 Aland 1978: 87–124.
73 cf. Ptolemaeus *Letter to Flora*.
74 See van den Broek 1983: 62–66.
75 Bianchi 1967.
76 See van den Broek 1983: 57–58.

2 TATIAN AND VALENTINIANISM

1 *Against the Heresies* I.28.1. In Book III, Irenaeus expands on Tatian's reputed teaching of the denial of the salvation of Adam, tracing Tatian's use of it back to Paul (*Against the Heresies* III.23.8 – citing 1 *Cor* 15:22). The reason that Irenaeus gives for Tatian's deviation is that he wished to gain a reputation as a teacher (*Against the Heresies* I.28.1).
2 Tatian's alleged rejection of marriage was commonly associated with Encratism, but Irenaeus does actually introduce Tatian as an Encratite (*Against the Heresies* I.28.1).
3 cf. *Eph* 4:22–24.
4 In view of Tatian's attitude towards the Hebrew Scriptures in his conversion account (*Or* 29) and his insistence on monotheism, it seems highly

likely that Clement's accusation is unfounded. Since this is the only non-Valentinian accusation to be made about Tatian, and as this chapter is primarily concerned with refuting Grant's Valentinian exegesis of the *Oration*, a fuller discussion of Clement's accusation can be found in the Appendix.

5 *Stromateis* III.92.1.

6 *Refutation of all Heresies* VIII.16; X.18.

7 *Ecclesiastical History* IV.29.

8 Epiphanius claims that Tatian established a school in Mesopotamia (*Panarion* 46.1.6), asserts that he led people astray 'like a rapacious wolf' using the guise of continence (*Panarion* 46.2.2), and that he replaced the Eucharistic wine with water (*Panarion* 46.2.3).

9 *Panarion* 46.1.7. It is pertinent to note that Epiphanius' information cannot always be trusted. He appears to have had his own personal agenda in writing this work; in order to fulfil a prophecy in *Canticles* 6:7, he needed to produce 80 sects (Young 1982: 202). Hence Epiphanius speaks of 'Tatianites' and 'Encratites' when, historically, if Tatian did have such a following the two would have been identical. Neither is Epiphanius' material always reliable, so we must treat his evidence with care.

10 cf. *Acts* 8.

11 Grant 1953: 99–101. Clarke rightly questions Grant's solution to the date problem (G.W. Clarke 1967: 123–126). See above, Introduction, p. 1 f.

12 Grant 1954: 62–68; Grant 1957b: 297–306; Grant 1964: 65–69.

13 Grant 1954: 63.

14 *Or* 20:2; M. Whittaker 1982: 41. Reprinted by permission of Oxford University Press.

15 e.g. One's time of life; a lifetime; a generation; an era; or an eternity. The word αἰών and its derivative αἰώνιος are used frequently throughout the New Testament with a wide variety of meanings (See Darton 1976: 164–166). In Philo, the word αἰών is used to describe an age (*On the Special Laws* I.282; *On Flight and Finding* 57), a person's age (*On Dreams* II.36), eternity or agelessness (*On the Unchangeableness of God* 32; *On the Sacrifices of Abel and Cain* 76), as well as the world (*Allegorical Interpretation of Genesis* III.25). He further uses αἰών as a technical term 'aeon', derived from Plato (*Timaeus* 37D). The *Shepherd of Hermas* also reflects this wide usage of the term; Hermas uses αἰών to describe the age to come (*Visions* 24.5), this world (*Similitudes* 52.2), and the world to come (*Similitudes* 53.2).

16 αἰών is used with its meaning of 'world' in the following New Testament passages; *Mt* 13:22; *Mk* 4:19; *Lk* 16:8; *Rom* 12:2; *2 Cor* 4:4; *Eph* 2:2; *1 Tim* 6:17; *2 Tim* 4:10; *Tit* 2:12; *Heb* 11:3 (Darton 1976: 165–166).

17 *Or* 5:2.

18 Grant 1954: 64.

19 cf. *Letter to Rheginos* 45.12; Theodotus, *Excerpts* 21.1; 67.1.

20 *Excerpts* 25.2; 54.2; 67.2–3; 80.1.

21 cf. *Or* 5.

22 *Or* 13:2; 15:1.

23 Grant 1954: 64.

24 cf. Irenaeus, *Against the Heresies* I.21.3.

25 *Or* 12:1; 15:2.

26 Grant 1954: 64–65.

27 *Or* 13:2. ἔναυσμα can also mean 'glimmer' or 'remnant'.

28 *Or* 6:1.

29 The word σάρξ is in fact used in *Or* 15:1.

30 Grant 1954: 65.

31 It has been suggested that the Valentinian Ptolemaeus may have been the Christian teacher mentioned by Justin in his second *Apology* (Lüdemann 1979: 97–114; see also Grant 1985: 461–472). If this is the case it highlights the flexible nature of Christianity in the mid-second century, since Justin does not call his Ptolemaeus a heretic or even a Valentinian, but rather a Christian teacher, and moreover presents him in a very favourable light.

32 *Panarion* 33.3–7

33 When I refer to 'Theodotus' in this section, I therefore mean the authors of the material contained in Clement's *Extracts of Theodotus*.

34 Grant 1954: 64. Ptolemaeus, *Letter to Flora* 3.4; 7.3; 7.5–6: Tatian *Or* 4:2; 12:4; 17:3; 25:2.

35 Grant 1954: 64. Ptolemaeus, *Letter to Flora* 7.8. Grant claims that Tatian also speaks of God as the sole principle in *Or* 4:1. Presumably, Grant is referring to the following passage: 'Our God has no origin in time, since he alone is without beginning and himself is the beginning of all things.' (M. Whittaker 1982: 9. Reprinted by permission of Oxford University Press).

36 Grant 1954: 64. This parallel, as we shall see, does not stand up to scrutiny, since although Tatian speaks of the law of the incorruptible father (*Or* 32:1), Ptolemaeus seems to differentiate between the incorruptible father (*Letter to Flora* 7.7) and the law as ordained by the Demiurge (*Letter to Flora* 7.2 f).

37 Ptolemaeus, *Letter to Flora* 7.5; Tatian, *Or* 7:1.

38 Ptolemaeus, *Letter to Flora* 7.6; Tatian, *Or* 4:1; cf. *Or* 5:3.

39 The roots of 'Perfect-being' theology are found in Plato (*Republic* II.381c). See Craig 1998: 96–97.

40 *Dial* 62.

41 *To Autolycus* II.10.

42 *Or* 5:1; M. Whittaker 1982: 11. Reprinted by permission of Oxford University Press.

43 Grant 1961a: 190.

44 Indeed, Grant's choice of Justin and Theophilus as 'orthodox' figures against whom Tatian's *Or* 4:1 and Ptolemaeus should be distinguished seems rather unfortunate.

45 Ptolemaeus, *Letter to Flora* 7.2–4.

46 *Or* 32:1.

47 Grant 1954: 63–66.

48 *Or* 18:2–3. NB: This information is not actually found within any of Justin's extant works.

49 *Or* 12:4; 14:1. The fact that Justin does not make this reference to demons in his extant works also begs the question of whether some other parts of Tatian's demonology might not be found in non-extant works of

Justin. Personally I do not think that this is the case, since the demonologies of Justin and Tatian do not seem to be closely related, but this possibility does not seem to have occurred to Grant.

50 *Excerpts* 72.2.

51 *Excerpts* 72.1–2 Theodotus says that this state of affairs exists because evil is unable to fight on the side of God (*Excerpts* 72.2).

52 *Or* 7:2–3; 12:3.

53 *Or* 12:4.

54 *Or* 20:1. This is a problematic passage; in her translation Whittaker distinguishes between demons and angels, although I believe that Tatian is talking about the same class of beings (see below, Chapter 5, p. 133 f).

55 Grant 1954: 64.

56 Grant 1954: 65.

57 *Or* 11:2; M. Whittaker 1982: 23. Reprinted by permission of Oxford University Press.

58 *Excerpts* 80.2.

59 *Excerpts* 77.1.

60 cf. *Eph* 4:22–24.

61 This is strongly implied since he talks of baptism on either side of this observation (Grant 1954: 65).

62 *Or* 15:4.

63 *Excerpts* 80.2.

64 i.e. That Tatian primarily appeals to the idea of dying to the old nature, whilst Theodotus turns to the idea of dying and rising with Christ.

65 Citing *Isaiah* 25:8.

66 *Or* 15:4.

67 Grant 1954: 65.

68 *Or* 12:1; 15:4. See below, Chapter 5, p. 139 f.

69 e.g. 1 *Cor* 3:16; 6:19; 2 *Cor* 3:18; 6:19.

70 Grant repeats this inference in his article 'Tatian and the Bible' when he says: 'Evidently Tatian, like Marcionites and Valentinians, was well acquainted with Paul.' (Grant 1957b: 301).

71 The Valentinian Heracleon was the first Christian author to write a commentary on the *Gospel of John*.

72 Grant 1954: 66.

73 *Excerpts* 34.1. NB: For Theodotus, the Light seems to be Christ.

74 cf. *Excerpts* 40.

75 *Or* 13:1–2.

76 cf. *Or* 15:4. This is another non-gnostic element in Tatian, which I shall discuss later in this chapter.

77 *Or* 15:2.

78 *Or* 15:3.

79 Grant 1954: 65–66 (*Excerpts* 3.1).

80 *Or* 21:1.

81 'The result of the Saviour's coming would have been to enable us to reject the "generation according to fate", the "old generation", by which "we brought forth evil". Now we have become "far from humanity and advance toward God himself". We conquer death by death through faith; we conquer the demons; we are masters of our passions and despise the things in the world.' (Grant 1954: 66).

82 i.e. The 'generation according to fate' (*Or* 11:1, 'fate-ordained nativity' in Whittaker) in fact relates to Tatian's rejection of the idea of fate, which is imposed upon men by demons, and which he does not in any case consider to be a reality but a fabrication. The word γένεσις can refer to human generation, but in this context does not seem to refer to human reproduction as Grant seems to imply. Although Grant refers to the 'old generation' (*Or* 11:2, 'old birth' in Whittaker) by which 'we brought forth evil' ('exhibited wickedness' in Whittaker), these phrases are actually separated by a large chunk of text, and the fact that men exhibited wickedness has nothing to do with 'bringing forth evil' (I suspect that Grant is again implying human reproduction here), but happened because men were created with free will.

83 i.e. The men that advance beyond humanity and towards God in *Or* 15:2 are in fact the prophets, and whilst it is true that this may be a model for Christians to aspire to at the resurrection (cf. *Or* 15:1; 6:1) it is not the realized eschatology of Valentinianism.

84 e.g. Baptism, Christ, and the Spirit.

85 Both use Paul and *John*, and therefore have a common Christian heritage.

86 *Or* 30:1–2; M. Whittaker 1982: 55. Reprinted by permission of Oxford University Press.

87 Grant 1964: 65–69; see also Grant 1954: 66–67; Grant 1957a: 298–300.

88 Grant 1964: 65. NB: Grant does acknowledge that οἱ ἡμῶν οἰκεῖοι (our own people) might be considered to refer merely to Christians in opposition to ὑμεῖς οἱ Ἕλληνες (you Greeks).

89 Grant 1964: 66–67; *Similitudes* 9.29.1–3; *Gospel of Thomas* log 21; 22; 37; 46.

90 *Mt* 13:32. NB: There is a precedent for Tatian's negative presentation of the seed in the parable of the wheat and tares (*Mt* 13:24–30; 36–43).

91 *Mt* 13:44.

92 *Mt* 13:45.

93 *Gospel of Thomas* log 20 (57 – the wheat and tares); 109; 76.

94 *Gospel of Thomas* log 21.

95 *Gospel of Thomas* log 3.

96 Epiphanius' *Gospel of Philip* speaks of collecting the scattered (*Panarion* 26.13.2), whilst the coptic *Gospel of Philip* contains a passage that is very similar indeed to Tatian: 'For so long as the root of wickedness is hidden, it is strong. But when it is recognized it is dissolved. When it is revealed it perishes. That is why the word says, "Already the ax is laid at the root of the trees" ... As for ourselves, let each one of us dig down after the root of evil which is within one, and let one pluck it out of one's heart from the root. It will be plucked out if we recognize it. But if we are ignorant of it, it takes root in us and produces fruit in our heart. It masters us. We are its slaves. It takes us captive, to make us do what we do [not] want to do. It is powerful because we have not recognized it. While [it exists] it is active.' (J.M. Robinson 1996: 158–159).

97 Grant 1964: 69.

98 Grant 1964: 67.

99 *Excerpts* 52–53. Here, Theodotus understands the bad tares to be the flesh.

100 Hippolytus, *Refutation of all Heresies* V.3. NB: Grant also highlights parallels with digging and wealth in *Thomas* in this paragraph. These Naasene parallels are not exegeses of *Matthew*, and can scarcely be considered as interpretations of *Thomas*. Why then does Grant include them here?

101 Grant 1964: 68.

102 e.g. Tatian's non-Valentinian exegesis of Paul discussed below, and the non-Valentinian elements in his thought also discussed below.

103 For a brief survey, see Bolgiani 1970: 226–235.

104 Maran 1742: 168 (cited in Bolgiani 1970: 229).

105 Elze 1960: 99.

106 Elze 1960: 13.

107 Bolgiani 1970: 230. NB: Bolgiani also perceives allusions to *Rom* 7:8, 11 and *Col* 3:3.

108 Bolgiani 1970: 234–235.

109 Bolgiani 1970: 232–235.

110 M. Whittaker 1982: 84–85. Reprinted by permission of Oxford University Press.

111 *Or* 30:1; M. Whittaker 1982: 55. Reprinted by permission of Oxford University Press.

112 *Or* 13:2.

113 cf. *Or* 13:3; 15:2. (See below, Chapter 6, p. 151 f).

114 *Or* 29:2; M. Whittaker 1982: 55. Reprinted by permission of Oxford University Press. NB: This is the passage that directly precedes Chapter 30.

115 Grant 1988.

116 Grant 1988: 115–130.

117 Grant 1988: 127–130.

118 For example, Grant once again parallels Tatian's 'perfect God' with Ptolemaeus, but admits that Ptolemaeus' perception of God is not the early theology of Tatian. Furthermore, in paralleling Tatian's idea of 'the Minister (διάκονος – translated "servant" in Whittaker) of the God who suffered' (*Or* 13:3) with the Basilidean concept of the Minister, he acknowledges that the expression does not prove that Tatian was a gnostic (Grant 1988: 130–131).

119 Grant 1988: 129.

120 cf. Grant 1988: 127, where Grant suggests that Tatian may have been influenced by the anti-Judaic polemicist Apion since 'we shall see later that Tatian came to consider the Creator an inferior god'; Grant 1988: 127, where Grant claims that 'in his later period Tatian certainly could not accept everything he found in the Gospels or the epistles; he had to "twist" some of the basic texts'; Grant 1988: 128, on Tatian's 'rewriting' of 1 *Cor* 7:2–5 Grant writes 'by this time Tatian was an avowed Encratite and could not accept such doctrine'. cf. Also Grant 1988: 131, where Grant criticizes Tatian's use of the term 'psychic', saying 'it can be claimed that his [i.e. Tatian's] language about some men as "psychic" is merely Pauline. It is at least unguarded, however, for Valentinian gnostics were using the term of ordinary Christians in his day'.

121 i.e. that he considered the creator to be an inferior god.

122 See Appendix, p. 179.

123 Grant 1954: 65.

124 In considering Tatian's use of Paul, I have chosen to include all of the Pauline Epistles that second century Christians like Tatian may have considered authentic. Thus, I include *Ephesians* and other Epistles which, although now considered to be spurious, were uncontested in our period. I have also included *Hebrews* within Tatian's Pauline corpus, despite concern often displayed until the fourth century about its authenticity.

125 *Or* 4:2; M. Whittaker 1982: 9. Reprinted by permission of Oxford University Press.

126 *Rom* 1:25: 'They exchanged the truth about God for a lie and worshipped and served the creature rather than the Creator.'

127 *Rom* 1:20: 'Ever since the creation of the world his invisible nature, namely, his eternal power and deity, has been clearly perceived in the things that have been made.' NB: This idea that the divine may be partly understood through the created world was also current amongst Platonic and Stoic philosophers.

128 *Or* 4:1.

129 *Rom* 1:26: 'For this reason [i.e. because they worshipped creature above Creator] God gave them up to dishonourable passions.'

130 *Or* 7:3; M. Whittaker 1982: 15. Reprinted by permission of Oxford University Press. NB: Those who turn from God are also described as foolish in *Rom* 1:22.

131 *Or* 7:2.

132 Physical impurity through sexual acts also plays a part in *Rom* 1:24, 26–27.

133 See *Or* 21:3 for Tatian's negative estimation of allegory.

134 This secret oral tradition was allegedly passed from Paul to his disciple Theudas, and thence to Valentinus. See Pagels 1992: 2. NB: For the following Valentinian exegesis of the Pauline Epistles, I am largely dependent upon this study by Pagels.

135 Pagels extrapolates this reading from Heracleon, *Commentary on John* 13.9 (1992: 17).

136 Theodotus, *Excerpts* 47.2.

137 Irenaeus, *Against the Heresies* I.17.2. NB: Pagels points out that Valentinus also acknowledges that God's image is seen by pneumatics in the visible cosmos (*Stromateis* IV.89.6–90.1; Pagels 1992: 9), although he does not seem concerned to explain why.

138 *Or* 15:2; M. Whittaker 1982: 31. Reprinted by permission of Oxford University Press.

139 1 *Cor* 3:16: 'Do you not know that you are God's temple and that God's spirit dwells in you?'; 1 *Cor* 6:19: 'Do you not know that your body is a temple of the Holy Spirit within you, which you have from God?'; 2 *Cor* 6:16: 'For we are the temple of the living God; as God said, "I will live in them and move among them".' cf. 1 *Cor* 12; *Eph* 2:19–22; *Acts of Paul and Thecla* 5.

140 NB: According to Tatian, the divine spirit is the 'image and likeness of God' (*Or* 12:1).

141 *Stromateis* III.81.1–3; J. Ferguson 1991: 306.

142 'Do not refuse one another except perhaps by agreement for a season, that you may devote yourself to prayer.'

143 *Or* 30:1; M. Whittaker 1982: 55. Reprinted by permission of Oxford University Press.

144 1 *Cor* 3:1: 'But I, brethren, could not address you as spiritual men, but as men of the flesh, as babes in Christ.'; 1 *Cor* 13:11: 'When I was a child, I spoke like a child, I thought like a child, I reasoned like a child; when I became a man, I gave up childish ways.'; 1 *Cor* 14:20: 'Brethren, do not be children in your thinking; be babes in evil, but in thinking be mature.' cf. *Gal* 4:1, 3; *Eph* 4:14; *Heb* 5:13.

145 Grant 1964: 66–67.

146 *Or* 20:2–3; M. Whittaker 1982: 41, 43. Reprinted by permission of Oxford University Press. cf. 2 *Cor* 5:2–4: 'Here indeed we groan, and long to put on our heavenly dwelling, so that by putting it on we may not be found to be naked. For while we are still in this tent, we sigh with anxiety; not that we would be unclothed, but that we would be clothed further, so that what is mortal may be swallowed up by life.'

147 See Brock 1992 XI.

148 There may be further correlations between Tatian and 1 and 2 *Corinthians* with the concepts of two kinds of spirit (*Or* 4:2; 1 *Cor* 2:12), and man as the likeness of God (*Or* 15:2; 2 *Cor* 3:18). However, since both of these ideas are found within philosophy, and as the latter also has a Scriptural basis in *Gen* 1:26 f, I think these particular parallels are more likely to be due to common backgrounds rather than direct dependency.

149 Pagels 1992: 61 (*Commentary on John* 10:33).

150 See Pagels (1992: 68), who points to Heracleon's treatment of this subject in *Commentary on John* 10:3.

151 The concept of pneumatic marriage is particularly significant in the *Gospel of Philip*, where it is represented by the Sacrament of the Bridal Chamber (cf. Grant 1961b: 129–140). According to Pagels (1992: 69), the Valentinians also related the concept of symbolic marriage to a union between psychics and pneumatics. This union relates to her suggestion that Valentinians considered psychic salvation possible, provided that pneumatic intervention was offered (cf. Pagels 1972: 241–258).

152 *Gospel of Philip* 56.28–34; 57.21–22. The Valentinians may also have offered an exegesis of 1 *Cor* 2:12, and the two spirits. According to Pagels (1992: 59), the Valentinians differentiated between the spirit of the cosmos (i.e. the Demiurge) and the spirit of God.

153 *Or* 12:1.

154 *Or* 13:2; M. Whittaker 1982: 27. Reprinted by permission of Oxford University Press.

155 NB: This interpretation of *Gal* 4 is disputed; some scholars envisage a gnostic background.

156 See below, Chapter 5, p. 133 f.

157 *Or* 13:3.

158 *Gospel of Philip* 54.31–55.1.

159 *Excerpts* 69–73. NB: Pagels (1992: 109) also mentions Heracleon's claim that the psychics worship 'angels, the months, and the moon' instead of the God whom they claim to know (*Commentary on John* 13.17).

160 *Or* 16:2–3; M. Whittaker 1982: 33. Reprinted by permission of Oxford University Press.

161 *Eph* 6:14: 'Stand therefore, having girded your loins with truth and

having put on the breastplate of righteousness.'; 1 *Thess* 5:8: 'let us . . . put on the breastplate of faith and love, and for a helmet the hope of salvation.'

162 *Or* 13:1; M. Whittaker 1982: 27. Reprinted by permission of Oxford University Press.

163 *John* 1:5.

164 *Eph* 5:8: 'For once you were darkness, but now you are light in the Lord; walk as children of light.' (cf. 1 *Thess* 5:5).

165 Pagels 1992: 115.

166 *Excerpts* 85:3.

167 cf. *Mt* 4:1–11.

168 *Excerpts* 35:1.

169 *Gospel of Truth* 18.16–19.

170 *Or* 15:4; M. Whittaker 1982: 31. Reprinted by permission of Oxford University Press. cf. *Heb* 2:7: 'Thou didst make him [i.e. Christ] for a little while lower than the angels.'

171 *Psalm* 8:5: 'Yet thou hast made him [i.e. man] little less than God.'

172 Tatian talks of men being lower than the angels, and not lower than God.

173 It is surely significant that Tatian uses the words 'repentance' and 'calling', which, according to Pagels, were words the Valentinians reserved solely for 'psychic' salvation (Pagels 1972: 257–258), and were, of course, also used frequently by non-Valentinians.

174 *Or* 12–13.

175 Pagels 1992: 141.

176 Although I am aware of the difficulties surrounding the concept of 'literal' exegesis, this term seems to be the most appropriate to use here.

177 Pagels 1972: 257.

178 Pagels 1972: 257.

179 Polycarp, *Epistle to the Philippians* 4; Theophilus, *To Autolycus* I.1; 11; II.16; III.14.

180 *Commentary on Titus* t. VII, p. 686 (cited by M. Whittaker 1982: 82). NB: Presumably Tatian rejected 1 and 2 *Timothy* because of their scathing comments towards asceticism, whilst *Titus* advocates sobriety and chastity (cf. *Tit* 2).

181 1 *Tim* 2:4: 'Who desires all men to be saved and to come to the knowledge of the truth.'; 2 *Tim* 3:7: '[Among them are weak women] who will listen to anybody and can never arrive at a knowledge of the truth.' cf. *Heb* 10:26.

182 *Or* 20:2.

183 1 *Tim* 6:16: 'Who alone has immortality and dwells in unapproachable light.'

184 *Or* 27:2: 'There is a saying that the Cretans are liars.' (M. Whittaker 1982: 51. Reprinted by permission of Oxford University Press). *Tit* 1:12: 'One of themselves, a prophet of their own said, "Cretans are always liars, evil beasts, lazy gluttons".'

185 cf. Callimachus, *Hymn to Zeus* 8.

186 *Or* 5:3; 6:1.

187 *Or* 4:2; 5:3; 12:1.

188 *Or* 5.

189 *Or* 17:2. NB: In the Syriac document *The Doctrine of Addai*, the act of

healing without the use of drugs is put forward as proof of the divinity of Jesus and the inspired work of his disciple Addai.

190 *Or* 17:4; M. Whittaker 1982: 35. Reprinted by permission of Oxford University Press.

191 *Or* 17:2.

192 *Or* 5:3; 12:1.

193 As we shall see, this is in line with Justin's cosmology.

194 *Or* 7:2–3.

195 *Refutation of all Heresies* VI.35, 5–7.

196 i.e. A non-hylic body.

197 *Or* 21:1; M. Whittaker 1982: 43. Reprinted by permission of Oxford University Press.

198 In criticizing the stories of the Greek gods, Tatian states that if the poets speak of the birth of the gods, they also represent them as mortal (*Or* 21:2). The implication of this is that if the Christian God has been born, then he has become mortal and must therefore be at least partly human.

199 As we noted earlier, the notion of psychic salvation through faith and works may have been present within some Valentinian circles.

200 *Or* 6:1; M. Whittaker 1982: 11. Reprinted by permission of Oxford University Press.

201 *Or* 6:2; M. Whittaker 1982: 13. Reprinted by permission of Oxford University Press.

202 *Or* 13:1: 'For if it is ignorant of the truth it [i.e. the soul] rises later at the end of the world along with the body.' (M. Whittaker 1982: 27. Reprinted by permission of Oxford University Press). cf. *Or* 15:1. NB: Grant (1954: 65) claims that the latter passage does not imply that the flesh rises at all, but from the other evidence it is clear that Tatian does envisage a resurrection of the flesh and not just of the soul. Furthermore, Grant's claim that the substance which is resurrected is only called σαρκίον can not be upheld in the light of *Or* 13:1, where Tatian uses the word σῶμα, and in *Or* 15:1, where he uses the word σάρξ.

203 *Or* 25:2.

204 Because Tatian is ascetically orientated, he puts conditions of purity on the flesh before such indwelling can occur. Yet the fact that such an arrangement is possible suggests that Tatian is definitely not Valentinian.

205 *Or* 12:1.

206 *Or* 15:4: 'After their loss of immortality men have overcome death by death in faith ... It is possible for everyone defeated to win another time, if he rejects the constitution making for death.' (M. Whittaker 1982: 31. Reprinted by permission of Oxford University Press).

207 *Or* 7:2–3.

208 *Or* 11:2; 15:4.

209 *Or* 15:1.

210 *Or* 12:1.

211 *Or* 15:2.

212 The word γνῶσις is used frequently in the *Stromateis*.

213 *Against the Heresies* II.19.5.

214 See Appendix, p. 179 f. NB: I have further argued, from evidence within the *Oration*, and especially from his understanding of the Hebrew

Scriptures as the foundation of his Christian philosophy, that Tatian could never have held the kind of gnostic position that Clement attributes to him.

215 The emergence of Montanism in the 160s or 170s may also reflect a rejection of the institutionalizing trends within Christianity of this period; see Trevett (1996: 44), where she also argues that Tatian's 'defection' to the East was a sign of the discontent within Graeco-Roman city states at this time.

216 For a more detailed discussion of Tatian's principle of internal consistency, see below p. 98 f.

3 TATIAN AND JUSTIN MARTYR

1 Irenaeus, *Against the Heresies* I.28.1; Hippolytus, *Refutation of all Heresies* VIII.16.1; Eusebius, *Ecclesiastical History* 4.29; Epiphanius, *Panarion* 46.1.1–5.

2 In considering Justin's use of Paul, I will include the same Pauline material that I did in Chapter 2 for Tatian. This means that I have again included *Ephesians* and other Epistles which are now considered spurious, along with *Hebrews*.

3 1 *Apol* 3.

4 NB: Tatian also uses *Rom* 1:20 in *Or* 4:2, although he focuses on a different phrase within the verse.

5 *Dial* 27; Falls 1977: 188.

6 '"No one understands, no one seeks for God./ All have turned aside, together they have gone wrong;/ no one does good, not even one."/ "Their throat is an open grave,/ they use their tongues to deceive."/ "Their mouth is full of curses and bitterness."/ "Their feet are swift to shed blood,/ in their paths are ruin and misery,/ and the way of peace they do not know."'

7 Skarsaune 1987.

8 a) In citing *Gen* 15:6, the texts of *Rom* 4:3 and *Dial* 92 are the same, and are close to the Septuagint version (Skarsaune 1987: 115).
b) In citing *Isaiah* 53:1, the texts of *Rom* 10:16 and *Dial* 42 are also identical, and also match the Septuagint version (Skarsaune 1987: 116).

9 a) In citing *Deut* 21:23, *Gal* 3:13 and *Dial* 96 are identical (Skarsaune 1987: 118).
b) In citing *Deut* 27:26, *Gal* 3:10 and *Dial* 95 are very similar (Skarsaune 1987: 118).

10 As we saw in the last chapter, there is only one instance where Tatian may be using Paul's citation of *Psalm* 8:5 (*Or* 15:4; *Heb* 2:7).

11 Holte 1958: 106–168 (especially 164).

12 Holte 1958: 125.

13 As Barnard suggests (Barnard 1967: 57).

14 W.L. Petersen 1990: 512–534.

15 The fact that Tatian makes no mention of gospel traditions in the *Oration* may be due to the importance of his chronological argument, which offers proof that Moses is more ancient than (and therefore superior to) Homer. The Greek audience whom he addresses would surely have dismissed such recent writings and accused him of hypocrisy.

16 See W.L. Petersen 1994: 35–65.

17 W.L. Petersen 1990: 512–534. cf. W.L. Petersen 1994: 27–29.

18 2 *Apol* 12.

19 Van Winden dives a detailed analysis of this account (van Winden 1971).

20 *Dial* 2.

21 *Dial* 3–8.

22 Von Engelhardt 1878; Hyldahl 1966. Both cited in Skarsaune 1976: 54.

23 It should also be noted that Justin does not claim immediate conversion following this incident.

24 Goodenough 1968: 58–59.

25 Several scholars have maintained the basic historicity of the account in *Dial* 1–8; Chadwick 1965: 275–297; Barnard 1967: 8; Skarsaune 1976: 67 f.

26 This has been widely accepted following the work of Andresen (Andresen 1952/53: 157–195).

27 *Or* 29:1; M. Whittaker 1982: 55.

28 *Or* 29:1–2; M. Whittaker 1982: 55. Reprinted by permission of Oxford University Press.

29 See *Or* 1:3; 35:1.

30 Justin, *Dial* 7: Tatian, *Or* 31:1.

31 See Swain 1996. NB: In his *Oration* Tatian mentions the Graeco-Roman dispute over linguistic purity that marks this period.

32 Justin states that he comes from Flavia Neapolis in Syrian Palestine (1 *Apol* 1.1). Tatian, on the other hand, calls himself 'Assyrian', and claims that he was educated in the Greek paideia (*Or* 42.1). Whilst the term 'Assyrian' is vague, it seems likely that Tatian originated from Mesopotamia. See Millar (1993) for an overview of hellenistic influence throughout the Near East; see especially 227–228 and 460, where Millar mentions both Tatian and Justin.

33 It should be noted that whilst Tatian attacks a predominantly Greek world with Greek gods, Justin attacks a predominantly Roman world, which uses Roman names for the gods. Yet the heritage still remains the same; the Romans took on board much from the Greeks, including myths and philosophy.

34 Tatian in particular is concerned to reject all things Greek, and his attack widens beyond that of Justin to include everything from Greek dialects to astrology, and from medicine to drama. In comparing Tatian with Justin, Tatian's attack on these aspects of Graeco-Roman culture goes beyond the boundaries of this chapter.

35 *Or* 21:1; M. Whittaker 1982: 43. Reprinted by permission of Oxford University Press.

36 *Or* 8. This underlines his belief that divinity and doctrines about divinity should be consistent.

37 *Or* 8; 10:2–3; 21:1; 22:1. The same is also true of Justin; 1 *Apol* 21; 25.

38 This demand was made especially because Christianity was 'new' in a time when what was considered most ancient was also considered most true.

39 1 *Apol* 54.

40 1 *Apol* 54.

41 This is a presupposition that Tatian goes to great lengths to prove (*Or* 31 f).

42 NB: This argument is very similar to his argument from prophecy.
43 Justin, 1 *Apol* 9; 18; *Dial* 22: Tatian, *Or* 4; 19.
44 Justin, *Dial* 18. In *Dial* 22, Justin directly denies the need for Christians to sacrifice to God.
45 See Young 1979b.
46 See Nahm 1992: 129–151.
47 Andresen 1952/53: 157–195; cf. Andresen 1955: 312–344.
48 Holte 1958: 106–168.
49 Hyldahl 1966: 272–292.
50 Nahm 1992: 151.
51 1 *Apol* 5; 2 *Apol* 10.
52 1 *Apol* 1.
53 1 *Apol* 3; Barnard 1997: 24. NB: This seems to be a loose quotation from Plato, *Republic* 5.18.
54 1 *Apol* 8. cf. Plato, *Gorg.* 523 E; *Phaedrus* 249 A; *Republic* 10.615 A: Tatian, *Or* 6:1.
55 1 *Apol* 20; Barnard 1997: 37.
56 1 *Apol* 60. Justin takes Plato's mention of the letter Chi to refer to the cross.
57 2 *Apol* 13; Barnard 1997: 83.
58 On the difficulties of classifying Justin's *Apologies* and Tatian's *Oration* as belonging to an apologetic 'genre', see Young 1999: 81–104.
59 Irenaeus, *Against the Heresies* I.28.1; Eusebius, *Ecclesiastical History* 4:29; Epiphanius, *Panarion* 46.1.6; 47.1.1.
60 *Or* 8:1; 11:2; 23:2; 33:1–2 (see below, Chapter 6, p. 151 f).
61 e.g. 1 *Apol* 14; 27; 29; 2 *Apol* 2 etc.
62 1 *Apol* 15.
63 Justin, 2 *Apol* 7: Tatian, *Or* 7:1.
64 Justin, 2 *Apol* 5: Tatian, *Or* 7.
65 *Or* 11:2.
66 1 *Apol* 43. NB: This method of arguing for free will by attacking the concept of predestination is one that both Justin and Tatian use on several occasions; Justin, 1 *Apol* 43–44; 2 *Apol* 7: Tatian, *Or* 8:1; 9; 10:1; 11:1.
67 *Or* 7:1–2.
68 *Or* 13:1–2.
69 1 *Apol* 46.
70 Justin and Tatian appear to have been involved in the process of defining 'demon' as a negative entity. Thus although Tatian reflects a primarily negative estimation of demons, as we shall see, his demonology is closely intertwined with his understanding of angels, and at one point he seems to state that the angels/demons are capable of 'turning to what is purer' (*Or* 12:3).
71 Justin, 1 *Apol* 5; 9; 2 *Apol* 5; *Dial* 73; 79: Tatian, *Or* 8:2; 9:1; 12:4.
72 E. Ferguson 1998: 259 f.
73 2 *Apol* 5.
74 cf. *On Dreams* I.141.
75 *Or* 7:2–3; M. Whittaker 1982: 13, 15. Reprinted by permission of Oxford University Press.
76 The figure of Satan is a development of a Jewish concept that can be

traced within the Old Testament, Rabbinic literature, and especially Jewish apocalyptic works (see Langton 1949).

77 1 *Apol* 28. cf. *Dial* 103; 125.
78 *Or* 18:2–3; M. Whittaker 1982: 37. Reprinted by permission of Oxford University Press; cf. *Or* 18:1–2; 14:1.
79 e.g. Plutarch (see below, Chapter 4, p. 74 f).
80 cf. Holte 1958: 106–168.
81 *Or* 13:3; 15:2.
82 *Dial* 61; Falls 1977: 244.
83 Justin, *Dial* 61: Tatian, *Or* 5:2–3.
84 Justin, *Dial* 127: Tatian, *Or* 4.
85 NB: Of the Middle Platonists I shall mention, only Plutarch makes use of the Logos concept to express divine immanence.
86 Justin, 2 *Apol* 6: Tatian, *Or* 5:2.
87 *Dial* 128. NB: In Justin, it is the Son who appears in the theophanies of the Old Testament and who relays God's commands to men.
88 *Dial* 61; Falls 1977: 244.
89 *Or* 5:1–3; M. Whittaker 1982: 11. Reprinted by permission of Oxford University Press.
90 *On Giants* 25.
91 *Against Praxeas* 8.
92 *Fragment* 14, Book 4/5 of *On the Good*. NB: Numenius only uses the fire metaphor here, and it is used to explain how philosophy (or knowledge) is passed from the giver to the receiver without diminishing the knowledge of the former.
93 2 *Apol* 10.
94 NB: From the Diatessaronic witnesses, it seems likely that Tatian included *John* 1:14 ('And the Word became flesh') in the *Diatessaron* (cf. Hamlyn Hill 1894: 54; McCarthy 1993: 78).
95 As we shall see, the Stoics perceived of the divine element as a material substance, permeating all of matter. The Logos was understood as the rational force within the divine element that structured and organized the universe, and the spermatic logos was the portion of this force that was within men. Thus for the Stoics, the spermatic logos was understood in entirely material terms. Andresen has also traced this concept to the 'semina justitiae' of Cicero. This is significant because it lends ethical overtones to the Stoic concept (Andresen 1952/53: 170 f).
96 A major characteristic of Middle Platonism was an eclectic tendency to appropriate Stoic and Peripatetic ideas. Several Middle Platonists incorporated the Stoic spermatic logos into their systems, understanding the concept in a purely incorporeal and ethical way. Andresen has traced the use of this concept in Arius Didymus, Albinus and Alcinous, and has concluded that Justin's spermatic logos theory is largely influenced by Middle Platonism (Andresen 1952/53: 172 f); cf. Barnard 1967: 98.
97 Philo was himself heavily influenced by Middle Platonism (see below, Chapter 5, p. 110 f), but Philo's Logos and spermatic logos theories are also dependent on the Old Testament concept of God's Word and the Jewish Wisdom tradition. Goodenough (1968: 162) has concluded that Philo's spiritualization of the Middle Platonic spermatic logos is closely

related to Justin's spermatic logos theory. This has been supported in part by Holte (1958: 106–168) and Trakatellis (1976).

98   2 *Apol* 8–13.

99   Holte has pointed out that Justin's whole understanding of the Logos may be based on the Prologue to *John* and the Pauline material. He concludes that Justin's use of spermatic logos terminology is not a synthesis of Christianity and Middle Platonism, but an attempt to translate Pauline theories on natural revelation to the language of contemporary philosophy (Holte 1958: 164).

100 *Or* 12–13.

101 *Or* 13:1–2.

102 This puzzle is heightened by Tatian's preoccupation with consistency.

103 1 *Apol* 59.

104 *Dial* 62.

105 1 *Apol* 59.

106 2 *Apol* 6. In 1 *Apol* 20, Justin even links his use of this concept with that of Plato. NB: Justin does not appear to have formulated the notion of creation out of nothing (cf. May 1994: 123).

107 cf. *Dial* 62, where Justin takes the use of the first person plural in *Gen* 1:26–28 and 3:22 as evidence that God was speaking to the pre-existent Logos.

108 *Or* 12:1.

109 *Or* 5:3: 'For matter is not without beginning like God, nor because of having beginning is it also of equal power with God; it was originated and brought into being by none other, projected by the sole creator of all that is.' (M. Whittaker 1982: 11. Reprinted by permission of Oxford University Press). NB: This is a significant element in Tatian's thought, and is discussed in full in Chapter 5.

110 Justin, 1 *Apol* 8; 12; 43; 52: Tatian, *Or* 6:1; 12:4.

111 Justin, 1 *Apol* 8; 18; 19: Tatian, *Or* 6:1.

112 Justin, 2 *Apol* 7: Tatian, *Or* 17:1; 25:2. NB: A further point of contact between Justin and Tatian may be in their use of the word παρουσία (advent); as Barnard indicates, Justin uses this word a total of 29 times in his extant works, whilst Tatian is the only other Greek apologist to use it in *Or* 39:3 (Barnard 1965: 87).

113 1 *Apol* 52; *Dial* 32; 52.

114 *Dial* 81.

115 1 *Apol* 12; 21; 43.

116 Barnard 1965: 86–98.

117 Epiphanius, *Panarion* 49.1.

118 Especially in the correlation between Justin's spermatic logos and Tatian's 'spark'.

119 *Dial* 8; *Or* 35:1.

4 TATIAN AND HELLENISTIC PHILOSOPHY

1   It should be noted that in the philosophy of the second century, lines distinguishing the various schools blur. For example, some Neopythagoreans claim the work of Plato (who was influenced by Pythagorean concepts) as part of Pythagorean teaching, whilst some Middle Platonists

claim the work of Aristotle (as Plato's pupil) to be part of the Platonic heritage. Schools also tend to borrow heavily from other schools, incorporating these ideas into their own. It should therefore be remembered that although I am considering individual schools separately, distinctions between them are not as clear as such a treatment might make them seem.

2 *Plutarch's Lives*; 11 volumes in the Loeb Classical Library.

3 *Plutarch's Moralia*; 15 volumes in the Loeb Classical Library. NB: Not all of the material contained within this collection is considered authentic.

4 *Isis and Osiris* 369B; *The Obsolescence of Oracles* 423D; *The E at Delphi* 393B, D.

5 *The E at Delphi* 392E; 393A.

6 *Isis and Osiris* 360F–361C. Plutarch was a priest of Apollo, which probably explains his interest in retaining the traditional gods. Dillon (1977: 199) suggests that for Plutarch the traditional gods became aspects of the godhead.

7 *Isis and Osiris* 361C. In *The Obsolescence of Oracles*, Plutarch expresses distress at the thought of denying the existence of demigods because this would make the relations of gods and men remote and alien by removing the interpretative and ministerial function provided by the demigods (*The Obsolescence of Oracles*, 416F). NB: Plutarch considered it possible for good demigods to be transformed into full gods (cf. *Isis and Osiris* 361E; 362E).

8 *On the Sign of Socrates* 591D–593D. This concept belongs within Plutarch's understanding of man, and I shall return to consider this shortly.

9 *Isis and Osiris* 371B. See also *Isis and Osiris* 373A, where the imperishable soul of Osiris is differentiated from his body, which is destructible. Thus, a dualistic tension exists within Plutarch's Logos.

10 *Isis and Osiris* 274A; 372E.

11 *Isis and Osiris* 373F. Plutarch also expresses this idea using the symbol of the triangle; the upright represents Osiris, the base Isis, and the hypotenuse the child of both (*Isis and Osiris* 374A).

12 *Isis and Osiris* 371B, where Osiris is presented as Intelligence and Reason and Typhon as the irrational soul. Throughout the myth Typhon actively moves against Osiris, firstly tricking Osiris into lying within a chest and sealing him in (*Isis and Osiris* 356C), and then dividing Osiris' body into pieces and scattering them (*Isis and Osiris* 358A). Osiris, Isis and Typhon are also presented as Monad, Dyad, and Indefinite Dyad.

13 *Isis and Osiris* 369A–B. This also explains why he denies that God was responsible for producing the stuff from which the cosmos was made (*The Obsolescence of Oracles* 430E). God's role is rather to bring order to the chaos (*Isis and Osiris* 362C).

14 *Isis and Osiris* 369D.

15 *Concerning the Procreation of the Soul* 5; 7. NB: Typhon is actually equated with Chaos in *Isis and Osiris* 374C.

16 In the light of *Special Laws* 10, Dillon considers Plutarch to have read the passages in the *Timaeus* relating to Necessity (Dillon 1977: 202–203). A passage in *Concerning the Procreation of the Soul* 6 certainly seems to bear this out; here Plutarch claims that Plato frequently calls the disorderly principle 'necessity'.

17 *Concerning the Procreation of the Soul* 3.

18 *On Moral Virtue* 441E; 450E; *On the Face in the Moon* 943A.

19 *On the Sign of Socrates* 591E; de Lacy and Einarson 1968: 471. He also says that the position of individual Intellects can be seen in the motions of stars (*On the Sign of Socrates* 591F). It is Socrates' exceptional concord with his daemon ('Sign' in the Loeb edition) that this treatise derives its name from (*On the Sign of Socrates* 588D–591E).

20 *On the Sign of Socrates* 593F–594A. NB: Punishment for wayward daemons was also embodiment within human flesh (*On the Face in the Moon* 944D).

21 *On the Face in the Moon* 942F. There are also a series of intermediate places for those souls awaiting punishment through reincarnation, or who aren't entirely perfect.

22 Plutarch calls this a 'second death' (*On the Face in the Moon* 942F; 943A).

23 *On the Face in the Moon* 245C; 943A–945A.

24 *Tabletalk* IX.5, 740C–D.

25 All of these are collected together in des Places 1977. I shall use des Places' numbering of the fragments in this chapter.

26 *Fragment* 12.

27 *Fragment* 34. Dillon (1977: 254–255) considers *Fragment* 9 to contradict Atticus' conception of the supreme God belonging above the realm of Ideas, although des Places (1977: 86) claims that *Fragment* 9 does not. In any case, *Fragment* 28 explicitly states that, for Atticus, the Ideas do exist outside of the divine intellect.

28 *Fragment* 8.

29 *Fragment* 23.

30 *Fragment* 7.

31 *Fragment* 15. Iamblichus in his work *On the Soul* (cited by Stobbaeus) confirms that Atticus conceived of a rational and irrational part of the soul, claiming that he considered a harmony to exist between the two parts (*Fragment* 10).

32 Dillon 1977: 256.

33 *Fragment* 3; 8.

34 Freudenthal 1879.

35 This is mainly due to the work of Guista (1960–61). John Whittaker offers a substantial overview of this debate in his article 'Platonic Philosophy in the Early Centuries of the Empire' (J. Whittaker 1987: 81–123). See also the introduction to his French translation of Alcinous' Handbook (J. Whittaker 1990: vii–xiii).

36 *Handbook* 10:165.5–17.

37 *Handbook* 10:165.17–19. Alcinous gives the geometrical example of conceiving of a point through considering a surface and a line, and then a point where two lines meet.

38 *Handbook* 10:165.21–23. Alcinous uses the example of viewing the sun.

39 *Handbook* 10:165.28–33. Alcinous gives the example of beauty here.

40 *Handbook* 10:164.31–36; 165.34–166.6.

41 *Handbook* 10:165.38–42.

42 *Handbook* 9:63.30–31; Dillon 1993: 16; cf. *Handbook* 10:164.27–31.

43 *Handbook* 10:164.22–24; 26:179.20–34.

44 *Handbook* 12:166.40–167.40. NB: Alcinous would seem to have merged the Platonic distinctions between the Good and the Demiurge.

45 *Handbook* 16:171.41–172.3. These gods, who are present in four of the five elements (*Handbook* 15:171.15–20), administer to the world as God's children, obeying his will. It is through these gods that omens and oracles appear (*Handbook* 15:171.23–27).

46 *Handbook* 14:169.32–37.

47 *Handbook* 23:176.7–19. NB: Plato proposed two alternative divisions of the soul; a bipartite division of rational and irrational (as we found in Plutarch), and a tripartite division of one rational and two irrational parts. The latter is reflected here in Alcinous.

48 *Handbook* 23:176.20–28.

49 *Handbook* 16:172.2–18.

50 *Handbook* 26:179.1–25. One of the examples he gives is of Paris stealing Helen, a voluntary action that necessitates the war to take her back.

51 Apuleius also wrote the rhetorical works *The Florida*, *Apology*, and *Cupid and Psyche*, and translated the Pseudo-Aristotelian work *On the Cosmos*, which we shall come across in the next section on Aristotelianism.

52 *Plato and his Doctrine* I.11:204.

53 *Plato and his Doctrine* I.5:190–191.

54 *On the God of Socrates* 3:124; *Plato and his Doctrine* I.5:190; 11:204.

55 *Plato and his Doctrine* I.5–6:191–192. cf. *On the God of Socrates* 3:124. NB: Since time would seem to belong solely to the visible realm (*Plato and his Doctrine* I.10:201), Apuleius no doubt intends that God uses the realm of Ideas as a model for the lower world.

56 *On the God of Socrates* 2:121. Apuleius names twelve of these celestial gods; Juno, Vesta, Minerva, Ceres, Diana, Venus, Mars, Mercury, Jupiter, Neptune, Vulcanus, and Apollo.

57 *On the God of Socrates* 3:123; 4–5:127–132.

58 *Plato and his Doctrines* I.11:204–205; *On the God of Socrates* 6:132–133; cf. *On the God of Socrates* 13:147.

59 *The Golden Ass* 11.

60 *On the God of Socrates* 12:147–148.

61 *On the God of Socrates* 15:150,152; 16:154.

62 *On the God of Socrates* 16:155–156. Apuleius goes on to describe Socrates' close relationship with his daemon, here called a god, from which this treatise, like that of Plutarch, takes its name.

63 *Plato and his Doctrine* I. 5:191; 7:194. In this section, Apuleius describes the relationship between God and matter by contrasting their two substances. The first (including God, the Forms and the soul) exists truly and provides the model for the second substance (which includes everything that is shaped and generated). The second substance is an image or shadow of the first, and is not only a reflection of the realm of Forms but an image of God himself (*Plato and his Doctrine* I.7:193–198).

64 *Plato and his Doctrine* I.8:198.

65 *Plato and his Doctrine* I.9:199.

66 *Plato and his Doctrine* I.9:199.

67 *On the God of Socrates* 4:126.

68 *Plato and his Doctrines* I.13:207.

69 *On the God of Socrates* 15:150–153; 16:155–156.

70 *Plato and his Doctrines* I.12:205.

71 *Oration* 11; 4; 9; 12.

72 *Oration* 41.4.
73 *Oration* 11.11–12.
74 *Oration* 11.9–10.
75 *Oration* 11.2.
76 *Oration* 8.8.
77 *Oration* 9.1–4.
78 *Oration* 9.6.
79 *Oration* 11.9.
80 *Oration* 10.9.
81 *Oration* 11.9.
82 *Oration* 9.6; 10.1.
83 *Oration* 5.4–6.
84 *Oration* 41.5.
85 *Oration* 13.4; 8.
86 All of these are collected together in des Places 1973. I shall use des Places' numbering of the fragments in this chapter.
87 See *Fragment* 20.
88 *Fragment* 4a; 5; 7; 16; 17.
89 *Fragment* 5; 15–19.
90 *Fragment* 11–12.
91 *Fragment* 13; 18.
92 *Fragment* 16.
93 *Fragment* 19–20.
94 *Fragment* 22.
95 Numenius actually speaks of two world souls in *Fragment* 52; one benevolent and the other maleficent.
96 *Fragment* 49. Numenius' metaphor of the Demiurge as the helmsman of matter would seem to express this.
97 *Fragment* 3.
98 *Fragment* 4a.
99 *Fragment* 52. There is no room for evil in his transcendent understanding of God. The second God is contaminated and divided only by his contact with matter.
100 *Fragment* 44.
101 *Fragment* 13.
102 *Fragment* 30–35; 48.
103 *Fragment* 39.
104 *Fragment* 14; 'This beautiful process occurs with knowledge by which the Receiver profits, as well as the Giver. This can be seen when one candle receives light from another by mere touch; the fire was not taken away from the other, but its component Matter was kindled by the fire of the other. Similar is the process with knowledge, which by both giving and taking remains with the Giver, while passing over to the Receiver' (V.29 in Guthrie 1917: 30, 32). NB: See below, Chapter 5, p. 116 f.
105 *On the Cosmos* 6 (398b.4–7; 399b.20–22).
106 *On the Cosmos* 6 (397b.33–398b.23).
107 *On the Cosmos* 6 (397b.25–28; 400a.6–16).
108 *On the Cosmos* 6 (397b.10–11; 20–23); Forster and Furley 1965: 384–385. NB: It is from the position of God as the cause that holds the world together that Pseudo-Aristotle embarks on his discussion of divinity.

109 This character of immutability suggests that God is also immutable.

110 *On the Cosmos* 6 (397b.28–33; 398b.20–25; 400a.20–24).

111 *On the Cosmos* 6 (400b.12–13).

112 *On the Cosmos* 7 (401a.13–401b.14). NB: The author is not concerned to address the problem of evil, since his supreme God is not the Platonic Good.

113 *On the Cosmos* 7 (401b.14–27).

114 Alexander's other genuine monographs include *On the Soul*; *On Mixture*; *On Providence*; and *Refutation of Galen's Attack on Aristotle's Doctrine That Everything That Moves is Set in Motion by a Mover*.

115 Although Alexander does not mention them by name, it seems likely that he understands the Stoics to be the proponents of the determinist position. As we shall see, the Stoic view on fate was not entirely deterministic, although this was the popular understanding of many non-Stoics.

116 *On Fate* 6.

117 *On Fate* 6. cf. Sharples 1983: 130, for an explanation of this anecdote.

118 *Or* 19:1; 2 *Apol* 3.

119 This could equally be expressed as a spiritualization of matter.

120 Panaetius and possibly Posidonius.

121 Some Stoics even called the divine 'Destiny'.

122 *Discourses* II.8.1–14; IV.11.3–4.

123 *Discourses* I.3.1.

124 *Discourses* I.15.

125 *Discourses* I.6.19; IV.1; 11.5–8.

126 1 *Apol* 1. Justin calls him by the name 'Verissimus', a nickname coined by Hadrian, and based on his surname before his adoption by Antoninus Pius, which was 'Verus'.

127 NB: In his first book, Marcus Aurelius claims to have read the *Discourses* of Epictetus (*Meditations* I.7).

128 *Meditations* II.11; V.27.

129 *Meditations* III.16.

130 *Meditations* II.17.

131 *Meditations* VIII.54 offers a fascinating insight into Marcus Aurelius' understanding of the cosmic soul; he likens the cosmic mind to the atmosphere and urges men to absorb it in the same way that the atmosphere is respired.

132 *Meditations* II.14; IV.14 describes the re-absorption of man's divine part into 'its generative reason'; *Meditations* IV.21 offers an explanation for how souls that might survive after death are gradually assumed into the Universal Nature, just as the matter of the body is absorbed into the ground; *Meditations* V.13 describes how the formal and material substances of which man is made are assigned to a be a new part of the universe after death; *Meditations* VII.32 suggests either atomic dispersal or assimilation into the unity of the world soul.

133 *Meditations* VII.75; Farquharson 1989: 67.

134 *Meditations* II.14.

135 *Meditations* II.3; IV.26; V.8.

136 *Meditations* III.6; XI.16.

137 *On the Nature of Things* I.418–421.

138 *On the Nature of Things* I.958–1051; II.1075 f.

139 *On the Nature of Things* II.132 f; 217–220; 251–260.

140 *On the Nature of Things* V.156 f (cf. II.167 f).

141 *On the Nature of Things* II.646–651.

142 *On the Nature of Things* III.94–273. NB: In this, Lucretius differs from Epicurus; Epicurus envisaged only body and soul.

143 *On the Nature of Things* III.140–281.

144 *On the Nature of Things* III.323–336; 455–458.

145 *On the Nature of Things* III.323–336; 455–458; 830–842.

146 *Outlines of Pyrrhonism* I.4; Bury 1933: 7.

147 *Outlines of Pyrrhonism* III.3.

148 This is compared with two Aristotelian treatises, two Stoics, one Epicurean (who does not even belong within the second century), and one Sceptic.

149 This is the emphasis of both Merlan (in Armstrong 1967: 14–132) and Dillon (1977).

150 Some philosophers would also have enjoyed patronage, living in the household of their patron.

151 For a further discussion of the modus operandi of Graeco-Roman philosophers, see Walden 1912; Wilken 1971.

152 It was believed that certain things, such as drugs, had a sympathetic, nourishing effect on the body, whilst others, such as poisons, had an antipathetic, destructive effect.

153 As M. Whittaker points out (1982: 33), when Bolus of Mendes (third century BCE) wrote a treatise on the sympathies and antipathies, this theory was already regarded as originating from Democritus.

154 *Or* 17:1.

155 *Or* 27:2.

156 As we shall see shortly, Tatian appears to have absorbed a great deal of Platonic thought, so it should not surprise us that his criticisms of Platonism are not wider ranging.

157 *Or* 3:2.

158 M. Whittaker 1982: 9.

159 *Or* 13:1; M. Whittaker 1982: 27.

160 *Or* 16:1; cf. *Or* 7:3.

161 *Or* 2:2; M. Whittaker 1982: 7; cf. *Or* 2:1.

162 *Or* 2:1–2.

163 As we saw earlier, the Stoics of the second century were moving away from this idea, but it was nonetheless still attributed to them in the popular view of Stoicism.

164 *Or* 3:1; 6:1.

165 *Or* 3:2.

166 *Or* 21:3.

167 *Or* 32–33.

168 *Or* 2:1; 19:1; 25:1.

169 *Or* 3:1. In one of his extant fragments, Heraclitus claims to have 'looked into' himself (cf. M. Whittaker 1982: 7), and his philosophy is based on introspection.

170 *Or* 3:1. NB: This accusation is especially significant when one remembers Tatian's negative estimation of medicine.

171 *Or* 3:2.

172 *Or* 2:1. The story of Plato's enslavement is recorded in *Quaest. Homericae* 78, which says that Plato was sold as a prisoner of war by a Spartan who had been given the philosopher by Dionysius I (see M. Whittaker 1982: 5). A possible motive is the influence that Plato exerted over Dionysius' son-in-law, Dion, who later went on to oppose Dionysius's son and successor, Dionysius II, in favour of a political system more in line with Plato's thought.

173 In his youth Alexander was the pupil of Aristotle, which explains why Tatian should classify Alexander as an Aristotelian.

174 *Or* 2:1. In view of the relationship between Aristotle and the Macedonian monarchy (Alexander's father destroyed Aristotle's home town), it is surprising that Aristotle even agreed to become the prince's tutor, and any such obsession seems unlikely.

175 *Or* 2:1. Callisthenes was the nephew of Aristotle, and historian of Alexander's campaigns. Following an assassination attempt on Alexander's life, Callisthenes was executed for his involvement, although Tatian makes no mention of this.

176 *Or* 2:1–2. Although Tatian does not mention Clitus by name, the story of Clitus' death corresponds with what Tatian says here. It is said that Clitus taunted Alexander, who threw his spear in anger and killed his friend. The remorse that Tatian relates was probably sincere and not, as Tatian claims, to ingratiate himself with his friends.

177 *Or* 2:1; M. Whittaker 1982: 5. Reprinted by permission of Oxford University Press.

178 *Or* 2:1.

179 *Or* 3:3.

180 Justin mentions Crescens in 2 *Apol* 3 (cf. Eusebius, *Ecclesiastical History* 4.16.3). Crescens is not otherwise known, although clearly Justin and Tatian came into direct contact with him.

181 *Or* 19:1.

182 *Or* 3:3; M. Whittaker 1982: 9. Reprinted by permission of Oxford University Press.

183 *Or* 25:1–2; M. Whittaker 1982: 49. Reprinted by permission of Oxford University Press.

184 *Or* 1:2; cf. *Or* 26:3–4.

185 *Or* 8:2. There follows a list of stories about the Graeco-Roman gods, which display conflicting behaviour.

186 *Or* 28:1; 31:4.

187 *Or* 12:2–3.

188 cf. Baarda 1994: 29–47; Elze 1960: 124–126 (see also 58–60 on the unity of Christianity versus the diversity and contradictions of Greek philosophy).

189 *Or* 31–33. The verb Tatian uses is φιλοσοφέω.

190 *Or* 42:1.

191 Strictly speaking, Tatian does not speak of 'Christian' philosophy, and indeed nowhere in the *Oration* does the title 'Christ' or its derivatives appear. However, as Barnard points out (1968a: 10), this does not mean anything, as the same is true of Theophilus of Antioch and Athenagoras.

When addressing the Greeks, the use of such a title would have been meaningless.
192 *Or* 29:1.
193 *Or* 31, 35–41. It is not necessary to include the details of this argument here, but it went on to influence later Christian writers (cf. Origen, *Contra Celsum* 1.16, where Origen praises Tatian's chronological argument). One cannot help but wonder whether the usefulness of this argument in part ensured the survival of Tatian's *Oration* after he was pronounced a heretic.
194 *Or* 40:1; M. Whittaker 1982: 73. Reprinted by permission of Oxford University Press.
195 See Droge 1989: 4–48.
196 Droge 1989: 84. Indeed a large proportion of the *Oration* is dedicated to this, and its structure pivots around Tatian's conversion story, which details his understanding of the history of culture most succinctly.
197 For a more detailed discussion, see Droge 1989: 82–101.
198 cf. M.L. Clarke 1971.
199 'Invisible' (*Or* 4:1); 'ineffable' (*Or* 4:3); 'incorruptible' (*Or* 7:1); 'fleshless' (*Or* 15:2).
200 *Or* 15:2.
201 *Or* 7:1; M. Whittaker 1982: 13. Reprinted by permission of Oxford University Press.
202 *Or* 5:2–3. Here, Tatian goes against conventional Platonism by denying the concept of pre-existent matter. Tatian's introduction of the creation out of nothing theory charts an important development within second century Christian doctrines, and will be discussed more fully in Chapter 5.
203 *Or* 7:1.
204 *Or* 5:3; M. Whittaker 1982: 11. Reprinted by permission of Oxford University Press.
205 It is interesting to note that although Tatian, Justin and Philo do not use this specific terminology, Theophilus of Antioch does (*To Autolycus* 2.10; 2.22).
206 *Or* 4:2; M. Whittaker 1982: 9. Reprinted by permission of Oxford University Press.
207 *Or* 12:1–2.
208 In *Or* 4:2, God is described as 'the constructor of material spirits and the shapes that are in matter' within the same breath (M. Whittaker 1982: 9. Reprinted by permission of Oxford University Press).
209 *Or* 12:3–5.
210 *Or* 5:2; 12:1.
211 *Or* 12:1.
212 *Or* 5:2–3.
213 *Or* 12:1.
214 *Or* 15.
215 *Or* 13:2.
216 *Or* 8 f.
217 cf. Rudolph 1987: 60; Edwards 1989: 26–47; Petrement 1991: 226.

5 TATIAN AND THE DEVELOPMENT OF A CHRISTIAN PHILOSOPHY

1 Links have been established between Philo and Clement of Alexandria (cf. van den Hoek 1988), and Philo and Origen (cf. Runia 1995). See Runia 1993 for a comprehensive survey of scholarly opinion on Philo's influence in the early church.

2 Philo, in his turn, was influenced by predecessors within Alexandrian hellenized Jewry. Unfortunately very little about them has survived, and we are left without any real evidence of how this synthesis of philosophy and Judaism emerged.

3 Holte 1958; Goodenough 1968; Edwards 1995.

4 *On the Account of the World's Creation; Allegorical Interpretation of Genesis II, III; On the Cherubim; On the Sacrifices of Abel and Cain; That the Worse is Wont to Attack the Better; On the Posterity of Cain and his Exile; On the Giants; On the Unchangeableness of God; On Husbandry; Concerning Noah's Work as a Planter; On Drunkenness; On the Prayers and Curses Uttered by Noah when he became Sober; On the Confusion of Tongues; On the Migration of Abraham; Who is the Heir of Divine Things?; On Mating with the Preliminary Studies; On Flight and Finding; On the Change of Names; On Dreams; On Abraham; On Joseph; On Moses; On the Decalogue; On the Special Laws; On the Virtues; On Rewards and Punishments; Every Good Man is Free; On the Contemplative Life; On the Eternity of the World; Flaccus; Hypothetica; On Providence; On the Embassy to Gaius; Questions and Answers on Genesis; Questions and Answers on Exodus.* (Loeb Edition in ten vols, plus two supplementary vols).

5 Philo reconciles philosophy with Judaism principally by claiming that the Greek philosophers were dependent on the Hebrew Scriptures (*Every Good Man is Free* 57; *On the Special Laws* IV.61; *Allegorical Interpretation* I.108; *Who is the Heir?* 214). However, his anthropological theory, where the human mind is an extension of the Logos (*Who is the Heir?* 235), may provide philosophers with the opportunity to grasp the truths of God independently, as too does his insistence on divine revelation and prophecy. Philo's method of reconciliation is familiar; the first two arguments are found in Justin (the second perhaps anticipating his spermatic logos theory), and, as we shall see, the last two are also found in Tatian. It is of course possible that Philo himself is the source from which Justin and Tatian take the argument that the philosophers have plagiarized Moses.

6 Wolfson 1947a, 1947b.

7 Dillon 1977: 182.

8 For a full survey, see Pearson 1984: 295–342.

9 Jonas 1954: 70–121 (cited in Pearson 1984: 304–309).

10 See Pearson's conclusions (1984: 340); cf. Stead 1969: 75–104; Wedderburn 1973: 301–326; Fallon 1976: 45–51.

11 cf. *On the Unchangeableness of God*, which concentrates on *Gen* 6:4–12. Here Philo argues that although God may appear to change his mind several times, this is not actually the case.

12 *On Rewards and Punishment* 40. Philo also says that God only wills the good (*Special Laws* IV.187) and that God is not responsible for creating evil (*On Husbandry* 128–129).

13 *On Rewards and Punishments* 162; *Allegorical Interpretation* II.3; III.48; *Special Laws* II.176; *Questions on Genesis* I.15.

14 *On Cherubim* 19; *Questions on Genesis* I.93; *On Dreams* II.220 The treatise *On the Unchangeableness of God*, as its name suggests, is devoted to the question of divine immutability.

15 *Who is the Heir of Divine Things?* 229; *On the Migration of Abraham* 183; *Questions on Genesis* IV.188; *Allegorical Interpretation* III.206; *Special Laws* I.32.

16 *Special Laws* I.20; *Questions on Genesis* IV.26.

17 *On the Change of Names* 7; *On the Unchangeableness of God* 62; *Question on Exodus* II.45.

18 *Who is the Heir of Divine Things?* 170; *On the Change of Names* 11; *On Dreams* I.230.

19 *On Cherubim* 49; cf. Radice 1991.

20 *On the Unchangeableness of God* 11 f; *Special Laws* II.176.

21 *On the Posterity of Cain and his Exile* 28.

22 In *On the Creation* 134, Philo clearly differentiates between a 'man' created in *Gen* 1:26 (the model) and a mortal man created in *Gen* 2:7.

23 *On the Creation* 9; 36; *On Dreams* I.241.

24 May 1994; Young 1991.

25 cf. *On Dreams* I.76; *Allegorical Interpretations* III.10.

26 So May (1994: 17–18), but cf. Wolfson (1956a: 303–309), who argues that Philo does present a creation out of nothing.

27 *On the Creation* 20; 24; 36; *On Dreams* II.45.

28 *On the Eternity of the World* 21; *That the Worse is Wont to Attack the Better* 154.

29 *Concerning Noah's Work as a Planter* 9–10; *Questions on Exodus* II.89; *Who is the Heir of Divine Things?* 156; 188; *On Flight and Finding* 112.

30 *On the Confusion of Tongues* 114; *On the Creation* 7; *On Dreams* II.283; *On the Decalogue* 58.

31 *Allegorical Interpretation* III.207; *Questions on Genesis* III.34.

32 *Questions on Exodus* 68. Then the 'power of mercy' is produced from the creative power and the 'law-making power' from the royal power. All five (Logos, creative power, royal power, power of mercy and law-making power) then create the world of Forms.

33 *On Giants* 25. Here, Philo adds the extra metaphors of sun and sunlight, and spring and streams (cf. *Questions on Genesis* II.40).

34 *On the Migration of Abraham* 103.

35 *Who is the Heir of Divine Things?* 230–231.

36 *On the Confusion of Tongues* 146.

37 Or 5:1. Tatian also uses the term 'firstborn' of the Logos.

38 *Who is the Heir of Divine Things?* 205; cf. *Questions on Exodus* II.68; *On Dreams* II.188.

39 *On Husbandry* 51; *On the Migration of Abraham* 102; *On Dreams* I.215; *On the Confusion of Tongues* 146; *Who is the Heir of Divine Things?* 79; *On Flight and Finding* 137.

40 *On the Sacrifices of Abel and Cain* 92.

41 *On Moses* II.147; *Special Laws* I.252; *On the Confusion of Tongues* 179; cf. *On Flight and Finding* 68; *On Abraham* 143.

42 *Questions on Genesis* I.55. The involvement of man's free will in the process

of the fall is highly reminiscent of Tatian (see below, p. 136 f). cf. *On the Virtues* 205.

43 *On the Creation* 135. NB: This concept is clearly Biblically orientated.

44 *On Giants* 12. Here, Philo also informs us that some of the souls remain above the earth and become 'ministering angels'. In *Concerning Noah's Work as a Planter* 14, Philo gives an alternative appellation for the angels of 'heroes', whilst in *On Dreams* I.141, he also calls them 'demons'.

45 *On Giants* 13–14; Colson and Whittaker 1929: 451, 453.

46 *On the Posterity of Cain and his Exile* 167; *Allegorical Interpretation* III.100.

47 *On Moses* II.6; *On Flight and Finding* 168.

48 *Who is the Heir of Divine Things?* 68 f.

49 Wolfson 1956b: 10.

50 This also has interesting implications for Tatian's understanding of prophecy.

51 Aune 1983: 147. NB: On p. 151, Aune writes: 'Philo was a prophet only in the sense that he consciously regarded the prophetic revelatory experience as the highest source of knowledge, and he himself had experienced the heightened vision into supranormal reality.'

52 *Who is the Heir of Divine Things?* 266; 249; *Special Laws* I.65. Philo frequently perceives of the prophet as an instrument upon which God plays (*On the Change of Names* 139; *Who is the Heir of Divine Things* 266), and once describes the Logos as a plectrum (*Questions on Genesis* IV.196).

53 cf. *Numbers* 11:25–29; *1 Samuel* 5–7; *1 Chronicles* 25:1.

54 See Aune 1983: 23–114; cf. also Winston 1990.

55 *Special Laws* IV.49; Colson and Whittaker 1939: 37, 39.

56 *Or* 15:2–3; 13:3.

57 *Allegorical Interpretation* I.108; III.69; *Questions on Genesis* I.93; *On Husbandry* 25. NB: σῶμα σῆμα was a common Greek proverb (cf. Plato, *Gorgias* 493A).

58 *Special Laws* II.225; *On the Decalogue* 107; *On the Creation* 152.

59 *Who is the Heir of Divine Things?* 285; *Questions on Genesis* III.16.

60 *That the Worse is Wont to Attack the Better* 19; *On Flight and Finding* 28.

61 *On the Change of Names* 32; *Special Laws* 20–21; *On Flight and Finding* 38.

62 *Special Laws* III.6–82.

63 Bianchi 1985: 296. NB: Bianchi accepts a very wide definition of the word 'Encratite'.

64 cf. Wolfson 1956a.

65 Norris 1966: 34.

66 Andresen 1952/53: 157–195. See above, Chapter 3, p. 58 f, for a discussion of the debate on Middle Platonic influence on Justin.

67 For a survey of this debate, see Runia 1993: 97–105.

68 This theme of Philonic influence runs throughout Goodenough's book, but is particularly concentrated in his investigation into Justin's doctrines of God and the Logos in Chapters 4 and 5 (Goodenough 1968: 123–175).

69 Goodenough 1968: 127–173.

70 Trakatellis 1976: 132.

71 Trakatellis 1976: 46. NB: Holte perceives a close link between Philo's spiritualization of the spermatic logos and Justin's own conception, although he also stresses the importance of the Pauline concept of a pre-

existent Christ (Holte 1958: 126). Waszink, meanwhile, concludes that Justin is dependent on Philo's use of sowing and planting imagery in his development of the spermatic logos theory (Waszink 1964: 389).

72 Barnard 1967: 92; cf. Shotwell 1965; Osborn 1973.
73 Runia 1993: 104.
74 Runia 1993: 104–105. NB: Runia wrongly assumes that Tatian was influenced by gnosticism, and therefore concludes: 'This brings him closer to the Gnostic teachers of Alexandria . . . but not to Philo.'
75 Runia 1993: 8–9.
76 Runia 1993: 98.
77 Edwards 1995: 263 f.
78 Goodenough 1968: 125–130.
79 e.g. 'Stone' or 'Rock'; 'Beginning'; 'Light'; 'Wisdom'; 'Israel' or 'Jacob'; 'Priest' or 'King' (Goodenough 1968: 168–172). Goodenough concludes: 'There can no longer be any doubt that in his titles for the Logos Justin has received much from a Philonic tradition. But even the impulse to speak of the Logos by many names has come through the same tradition. Philo, like Justin, is not only always interested in finding new names which he can apply to the Logos, but is fond of drawing up lists of such names.'
80 *On Giants* 25; Colson and Whittaker 1929: 457. Philo also uses the metaphor of water from a spring in *On Giants* 25–26. cf. *Questions on Exodus* II.40.
81 *Or* 5:1; Grant 1958: 126–127.
82 *Questions on Exodus* II.68; Marcus 1953: 116.
83 *Fragment* 14; V.29 in Guthrie 1917: 30, 32.
84 Runia 1993: 8–9.
85 *Dial* 61; Falls 1977: 244.
86 *Against Praxeas* 8; Heine 1989: 9.
87 *Dial* 61; Falls 1977: 244.
88 *On Moses* II.127; Goodenough 1968: 152.
89 Holte 1958: 127–128.
90 Trakatellis 1976: 122–123.
91 Runia 1993: 104.
92 Martín 1988: 263–294.
93 Elze 1960: 11–13.
94 Elze 1960: 20, 14. NB: Elze presupposes that Tatian's now lost philosophical works (e.g. *On Animals*) were written before his conversion, and represent his pre-Christian phase. Elze further argues that esoteric passages, like *Or* 30, were imported from these pre-Christian works.
95 In his conversion account, Tatian himself states that he sought the truth (*Or* 29:1).
96 See above, Chapter 4, p. 98 f.
97 See *Or* 5:3; 29:1–2 (cf. Elze 1960: 32).
98 Elze 1960: 33.
99 *Or* 17:1; M. Whittaker 1982: 35. Reprinted by permission of Oxford University Press.
100 *Or* 13:3; 15:2; 20:2–3.
101 Elze 1960: 14.
102 Elze 1960: 29–31.

103 Throughout this book, I have argued for caution when using isolated parallels.

104 Tatian tells us this in *Or* 42.

105 cf. The popularized (and stereotyped) philosophy expressed by Cicero some 200 years earlier.

106 *Or* 19:4; 29:2.

107 Tatian calls his God invisible and impalpable (*Or* 4:1–2), incomprehensible (*Or* 4:1), ineffable (*Or* 4:3), incorruptible (*Or* 7:1; 32:1), and fleshless (*Or* 15:2; 25:2). Tatian also rejects the notion of sacrificial offerings when he claims that his God is free of needs and is therefore not to be bribed (*Or* 5:3), and he further expresses his God's transcendence by claiming that he belongs beyond temporal bounds; he says that God has no origin in time and that he is without beginning (*Or* 4:1; 5:3).

108 Tatian calls his God 'God the creator' (*Or* 6:1), claims that he is responsible for constructing material spirits and shapes that are in matter (*Or* 4:2), that he is the originator of matter itself (*Or* 12:1), and that he is 'the sole creator' of the universe (*Or* 5:3).

109 *Or* 5:1–2.

110 *Or* 4:2; *Rom* 1:20.

111 *Or* 6:1; 12:4; 18:2; 25:2; 32:2.

112 *Or* 5:1; 6:2; 12:4; 18:2; 29:2.

113 *Or* 4:2; 7:1; 32:1.

114 *Or* 4:2.

115 Justin, 1 *Apol* 16; *Dial* 4: Philo, *On Rewards and Punishments* 40; *Special Laws* IV.187; *On the Posterity and Exile of Cain* 2; 9; *On Giants* 52; *On Dreams* II.237.

116 *Or* 5:1; M. Whittaker 1982: 11. Reprinted by permission of Oxford University Press.

117 NB: The designations 'Beginning' and 'Firstborn' are also used by Justin (*Dial* 129; 1 *Apol* 23; *Dial* 138) and Philo (*On the Confusion of Tongues* 146). It is also interesting to note that Tatian indicates that the notion of the Logos as the Beginning is an inherited concept by his use of the verb παραλαμβάνω (to receive).

118 *Or* 5:1–2; M. Whittaker 1982: 11. Reprinted by permission of Oxford University Press.

119 It is clear that Tatian does not understand the Logos to fulfil a gnostic-type Demiurge role in creation.

120 *Or* 5:3.

121 *Or* 5:2; 'The Word begotten in the beginning in turn begot our creation by fabricating matter.' (M. Whittaker 1982: 11. Reprinted by permission of Oxford University Press).

122 *Or* 7:1; M. Whittaker 1982: 13. Reprinted by permission of Oxford University Press.

123 πατρός is found in manuscripts MVP. This was emended to πνεύματος by Schwartz in his 1888 edition of the text, and has been followed by both Whittaker (1982: 12) and Marcovich (1995: 17, line 1).

124 *Or* 7:2.

125 *Or* 12:1.

126 *Or* 7:3.

127 *Or* 13:3.

128 i.e. The prophets; *Or* 13:3; 15:2; 20:2–3.
129 *Or* 5:1–2.
130 This is probably due to the genre of the *Oration*.
131 *Or* 21:1; M. Whittaker 1982: 43. Reprinted by permission of Oxford University Press.
132 *Or* 13:3; M. Whittaker 1982: 29. Reprinted by permission of Oxford University Press.
133 NB: πεπονθότος is found only in M and P. Marcovich has emended it to πεποιηκότος (Marcovich 1995: 30, line 26).
134 *Or* 29:2.
135 *Or* 12:1–2; M. Whittaker 1982: 23, 25; cf. *Or* 5:2–3. Reprinted by permission of Oxford University Press.
136 Philo, *On the Creation* 9; *On Dreams* I.241: Justin, 1 *Apol* 20; 59; 2 *Apol* 6.
137 Berlin: Walter de Gruyter, 1978. Translated into English by A.S. Worrall (May 1994).
138 May 1994: 17–18.
139 May 1994: 1–6.
140 May 1994: 62–84.
141 Hippolytus, *Refutation of all Heresies* VII.20–27.
142 Irenaeus, *Against the Heresies* I.24.3–7.
143 *Refutation of all Heresies* VII.20.2–21.1; Young 1991: 147–150.
144 May even tentatively suggests a common Syriac background for Basilides, Theophilus and Tatian (May 1994: 77). In view of the different directions each took to reach the theory of creation out of nothing, such a common source seems unlikely, as May himself admits.
145 *To Autolycus* II.4.
146 *Or* 5:3; M. Whittaker 1982: 11. Reprinted by permission of Oxford University Press.
147 May 1994: 77.
148 *Or* 6:2.
149 May 1994: 151–154. May concludes: 'Tatian stands between the two fronts of orthodoxy and heresy, neither of which was yet firmly established, but certainly his view that matter was directly created by God was ungnostic and probably developed in his controversies with gnostic theologians. It constitutes the decisive step to the final formulation of "creatio ex nihilo".'
150 *Or* 12:2–4.
151 *Or* 4:2; cf. *Or* 26:1.
152 *Or* 7:1–3.
153 *Or* 20:1; M. Whittaker 1982: 41. Reprinted by permission of Oxford University Press.
154 *Or* 20:1; M. Whittaker 1982: 40. Reprinted by permission of Oxford University Press.
155 *Or* 13:2; 15:3; 16:2; cf. Especially *Or* 17:3; 18:2.
156 *Or* 16:1.
157 *Or* 15:3; M. Whittaker 1982: 31. Reprinted by permission of Oxford University Press.
158 *Or* 12:3; M. Whittaker 1982: 25. Reprinted by permission of Oxford University Press.
159 In the face of this apparent contradiction (namely Tatian's negative

portrayal of demons and this claim that some 'turn to what is purer')
Marcovich changes the position of ὕλης so that it follows on from
τραπέντες and would therefore read, 'some of them turning to what is
purer *in matter*' (Marcovich 1995: 28, line 30). This is a subtle but
significant change, which highlights an important ambiguity in Tatian;
what does Tatian mean by τὸ καθαρώτερον? Is it, as Marcovich suggests, what is purer in matter, or is it what is purer and beyond matter
(i.e. the divine)? Whatever Tatian means when he refers to τὸ
καθαρώτερον, clearly the word has a positive connotation.

160 *Or* 7:2; M. Whittaker 1982: 13. Reprinted by permission of Oxford University Press.
161 It is interesting to note similarities between Tatian's portrayal of the
arch-rebel and the myth of Lucifer, which became popular in the Middle
Ages.
162 Especially in *Or* 12:4.
163 *Or* 13:2.
164 NB: This assertion may be in refutation of Platonic views.
165 *Or* 12:3–16:1.
166 *Or* 12:4–16:2.
167 *Or* 16:3; 17:2–3; 18:2–3.
168 *Or* 8:1; 9:2; 15:4.
169 *Or* 18:2–3; 14:1.
170 i.e. That demons are reflections of evil and matter, and have no 'room for
repentance' (*Or* 15:3).
171 *Or* 14:1–2.
172 *Or* 7:1; M. Whittaker 1982: 13. Reprinted by permission of Oxford University Press. cf. *Or* 7:3; 15:1.
173 *Or* 15:2; M. Whittaker 1982: 31. Reprinted by permission of Oxford
University Press. NB: This passage is central to Tatian's anthropology,
and we will return to it again shortly.
174 *Or* 12:1.
175 *Or* 7:1.
176 *Or* 12:1.
177 *Or* 7:1–2; cf. *Or* 11:2. NB: The notion that man is responsible for the fall
through his free will is also proposed by Philo (*Questions on Genesis* I.55;
On the Virtues 205).
178 *Or* 7:3; 13:2. NB: It is interesting to note that in *Or* 20:1, Tatian actually
uses a metaphor from Plato's *Phaedrus* (246c1) to describe the dissolution of
this union: 'The soul's wings are the perfect spirit, but the soul cast it away
because of sin, fluttered like a nestling and fell to the ground.' (M. Whittaker 1982: 41. Reprinted by permission of Oxford University Press).
179 *Or* 13:2–3; 20:1.
180 *Or* 11:2; 15:4.
181 *Or* 15:1; 20:1.
182 *Or* 13:1–2.
183 *Or* 13:2.
184 *Or* 13:3; 20:2–3; cf. Philo, who also asserts that prophecy is necessary to
reveal what the human mind is incapable of achieving alone (*On Moses*
II.6; *On Flight and Finding* 168). *Or* 15:2 also appears to explain the
method of prophetic inspiration.

185 *Or* 6:1–2. NB: In this passage, I believe that the section where Tatian speaks of the nature of existence before and after death should be understood literally, although it may sound esoteric; here Tatian is justifying his belief in the resurrection by comparing it with man's state prior to birth. (cf. 1 *Apol* 19, where Justin is dealing with the same issue.)

186 *Or* 17:1; 25:2.

187 *Or* 14:2.

188 cf. *Or* 13:1.

189 *Or* 20:2.

190 *Or* 26:1–2.

191 *Or* 8:1.

192 *Or* 2:1–2.

193 *Or* 7:1.

194 *Or* 7:2; M. Whittaker 1982: 13. Reprinted by permission of Oxford University Press.

195 *Or* 15:3; M. Whittaker 1982: 31. Reprinted by permission of Oxford University Press.

196 *Or* 20:2–3; M. Whittaker 1982: 41, 43. Reprinted by permission of Oxford University Press. cf. *Or* 12:2; 15:1.

197 *Or* 13:3; M. Whittaker 1982: 27. Reprinted by permission of Oxford University Press.

198 *Or* 15:2; M. Whittaker 1982: 31. Reprinted by permission of Oxford University Press.

199 *Or* 15:1.

200 *Or* 12:1.

201 *Or* 13:1–2.

202 *Or* 20:1; M. Whittaker 1982: 41. Reprinted by permission of Oxford University Press.

203 Chapter 15 even opens with the words: 'Well then, we ought now to search for what we once had and have lost, and link the soul and the Holy Spirit and busy ourselves with the union ordained by God.' (M. Whittaker 1982: 29. Reprinted by permission of Oxford University Press).

204 *Or* 12:1.

205 *Or* 15:3; M. Whittaker 1982: 31. Reprinted by permission of Oxford University Press.

206 *Or* 13:3; M. Whittaker 1982: 27. Reprinted by permission of Oxford University Press.

207 *Or* 29:1.

208 *On Moses* II.6; cf. *Or* 20:2; 13:3.

209 *Special Laws* IV.49. cf. *Or* 15:2.

210 See Wolfson 1947b: 10.

6 TATIAN AND SYRIAC CHRISTIANITY

1 Clement of Alexandria, *Stromateis* 3.81.1; Epiphanius, *Panarion* 46.1.6; *Or* 42:1.

2 cf. *Or* 29:1.

3 Although the heresiologists claim that Tatian's return was motivated by his apostasy from the church (Irenaeus, *Against the Heresies* I.28.1), it may be that, like the Montanists, Tatian became disillusioned by the

increasing conservatism of the mainstream church. The precise location where Tatian settled is rather uncertain. Several suggestions have been made: Zahn and Harnack have suggested that Tatian settled in Edessa; Kukula that he went to Asia Minor; Ponschab that he went to Antioch in Syria; and Kahle and Vööbus that he settled in 'his Assyrian homeland' (cited in W.L. Petersen 1994: 71–72). Although I think it very likely that he returned to eastern Syria, there is little evidence to support this.

4 Epiphanius, *Panarion* 46.1.6.

5 Burkitt 1939: 492–496.

6 NB: The name given for Addai in Eusebius is in fact 'Thaddaeus'.

7 The *Gospel of Thomas* seems to reflect a non-gnostic Syriac Christian tradition that was in existence before the time of Tatian (cf. Koester 1965: 279–318), and Vööbus, who perceives a Jewish origin to Syriac Christianity, even places the beginning of Christianity's spread to the East as early as the start of the second century (Vööbus 1958: 5).

8 Drijvers 1990: 492–499. Addai (or 'Adda') was the name of one of Mani's disciples, whose missionary work largely concentrated on the area around Syria. Letters, from Jesus and from Mani, were common coin within Manicheism, forming part of their canon. Moreover, certain parallels between the *Doctrine of Addai* and the Manichean texts suggest a link between these two traditions (Drijvers 1990: 495), and the fact that at this period Manicheism (along with other so-called 'heretical' groups) had marginalized 'orthodox' Christianity means that there was a motive for this appropriation; a defence against the threat the Manichees posed. NB: We recall that other scholars (e.g. Bauer 1972: 36) consider the *Doctrine of Addai* to be a fourth century propagandist work designed to give apostolic roots to Syriac orthodoxy.

9 *Against the Heresies* I.28.1.

10 *Ecclesiastical History* IV.29.6. NB: Some translate πρότερος as 'founder' rather than 'leader'.

11 *Panarion* 47.1.1.

12 It is difficult to distinguish an Encratite sect within Syriac Christianity, since asceticism was very popular in the East. I suspect that the notion of an Encratite sect is actually the invention of western heresiologists in their attempt to define 'orthodoxy'.

13 The *Gospel of Thomas* or the *Gospel of the Hebrews* may well have circulated in Syria before Tatian's return, but their impact, compared to the huge success of the *Diatessaron*, was negligible.

14 W.L. Petersen 1994: 2.

15 Theodoret of Cyrrhus, *History of Heresies* I.20; Rabulla, *Canon* 43.

16 This variant was first identified by Vööbus (1958: 42), and although Vööbus introduces it somewhat hesitantly, Petersen appears to cite Vööbus' inclusion of this variant with some conviction (W.L. Petersen 1994: 81). Metzger adds Ephrem's citation of the *Diatessaron* as a witness here (Metzger 1977: 34).

17 Vööbus 1958: 42 (cited in W.L. Petersen 1994: 81).

18 This variant was first identified by Plooij, who concludes: 'The author of this redaction evidently was prepared to accept marriage as a divine institution, but only in the sense of a spiritual union into which God has united husband and wife; but it was Adam who said that they should be

one flesh.' (Plooij 1923b: 54 – cited in W.L. Petersen 1994: 79–80). Vööbus also points out this variant in the Liège Harmony (Vööbus 1958: 42–43. NB: he appears to have discovered this variant independently, since he makes no reference to Plooij), and Metzger claims that this variant is also present in the Stuttgart, Gravenhage and Theodiscum harmonies (Metzger 1977: 34).

19 Vogels (1913: 168–171) was the first scholar to identify this variant in the Persian Harmony. However, it was Vööbus who discovered the parallel variant in the Stuttgart Harmony (Vööbus 1958: 42), and Metzger who pointed out the parallel in the German Zürich Harmony (Metzger 1977: 34) (cited in W.L. Petersen 1994: 80–81).

20 Vogels 1913: 168–171 (cited in W.L. Petersen 1994: 81).

21 *Luke* 20:35–36.

22 Vööbus 1958: 43 (cited in W.L. Petersen 1994: 81–82).

23 Leloir 1966: 12 (cited in W.L. Petersen 1994: 82). As Petersen notes, Metzger points out that this verse is not included in Ephrem's citations from the *Diatessaron* (Metzger 1977: 33–35).

24 Vööbus 1958: 41–42 (cited in W.L. Petersen 1994: 81).

25 Leloir 1966: 12 (cited in W.L. Petersen 1994: 82).

26 Leloir 1966: 12 (cited in W.L. Petersen 1994: 82). Metzger also points out the omission of this verse (Metzger 1977: 35).

27 Vööbus 1958: 41 (cited in W.L. Petersen 1994: 82).

28 Vööbus 1958: 40–41 (cited in W.L. Petersen 1994: 81).

29 Vööbus 1958: 40 (cited in W.L. Petersen 1994: 81).

30 Vööbus 1958: 41 (cited in W.L. Petersen 1994: 81).

31 cf. Justin's asceticism outlined earlier.

32 *Or* 11:2; M. Whittaker 1982: 23. Reprinted by permission of Oxford University Press.

33 cf. *Rom* 6:10; *Col* 2:20.

34 *Or* 11:1. NB: Tatian also here states 'I hate fornication' (M. Whittaker 1982: 23).

35 The passage cited above is immediately followed by the words; 'We were not born to die, but die through our own fault. Free will has destroyed us ... it was we who exhibited wickedness; but we who exhibited it are still capable of rejecting it.' (*Or* 11:2; M. Whittaker 1982: 23. Reprinted by permission of Oxford University Press).

36 *Or* 8:1–2; M. Whittaker 1982: 15. Reprinted by permission of Oxford University Press. NB: Battle imagery was frequently used in the early church to express the ascetic's fight against the things of this world (cf. *Or* 16:2–3). One who deserted the battlefield would have been a failed ascetic. Whilst this concept may have been at the back of Tatian's mind, in this passage, he is primarily denouncing examples of demonic cowardice.

37 Hawthorne 1964: 166.

38 *Or* 13; 15.

39 *Or* 23:2; M. Whittaker 1982: 47. Reprinted by permission of Oxford University Press.

40 *Or* 33:2; M. Whittaker 1982: 61, 63. Reprinted by permission of Oxford University Press.

41 This passage stands out from the rest of the *Oration* because of the almost

misogynistic way in which Tatian refers to women elsewhere (cf. especially *Or* 34:1).

42 *Or* 15:2; M. Whittaker 1982: 31. Reprinted by permission of Oxford University Press.

43 See above, Chapter 5, p. 139 f. NB: As we have seen, this passage contains echoes of several Pauline passages (1 *Cor* 3:16; 6:19; 2 *Cor* 6:16; *Eph* 2:19–22).

44 *Or* 13:3; M. Whittaker 1982: 27. Reprinted by permission of Oxford University Press.

45 *Stromateis* 3.81.1–2; J. Ferguson 1991: 306.

46 See below, p. 170 f.

47 Epiphanius claims that the *Acts of Andrew*, the *Acts of John*, and the *Acts of Thomas* were Encratite texts (*Panarion* 47.1.5).

48 e.g. Epiphanius appears to have been driven by a desire to fulfil a prophecy in *Canticles* 6:7, which meant that he had to present 80 sects (see Young 1982: 199–205).

49 See Drijvers 1992: 323.

50 cf. Widengren 1945; 1946; Adam 1959 (cited in Drijvers 1992: 322).

51 NB: Klijn rejects a gnostic interpretation, and sees the 'Hymn of the Pearl' as the tale of the human soul, from its pre-existence with God until its return to God (Klijn 1960: 154–164). Klijn also cites Peterson's suggestion that the 'Hymn of the Pearl' reflects the relationship between soul and spirit in Tatian's *Oration* (E. Peterson 1949: 160 – cited in Klijn 1960: 161).

52 Klijn 1965: 49.

53 Drijvers 1984: I.7. NB: Although Klijn and Drijvers have pointed out parallels between Tatian and the *Acts of Thomas*, neither has explored those parallels in great detail. This section therefore expands and builds on their work.

54 *Or* 12:1; 13:2.

55 *Or* 13:1–3; 15:2.

56 *Acts of Thomas* 11; 31; 39.

57 *Acts of Thomas* 34; 54.

58 *Acts of Thomas* 45.

59 *Acts of Thomas* 11; Drijvers 1992: 343.

60 *Acts of Thomas* 160.

61 NB: Drijvers sees the imitation of Christ as central to Tatian's theology, and even interprets the difficult passage in *Or* 30 in this light (Drijvers 1984: I.13 f). This is surprising given the sparsity of references to Christ in Tatian, but what Drijvers appears to have done during his comparison of the *Oration* and the *Acts of Thomas* is to read into Tatian the kind of imitation of Christ that is present in the *Acts of Thomas*. He also points out the more general parallel between twinning in the *Acts of Thomas* and the union of soul and divine in Tatian (Drijvers 1984: I.16).

62 In *Acts of Thomas* 34, Judas Thomas appears to be imitating the passion of Christ by wearing a crown and holding a reed branch (cf. *Mt* 27:29); in *Acts of Thomas* 8, Judas Thomas's appearance changes, possibly mimicking the transfiguration; in *Acts of Thomas* 40, Judas Thomas rides on a colt to the city and an explicit link with Jesus' journey into Jerusalem is expressed.

63 cf. The two princes in the 'Hymn of the Pearl' (*Acts of Thomas* 108–113).

64 Or 15:2: *Acts of Thomas* 20; 144.
65 NB: Drijvers also points out the parallel between spiritual marriage in the *Acts of Thomas* and the divine union in Tatian (1984: I.10; 1992: 335).
66 *Acts of Thomas* 12.
67 *Acts of Thomas* 14. The bridegroom's response is a little more esoteric, and we shall return to it shortly.
68 *Acts of Thomas* 124. NB: The breaking up of sexual relations is not solely restricted to those between humans; in *Acts of Thomas* 43, a woman begs Judas Thomas to relieve her of a demon who has been forcing intercourse on her.
69 *Acts of Thomas* 150.
70 Although there is evidence that suggests that the bridal hymn and the hymn of the pearl, which appears later in the *Acts of Thomas* (108–113) circulated separately and were probably even composed independently, Drijvers has argued convincingly that the redactor of the *Acts of Thomas* has incorporated the hymns in such a way that they are an integral part of the narrative, and that the *Acts* should be considered as a literary unit (Drijvers 1992: 327).
71 cf. Murray, who states that the use of bridal imagery in the *Acts of Thomas* and the *Odes of Solomon* are expressions of personal devotion rather than of teaching about the church (Murray 1975: 132).
72 *Acts of Thomas* 15.
73 *Acts of Thomas* 43.
74 Indeed, the woman in *Acts of Thomas* 5 may merely be referring to a wish to return to continence, although what the 'gift' would therefore be then becomes problematic.
75 *Acts of Thomas* 108–113.
76 cf. Drijvers 1984: I.335.
77 *Acts of Thomas* 112.
78 Or 20:2–3.
79 cf. Tatian's use of the concept of the image and likeness of God in *Or* 15:2.
80 *Acts of Thomas* 7.
81 *Acts of Thomas* 142; 146.
82 *Acts of Thomas* 135; Drijvers 1992: 392.
83 Brock points out that the clothing imagery used by Syriac writers has a strong Biblical basis, and also traces possible influences from Mesopotamian and Iranian religion (Brock 1992: XI).
84 On the relationship between celibacy and baptism, see Vööbus, 1951; Murray 1974.
85 *Acts of Thomas* 51.
86 *Acts of Thomas* 28.
87 *Acts of Thomas* 87–88; 136.
88 *Acts of Thomas* 131.
89 *Acts of Thomas* 121.
90 *Acts of Thomas* 132; Drijvers 1992: 391.
91 Drijvers 1992: 335.
92 cf. Diatessaronic variant of *Mt* 27:34 in the Armenian version of Ephrem's *Commentary on the Diatessaron* (see above, p. 145 f).

93 *Acts of Thomas* 158. cf. *Odes of Solomon* 1. It may be possible that the concept of the crown (of truth) is a development of Tatian's union of soul and spirit, and reflects a Tatianic tradition present in the *Acts of Thomas* and the *Odes of Solomon*.

94 cf. *Acts of Thomas* 79, which shows the relevance of Christ's life and birth for Christians.

95 *Or* 13:1.

96 *Or* 13:1.

97 *Acts of Thomas* 14; 117.

98 *Or* 30:1; M. Whittaker 1982: 55. Reprinted by permission of Oxford University Press.

99 Drijvers 1992: 335.

100 *Acts of Thomas* 136.

101 *Acts of Thomas* 12.

102 *Acts of Thomas* 127–130.

103 Drijvers 1992: 12; cf. *Acts of Thomas* 44.

104 *Or* 15:3.

105 Drijvers also points out this parallel (Drijvers 1992: 13).

106 *Or* 15:2; M. Whittaker 1982: 31. Reprinted by permission of Oxford University Press.

107 cf. *Acts of Thomas* 12; 86; 94; 156.

108 *Acts of Thomas* 94.

109 Although Harnack has suggested that the *Odes* are a Jewish work with later Christian interpolations (Harnack 1910), it seems most likely that the *Odes* are actually Christian in origin (see Connolly 1912).

110 *Ode* 11 exists in Greek in the third century Papyrus Bodmer XI. The ambiguity may best be explained by the suggestion that the author was bilingual.

111 See Charlesworth 1985: 726.

112 See Charlesworth 1985: 726–727.

113 Drijvers 1984: IX.355.

114 Bauer, taking a late date for the *Odes*, has suggested that they are a product of second century gnosticism (Bauer 1964: 577; cf. Grant 1957a: 145–151), whilst Charlesworth has argued that they are too early to be considered gnostic, and points out that they contain many non-gnostic elements (Charlesworth 1969: 357–369; cf. Chadwick 1970: 266–270).

115 The *Odes* repeatedly refer to the concept of 'knowledge', and traces of docetism can be found (cf. especially *Ode* 42).

116 Charlesworth (1969: 366–368) mentions the following non-gnostic elements in the *Odes*:

1 A positive evaluation of the creator.

2 No characteristic dualism.

3 No spark or elite group.

4 The Old Testament is not rejected, but used as pattern for prophecy.

5 An open declaration of God's revelation.

6 No divine redeemer to release the pneumatics and lead them back to the realm of light.

117 Aune shares this view: 'Though they contain some features of a docetic character, the anachronistic use of labels from a later period serves no

useful purpose in understanding and interpreting the Odes.' (Aune 1982: 436).

118 If we were to suppose that the *Odes* predate Tatian, we would run into several difficulties. If the provenance of the *Odes* is Syriac, it is doubtful that Tatian could have come across the *Odes* in his homeland; by his own admission (*Or* 29) Tatian's conversion took place after extensive travel, and there is no evidence to suggest that he returned to Syria at all until after Justin's martyrdom. Although it is possible that Tatian came across the *Odes* elsewhere on his travels, this clearly weakens the argument for an early date for the *Odes*. An early date also fails to take into account the similar thought world found in the *Acts of Thomas* and other Syriac texts. This milieu seems peculiarly Syriac, and I will argue that the *Odes* reflect a stream of tradition within Syriac Christianity, which was heavily influenced by Tatian. However, the *Odes* did not remain a solely Syriac document; a Latin citation of the *Odes* by Lactantius (*c*.300 CE) provides evidence that the *Odes* had travelled well beyond Syria's borders by the end of the third century, and were extant in translation.

119 Drijvers 1984: I.7 (for Drijvers' comparison of Tatian and the *Odes*, see 14–15). NB: Drijvers also correctly sees a Platonic background to the Christological and anthropological theories in Tatian and the *Odes*.

120 cf. *Or* 13:1–2.

121 *Ode* 15.3–6.

122 *Ode* 8.8; Charlesworth 1985: 741.

123 This is not unusual since, although the *Odes* display clear evidence of prophetic activity, nowhere does the Odist use the word 'prophet'.

124 This is most clearly expressed in *Ode* 15.4–5; cf. *Ode* 8.8; 12.1, 3.

125 *Ode* 7.21; 23.4; cf. *Ode* 6.6; 7.13; 8.8; 12.3.

126 *Ode* 33.5 f.

127 *Ode* 1.1–5.

128 *Ode* 3.7.

129 *Ode* 13.1–4; cf. *Ode* 7.4.

130 *Ode* 3.7; cf. *Ode* 1.5; 28.7–8.

131 *Ode* 12.10–12; cf. *Ode* 10.1–2.

132 cf. Rudolph, who still maintains Bardaisan's gnosticism (Rudolph 1987: 327–329).

133 *The Book of the Laws of the Countries*, Drijvers 1967: 5; 13; 23; 25.

134 NB: In his incorporation of astrology (*The Book of the Laws of the Countries*, Drijvers 1967: 40 f), Bardaisan differs greatly to Tatian, who was extremely hostile towards such practices (cf. *Or* 8).

135 *Or* 13:1.

136 *The Book of the Laws of the Countries*, Drijvers 1967: 9.

137 *Or* 7:1–2.

138 *The Book of the Laws of the Countries*, Drijvers 1967: 11; 13; 15.

139 *The Book of the Laws of the Countries*, Drijvers 1967: 19.

140 *Or*: 1–2; M. Whittaker 1982: 13. Reprinted by permission of Oxford University Press. cf. Justin, 1 *Apol* 43, who puts forward a similar argument.

141 *The Book of the Laws of the Countries*, Drijvers 1967: 13.

142 *Or* 11:1–2.

143 *The Book of the Laws of the Countries*, Drijvers 1967: 23; 31–33.

144 *Or* 15:1–3.

145 *The Book of the Laws of the Countries*, Drijvers 1967: 23; 25.

146 *Hymns on Faith* 69:11; cf. Philo, *On the Sacrifices of Abel and Cain* 92.

147 *Hymns on Virginity* 20:12; *Hymns on Paradise* 5:2.

148 *Or* 4:2.

149 *Or* 20:2–3.

150 *Hymns against Heresies* 32:9.

151 See Brock 1985: 36. NB: A similarly positive view of the body, fuelling a positively motivated asceticism is found in the *Acts of Paul and Thecla*.

152 *Commentary on the Pauline Epistles* p. 62 = p. 59; *Hymns on Faith* 14:5.

153 NB: The details of Ephrem's history are different; he begins with the creation of Adam and Eve and their expulsion from Paradise, and ends with Christ's reversal of the fall and mankind's restoration in the eschatological Paradise. (See Brock 1985: 31–34).

154 *Hymns on Paradise* 12:18; *Hymns against Heresies* 11:4.

155 *Hymns on Paradise* 6:9; *Hymns on Virginity* 16:9.

156 *Hymns on the Epiphany* 12:1. NB: Although this hymn may not be authentic (see Brock 1985: 94), it was attributed to Ephrem, and probably represents a tradition which was heavily influenced by him.

157 *Discourse on Our Lord* 53.

158 See Brock 1992: XI.

159 NB: Elsewhere Ephrem speaks of Christians putting on Christ, as too does Aphrahat (*Demonstration* 14:39).

160 *Hymns on Faith* 14:5.

161 According to Ferguson, an English translation of all 23 *Demonstrations*, with Syriac text, is being prepared by R. Murray and R.J. Owen, but has not yet been published at the time of writing (E. Ferguson 1998: 72). I shall be using Gwynn 1898: 115–433 for *Demonstrations* 1, 5, 6, 8, 10, and 22; and Neusner 1971 for *Demonstrations* 11, 12, 13, 15, 16, 17, 18, 19, 21, and 23.

162 *Or* 4:2; 5:3; 6:1; 12:1–3.

163 *Demonstrations* 18:8; Neusner 1971: 81.

164 *Or* 17:1–4.

165 *Or* 5:2; M. Whittaker 1982: 11. Reprinted by permission of Oxford University Press.

166 *Demonstrations* 5:25; Gwynn 1898: 361–362. Aphrahat also uses the following metaphors in this passage; taking water from the sea, or sand from the seashore; counting the stars; and sunlight shining from the sun (cf. Philo, *Questions on Genesis* II.40).

167 *Demonstrations* 6:11; Gwynn 1898: 370. Aphrahat also uses the metaphors of sunlight and dust in this passage.

168 *Demonstrations* 10:8; Gwynn 1898: 386. Aphrahat uses further metaphors in this passage; one man does not receive all of a King's treasures; drinking from a fountain does not deplete it; the vision of near and far; and counting stars.

169 *Or* 13:1–2.

170 *Demonstrations* 6:1; 12; 14.

171 *Or* 15:2–3.

172 *Demonstrations* 1:4. The other conditions mentioned in this passage are prayer, love, alms, meekness, wisdom, hospitality, simplicity, patience,

long-suffering and mourning, although clearly Aphrahat's focus is on asceticism.
173 *Demonstrations* 17:7.
174 *Demonstrations* 6:12; 14; Gwynn 1898: 370–371.
175 *Or* 7:2–3; 15:3.
176 *Demonstrations* 6:2.
177 *Or* 20:1.
178 *Or* 6:1.
179 *Demonstrations* 8:1–3.
180 *Or* 13:1.
181 *Demonstrations* 6:14.
182 *Demonstrations* 6:14.
183 Vööbus 1951; 1961; Nedungatt 1973; Murray 1974.
184 *Demonstrations* 6:1.
185 Especially Aphrahat's mention of the pearl in *Demonstrations* 6:1.
186 Given the bilingual nature of the area, however, it is certainly possible that the *Oration* was read by Syriac Christians.

CONCLUSION

1 cf. Gero 1986.

APPENDIX

1 *Stromateis* III.82.2; J. Ferguson 1991: 307.
2 *Or* 29:1.
3 *Or* 31 f.
4 *Or* 19:4. NB: Tatian even gives the monotheistic doctrine of the 'barbarian writings' as a reason for his conversion (*Or* 29:2).
5 Tatian allows this without compromising God's transcendence by introducing the Word as the instrument of creation (*Or* 5).

223

BIBLIOGRAPHY

Adam, A. (1959) *Die Psalmen des Thomas und das Perlenlied als Zeugnisse vorchristlicher Gnosis*, Beihefte zur Zeitschrift für die neutestamentliche Wissenschaft 24, Berlin: A. Töpelmann.

Aland, B. (ed.) (1978) *Gnosis: Festschrift für Hans Jonas*, Göttingen: Vandenhoeck und Ruprecht.

Amidon, P.K. (trans.) (1990) *The Panarion of St. Epiphanius, Bishop of Salamis*, Oxford: Oxford University Press.

Andresen, C. (1952/1953) 'Justin und der mittlere Platonismus', *ZNTW* 44: 157–195.

—— (1955) *Logos und Nomos: Die Polemik des Kelsos Wider das Christentum*, Arbeiter zur Kirchengeschichte 30, Berlin: Walter de Gruyter & Co.

Armstrong, A.H. (1947) *An Introduction to Ancient Philosophy*, London: Methuen & Co. Ltd.

—— (ed.) (1967) *The Cambridge History of Later Greek and Early Medieval Philosophy*, Cambridge: Cambridge University Press.

—— (1984) 'Greek Philosophy and Christianity', in M.I. Finley (ed.), *The Legacy of Greece: A New Appraisal*, Oxford: Oxford University Press, pp. 347–375.

Asmis, E. (1989) 'The Stoicism of Marcus Aurelius', in W. Haase (ed.), *ANRW* II.36.3: 2228–2252.

Aune, D.E. (1982) 'The Odes of Solomon and Early Christian Prophecy', *NTS* 28: 435–460.

—— (1983) *Prophecy in Early Christianity and the Ancient Mediterranean World*, Grand Rapids, Michigan: William B. Eerdmans Publishing Co.

Baarda, T. (1983) *Early Transmission of Words of Jesus: Thomas, Tatian and the Text of the New Testament*, Amsterdam: V.U. Bockhandel/Uitgeverij.

—— (1994) 'Διαφωνία and Συμφωνία: factors in the harmonization of the gospels, especially in the Diatessaron of Tatian', *Essays on the Diatessaron*, Contributions to Biblical Exegesis and Theology 11, Kampen: Kok Pharos Publishing House, pp. 29–47.

Babcock, W.S. (ed.) (1990) *Paul and the Legacies of Paul*, Dallas: Southern Methodist University Press.

Barnard, L.W. (1965) 'Justin Martyr's Eschatology', *VChr* 19: 86–98.

—— (1967) *Justin Martyr: His Life and Thought*, Cambridge: Cambridge University Press.

—— (1968a) 'The Heresy of Tatian – Once Again', *JEH* 19: 1–10.

—— (1968b) 'The origins and emergence of the church in Edessa during the first two centuries AD', *VChr* 22: 161–175.

—— (trans.) (1997) *Saint Justin Martyr: The First and Second Apologies*, ACW 56, New York: Paulist Press.

Barrett, C.K. (1974) 'Pauline Controversies in the Post-Pauline Period', *NTS* 20: 229–245.

Bauer, W. (1972) *Rechtgläubigkeit und Ketzerei im ältesten Christentum*, Beiträge zur historischen Theologie 10, Tübingen, J.C.B. Mohr (Paul Siebeck) 1934; trans. R.A. Kraft and G. Krodel (eds), *Orthodoxy and Heresy in Earliest Christianity*, London: SCM Press Ltd.

—— (1964) 'Die Oden Salomos', in E. Hennecke and W. Schneemelcher (eds), *Neutestamentliche Apokryphen in deutscher Übersetzung vol 2*, Tübungen: J.C.B. Mohr (Paul Siebeck), pp. 576–625.

Beaujeu, J. (1973) *Apulée: Opuscules Philosophiques*, Collection des Universités de France, Paris: Société d'Édition 'Les Belles Lettres'.

Berchman, R.M. (1984) *From Philo to Origen: Middle Platonism in Transition*, Brown Judaic Studies 69, Chicago: Scholars Press.

Betz, H.D. (ed.) (1975) *Plutarch's Theological Writings and Early Christian Literature*, Studia ad Corpus Hellenisticum Novi Testamenti 3, Leiden: E.J. Brill.

Bianchi, U. (ed.) (1967) *Le Origini dello Gnosticismo: Colloquio di Messina 13–18 Aprile 1966*, Leiden: E.J. Brill.

—— (ed.) (1985) *La Tradizione dell' Enkrateia: Motivazioni ontologiche e proto-logiche*, Atti del Colloquio Internazionale Milano, 20–23 aprile 1982, Rome: Edizione dell' Ateneo.

Boismard M.E. (1992) *Le Diatessaron de Tatien à Justin*, Études Bibliques, Nouvelle série 15, Paris: Librarie Lecoffre.

Bolgiani, F. (1970) 'Taziano *Oratio ad Graecos* cap 30.1', in P. Granfield and J.A. Jungmann (eds), *Kyriakon: Festschrift Johannes Quasten vol 1*, Münster: Verlag Aschendorff, pp. 226–235.

Bovon, F. (ed.) (1981) *Les Actes Apocryphes des Apôtres: Christianisme et monde païen*, Geneva: Labor et Fides.

Brenk, F.E. (1986) 'In the light of the moon: demonology in the Early Imperial Period', in W. Haase (ed.), *ANRW* II.16.3: 2068–2145.

Brent, A. (1995) *Hippolytus and the Roman Church in the third century: communities in tension before the emergence of a monarch-bishop*, VChr (Suppl. 31), Leiden: E.J. Brill.

Brock, S.P. (1973) 'Early Syrian Asceticism', *Numen* 20: 1–19.

—— (1979b) 'Jewish Traditions in Syriac Sources', *Journal of Jewish Studies* 30: 212–232.

—— (1979b) *The Holy Spirit in the Syrian Baptismal Tradition*, The Syrian Churches Series 9, Kerala: Deepika.

—— (trans.) (1983) *The Harp of the Spirit: 18 Poems of Saint Ephrem*, Studies

Supplementary to Sobornost 4, London: Fellowship of St Alban and St Sergius.

Brock, S.P. (1984) *Syriac Perspectives on Late Antiquity*, London: Variorum.

—— (1985 2nd rev. 1992) *The Luminous Eye: The Spiritual World Vision of Saint Ephrem*, Cistercian Studies Series 124, Kalamazoo, Michigan: Cistercian Publications.

—— (trans.) (1990) *Saint Ephrem: Hymns on Paradise*, New York: St Vladimir's Seminary Press.

—— (1992) *Studies in Syriac Christianity: History, Literature and Theology*, Aldershot: Variorum.

Brown, P. (1982) *Society and the Holy in Late Antiquity*, London: Faber & Faber.

—— (1989) *The Body and Society: Men, Women and Sexual Renunciation in Early Christianity*, London: Faber & Faber.

Brown, R.E. and Meier, J.P. (1983) *Antioch and Rome: New Testament Cradles of Catholic Christianity*, London: Geoffrey Chapman.

Burkitt, F.C. (1904) *Early Eastern Christianity*, London: John Murray.

—— (1939) 'Syriac-Speaking Christianity', in *The Cambridge Ancient History, vol 12: The Imperial Crisis and Recovery AD 193–324*, Cambridge: Cambridge University Press.

Burney, C.F. (1926) 'Christ as the ΑΡΧΗ of Creation', *JThS* 27: 160–177.

Bury, R.G. (1933) *Sextus Empiricus 1: Outlines of Pyrrhonism*, LCL 273, Cambridge, Massachusetts: Harvard University Press.

Carroll, K. (1961–62) 'Toward a commonly received New Testament', *BJRL* 44: 327–349.

Casey, R.P. (1934) *The Excerpta Ex Theodoto of Clement of Alexandria*, Studies and Documents 1, London: Christophers.

Chadwick, H. (1965) 'Justin Martyr's defence of Christianity', *BJRL* 47: 275–297.

—— (1970) 'Some reflections on the character and theology of the Odes of Solomon', in P. Granfield and J.A. Jungmann (eds), *Kyriakon: Festschrift Johannes Quasten, vol 1*, Münster: Verlag Aschendorff, pp. 266–270.

Charlesworth, J.H. (1969) 'The Odes of Solomon – not gnostic', *CBQ* 31: 357–369.

—— (1974) 'Tatian's dependence upon apocryphal traditions', *The Heythrop Journal* 15: 5–17.

—— (1985) 'Odes of Solomon', in *The Old Testament Pseudepigrapha, vol 2: Expansions of the 'Old Testament' and Legends, Wisdom and Philosophical Literature, Prayers, Psalms and Odes, Fragments of Lost Judeo-Hellenistic Works*, London: Doubleday, pp. 725–771.

Clarke, G.W. (1967) 'The date of the Oration of Tatian', *HThR* 60: 123–126.

Clarke, M.L. (1971) *Higher Education in the Ancient World*, London: Routledge and Kegan.

Colson, F.H. and Whittaker, G.H. (1929) *Philo II*, LCL 227, Cambridge, Massachusetts: Harvard University Press.

—— (1939) *Philo VIII*, LCL 341, Cambridge, Massachusetts: Harvard University Press.

Connolly, R.H. (1912) 'The Odes of Solomon: Jewish or Christian', *JThS* 13: 298–309.

Craig, E. (ed.) (1998) *Routledge Encyclopedia of Philosophy*, 10 vols, London: Routledge.

Danielou, J. (1973) *A History of Early Christian Doctrine Before the Council of Nicaea, vol 2: Gospel Message and Hellenistic Culture*, trans. J.A. Baker, London: Darton, Longmann & Todd.

Darton, M. (ed.) (1976) *Modern Concordance to the New Testament*, London: Darton, Longmann & Todd.

Davies, J.G. (1960) *The Making of the Church*, London: Skeffington.

de Lacy, P.H. and Einarson, B. (1968) *Plutarch's Moralia VII*, LCL, Cambridge, Massachusetts: Harvard University Press.

Desjardins, M. (1991) 'Bauer and beyond: on recent scholarly discussions of Αἵρεσις in the early Christian era', *SCent* 8: 65–82.

des Places, É. (1973) *Numénius: Fragments*, Collection des Universités de France (Budé), Paris: Société d'Édition 'Les Belles Lettres'.

—— (1977) *Atticus: Fragments*, Collection des Universités de France (Budé), Paris: Société d'Édition 'Les Belles Lettres'.

De Vogel, C.J. (1985) 'Platonism and Christianity: a mere antagonism or a profound common ground?', *VChr* 39: 1–62.

Dillon, J.M. (1977) *The Middle Platonists: A Study of Platonism from 80 BC to AD 220*, London: Duckworth.

—— (1988) '"Orthodoxy" and "Eclecticism": Middle Platonists and Neopythagoreans', in J.M. Dillon and A.A. Long (eds), *The Question of Eclecticism: Studies in Later Greek Philosophy*, Berkeley: University of California Press, pp. 103–125.

—— (1989) 'Plutarch and second century Platonism', in A.H. Armstrong (ed.), *Classical Mediterranean Spirituality*, World Spirituality: An Encyclopedic History of the Religious Quest 15, London: SCM Press Ltd, pp. 214–229.

—— (trans.) (1993) *Alcinous: The Handbook of Platonism*, Clarendon Later Ancient Philosophers, Oxford: Clarendon Press.

Dodds, E.R. (1965) *Pagan and Christian in an Age of Anxiety: Some Aspects of Religious Experience from Marcus Aurelius to Constantine*, Cambridge: Cambridge University Press.

Drijvers, H.J.W. (1966) *Bardaisan of Edessa*, Studia Semitica Neerlandica, Assen: Von Gorcum.

—— (1967) *The Book of the Laws of Countries: Dialogue on Fate of Bardaisan of Edessa*, Assen: Van Gorcum.

—— (1984) *East of Antioch: Studies in Early Syriac Christianity*, London: Variorum.

—— (1990) 'The Abgar Legend', in W. Schneemelcher (ed.), *New Testament Apocrypha I: Gospels and Related Writings*, Cambridge: James Clarke and Co. Ltd, pp. 494–496.

—— (1992) 'The Acts of Thomas', in W. Schneemelcher (ed.), *New Testament Apocrypha II: Writings Related to the Apostles, Apocalypses and Related Subjects*, Cambridge: James Clarke and Co. Ltd, pp. 322–411.

Drijvers, H.J.W. and Reinink, G.J. (1988) 'Taufe und Licht: Tatian, Ebionäerevangelium und Thomasakten', in T. Baarda (ed.), *Text and Testimony: Essays on New Testament and Apocryphal Literature in Honour of A.F.J. Klijn*, Kampen: Uitgeversmaatschappij J.H. Kok.

Droge, A.J. (1987) 'Justin Martyr and the restoration of philosophy', *ChHist* 56: 303–319.

—— (1989) *Homer or Moses? Early Christian Interpretations of the History of Culture*, Hermeneutische Untersuchungen zur theologie, Tübingen: J.C.B. Mohr (Paul Siebeck).

Dunn, J.D.G. (1977) *Unity and Diversity in the New Testament: An Inquiry into the Character of Early Christianity*, Philadephia: Westminster Press.

Edwards, M.J. (1989) 'Gnostics and Valentinians in the Church Fathers', *JThS* 40: 26–47.

—— (1995) 'Justin's Logos and the Word of God', *JECS* 3: 261–280.

Ehrhardt, A. (1962) 'Christianity before the Apostle's Creed', *HThR* 55: 73–119.

Elze, M. (1960) *Tatian und seine Theologie*, Forschungen zur Kirchen und Dogmengeschicte 9, Göttingen: Vandenhoeck und Ruprecht.

Fallon, F.T. (1976) 'The law in Philo and Ptolemy: a note on the letter to Flora', *VChr* 30: 45–51.

Falls, T.B. (trans.) (1977) *Writings of Saint Justin Martyr*, The Fathers of the Church 6, Washington DC: The Catholic University of America Press.

Farquharson, A.S.L. (trans.) (1989) *The Meditations of Marcus Aurelius Antoninus*, Oxford: Oxford University Press.

Ferguson, E. (ed.) (1997; 2nd edn 1998) *Encyclopedia of Early Christianity*, London: Garland Publishing.

Ferguson, J. (trans.) (1991) *Clement of Alexandria: Stromateis Books 1–3*, The Fathers of the Church 85, Washington DC: The Catholic University of America Press.

Filoramo, G. (1990) *A History of Gnosticism*, Oxford: Basil Blackwell.

Flora, J.R. (1972) 'A critical analysis of Walter Bauer's theory of early Christian orthodoxy and heresy', unpublished thesis, Southern Baptist Theological Seminary.

Forster, E.S. and Furley, D.J. (1965) *Aristotle: On Sophistical Refutations, On Coming-to-be and Passing Away, On the Cosmos*, LCL, Cambridge, Massachusetts: Harvard University Press.

Fox, R.L. (1986) *Pagans and Christians in the Mediterranean World from the Second Century AD to the Conversion of Constantine*, London: Penguin Books.

Frend, W.H.C. (1965) *Martyrdom and Persecution in the Early Church: A Study of a Conflict from the Maccabees to Donatus*, Oxford: Basil Blackwell.

Freudenthal, J. (1879) *Hellenistische Studien 3: Der Platoniker Albinos und der falsche Alkinoos*, Berlin: Verlag von S. Calvary & Co.

Froidefond, C. (1987) 'Plutarque et le Platonisme', in W. Haase (ed.), *ANRW* II.36.1: 184–233.

Gero, S. (1986) 'With Walter Bauer on the Tigris: Encratite orthodoxy and Libertine heresy in Syro-Mesopotamian Christianity', in C.W. Hedrick and

R. Hodgson Jr. (eds), *Nag Hammadi, Gnosticism and Early Christianity*, Peabody, Massachusetts: Hendrickson Publishers, pp. 287–307.

Goodenough, E.R. (1923; reprinted 1968) *The Theology of Justin Martyr: An Investigation into the Conceptions of Early Christian Literature and its Hellenistic and Judaistic Influences*, Amsterdam: Philo Press.

—— (1940; 2nd edn 1962) *An Introduction to Philo Judaeus*, Oxford: Basil Blackwell.

Grant, R.M. (1953) 'The date of Tatian's Oration', *HThR* 46: 99–101.

—— (1954) 'The heresy of Tatian', *JThS (NS)* 5: 62–68.

—— (1957a) 'Notes on Gnosis', *VChr* 11: 145–151.

—— (1957b) 'Tatian and the Bible', *SP* 1: 297–306.

—— (1958) 'Studies in the Apologists', *HThR* 51: 123–134.

—— (1959; 2nd edn 1966) *Gnosticism and Early Christianity*, New York, Columbia University Press.

—— (trans.) (1961a) 'Letter to Flora', *Gnosticism: An Anthology*, London: Collins, pp. 184–190.

—— (1961b) 'The mystery of marriage in the Gospel of Philip', *VChr* 15: 129–140.

—— (1964) 'Tatian (*Oratio* 30) and the Gnostics', *JThS (NS)* 15: 65–69.

—— (1970) *Theophilus of Antioch: Ad Autolycum*, Oxford Early Christian Texts, Oxford: Clarendon Press.

—— (1985) 'A woman of Rome: the matron in Justin, 2 *Apol* 2.1–9', *ChHist* 54: 461–472.

—— (1986) *Gods and the One God: Christian Theology in the Graeco-Roman World*, London: SPCK.

—— (1988) *Greek Apologists of the Second Century*, Philadelphia: The Westminster Press.

Guerra, A.J. (1992) 'The Conversion of Marcus Aurelius and Justin Martyr: the purpose, genre and content of the First Apology', *SCent* 9: 171–187.

Guista, M. (1960–61) ''Αλβίνου 'Επιτομὴ ο 'Αλκινόου Διδασκαλικός?', *Atti della Accademia delle Scienze di Torino, Classe de Scienze morali, storiche e filologiche*, 95: 167–177.

Gunther, J.J. (1980) 'The meaning and origin of the name Judas Thomas', *Le Museon* 93: 113–148.

Guthrie, K.S. (1917) *Numenius of Apamea, The Father of Neo-Platonism: Works, Biography, Message, Sources and Influence*, London: George Bell and Sons.

Gwynn, J. (trans.) (1898) 'Selections translated into English from the Hymns and Homilies of Ephraim the Syrian, and from the Demonstrations of Aphrahat the Persian Sage', in *A Select Library of Nicene and Post-Nicene Fathers of the Christian Church, 2nd Series, vol 13*, Oxford: James Parker & Co, pp. 115–433.

Harnack, A. (1882) *Die Überlieferung der griechischen Apologeten des zweiten Jahrhunderts in der alten Kirche und im Mittelalter*, TU 2, Leipzig: Akademie.

—— (1908) *The Mission and Expansion of Christianity in the First Three Centuries, vol 1*, trans. J. Moffatt, Theological Translations Library 19, London: Williams and Norgate.

Harnack, A. (1910) *Ein jüdisch-christlichen Psalmbuch aus dem ersten Jahrhundert*, TU 35.4, Leipzig: J.C. Hinrichs.

Harrington, D.J. (1980) 'The reception of Walter Bauer's *Orthodoxy and Heresy in Earliest Christianity* during the last decade', *HThR* 73: 289–298.

Harris, J.R. (1924) 'Tatian: Perfection According to the Saviour', *BJRL* 8: 15–51.

—— (1931) 'The mentality of Tatian', *Bulletin of the Bezan Club* 9: 8–10.

Hawthorne, G.F. (1964) 'Tatian and his Discourse to the Greeks', *HThR* 57: 161–188.

Heard, R.G. (1954) 'The ΑΠΟΜΝΗΜΟΝΕΥΜΑΤΑ in Papias, Justin and Irenaeus', *NTS* 1: 122–134.

Heine, R.E. (1989) *The Montanist Oracles and Testimonia*, North American Patristic Society, Patristic Monograph Series 14, Macon: Mercer University Press.

Hill, D. (1979) *New Testament Prophecy*, London: Marshall, Morgan & Scott.

Hill, J. Hamlyn (trans.) (1894) *The Earliest Life of Christ Ever Compiled from the Four Gospels*, Edinburgh: T & T Clarke.

Holte, R. (1958) 'Logos spermatikos: Christianity and ancient philosophy according to St. Justin's Apologies', *STh* 12: 106–168.

Honderich, T. (ed.) (1995) *The Oxford Companion to Philosophy*, Oxford: Oxford University Press.

Hyldahl, N. (1966) *Philosophie und Christentum: Eine Interpretation der Einleitung zum Dialog Justins*, Acta Theologica 9, Copenhagen: Munksgaard.

Jeffers, J.S. (1991) *Social Order and Hierarchy in Early Christianity: Conflict at Rome*, Minneapolis: Fortress Press.

Joly, R. (1973) *Christianisme et Philosophie: Études sur Justin et les Apologistes Grecs du deuxième siècle*, Université Libre de Bruxelles, Faculté de Philosophie et Lettres 52, Brussels: Editions de l'Université de Bruxelles.

—— (1979) 'Notes pour le Moyen Platonisme', in A.M. Ritter (ed.), *Kerygma und Logos: Beiträge zu den geistesgeschichtlichen Beziehungen zwischen Antike und Christentum, Festschrift für Carl Andresen*, Göttingen: Vandenhoeck und Ruprecht, pp. 311–321.

Jonas, H. (1954) *Gnosis und spätaniker Geist, Band 2¹: Von der Mythologie zur mystischen Philosophie*, Forschungen zur Religion und Literatur des Alten und Neuen Testaments 159, Göttingen: Vandenhoeck und Ruprecht.

Klijn, A.F.J. (1960) 'The so-called Hymn of the Pearl (Acts of Thomas Ch. 108–113)', *VChr* 14: 151–164.

—— (1965) *The Acts of Thomas*, Suppl. NovTest 5, Leiden, E.J. Brill.

—— (1972) 'Christianity in Edessa and the Gospel of Thomas', *NovTest* 14: 70–77.

—— (1973) 'Baptism in the Acts of Thomas', in J. Vellian (ed.), *Studies on Syrian Baptismal Rites*, The Syrian Churches Series 6, Kottayam: J. Vellian.

Kukula, R.C. (1900) *Tatians Sogenannte Apologie*, Leipzig: Bruck und Verlag von B.G. Teubner.

La Piana, G. (1925) 'The Roman Church at the end of the second century', *HThR* 18: 201–277.

Lake, K. (1975) *Eusebius: The Ecclesiastical History, vol 1*, LCL 153, Cambridge, Massachusetts: Harvard University Press.

Lampe, P. (1987) *Die stadtrömischen Christen in dem ersten beiden Jahrhunderten*, Wissenschaftliche Untersuchungen zum Neuen Testament II.18, Tübingen: J.C.B. Mohr (Paul Siebeck).

Langton, E. (1949) *Essentials of Demonology: A Study of Jewish and Christian Doctrine, its Origin and Development*, London: Epworth Press.

Layton, B. (ed.) (1980) *The Rediscovery of Gnosticism: Proceedings of the International Conference on Gnosticism at Yale New Haven, Connecticut, March 28–31, 1978, vol 1: The School of Valentinus*, Studies in the History of Religions, (Supplements) Numen 41, Leiden: E.J. Brill.

Leloir, L. (1966) *Commentaire de l'Évangile concordant ou Diatessaron*, SC 121, Paris: Les Éditions du Cerf.

Lieu, J., North, J. and Rajak, T. (eds) (1992) *The Jews Among Pagans and Christians in the Roman Empire*, London: Routledge.

Logan, A.H.B. (1996) *Gnostic Truth and Christian Heresy: A Study in the History of Gnosticism*, Edinburgh: T & T Clark.

Lüdemann, G. (1979) 'Zur Geschichte des altesten Christentums in Rome', *ZNTW* 70: 97–114.

—— (1996) *Heretics: The Other Side of Christianity*, London: SCM Press Ltd.

McCarthy, C. (trans.) (1993) 'Saint Ephrem's commentary on Tatian's Diatessaron: an English translation of "Chester Beatty" Syriac MS 709', *Journal of Semitic Studies Supplement 2*, Oxford: Oxford University Press.

McGehee, M. (1993) 'Why Tatian never "Apologized" to the Greeks', *JECS* 1, 2: 143–158.

McVey, K.E. (trans.) (1989) *Ephrem the Syrian: Hymns*, The Classics of Western Spirituality, New York: Paulist Press.

Mansfield, J. (1988) 'Philosophy in the service of Scripture: Philo's exegetical strategies', in J.M. Dillon and A.A. Long (eds), *The Question of 'Eclecticism': Studies in Later Greek Philosophy*, Hellenistic Culture and Society 3, Berkeley: University of California Press, pp. 70–102.

Manson, T.W. (1945) 'The Argument from Prophecy', *JThS* 46: 129–136.

Maran, P. (1742) *S.P.N. Justini Philosophi et Martyris Opera quae extant omnia necnon Tatiani Adversus Graecos oratio . . . opera et studio unius ex monachis Congregationis S. Mauri*, Paris.

Marcovich, M. (1995) *Tatiani Oratio Ad Graecos*, Patristische texte und Studien 43, Berlin: Walter de Gruyter.

Marcus, R. (1953) *Philo Supplement II: Questions and Answers on Exodus*, LCL 401, Cambridge, Massachusetts: Harvard University Press.

—— (1974) *Christianity in the Roman World: Currents in the History of Culture and Ideas*, London: Thames & Hudson.

Martín, J.P. (1987) 'Taciano de Siria y el Origen de la Oposicion de Materia y Espiritu', *Stromata* 43: 71–107.

—— (1988) 'Filon y las Ideas Christianas del Siglo II: Estado de la Cuestion', *Revista Biblica* 50: 263–294.

May, G. (1994) *Schöpfung aus dem Nichts*, Berlin, Walter de Gruyter, 1978;

trans. A.S. Worral, *Creatio ex Nihilo: The Doctrine of 'Creation Out of Nothing' in Early Christian Thought*, Edinburgh: T & T Clark.

Metzger, B.M. (1977) *The Early Versions of the New Testament, Their Origin, Transmission and Limitations*, Oxford: Oxford University Press.

Millar, F. (1993) *The Roman Near East: 31 BC–AD 337*, Cambridge, Massachussets: Harvard University Press.

Munier, C. (1994) *L'Apologie de Saint Justin, Philosophe et Martyr*, Paradosis: Études de Littérature et de Théologie Anciennes 38, Fribourg Suisse: Éditions Universitaires Fribourg Suisse.

Murray, R. (1969) 'Reconstructing the Diatessaron', *The Heythrop Journal*, 10: 43–49.

—— (1974) 'The exhortation to candidates for ascetical vows at baptism in the Ancient Syriac Church', *NTS* 21: 59–80.

—— (1975) *Symbols of Church and Kingdom: A Study in Early Syriac Tradition*, Cambridge: Cambridge University Press.

Myers, J.M. and Freed, E.D. (1966) 'Is Paul also among the prophets?', *Interpretation* 20: 40–53.

Nahm, C. (1992) 'The debate on the 'Platonism' of Justin Martyr', *SCent* 9, 3: 129–151.

Nedungatt, G. (1973) 'The covenanters of the early Syriac-speaking Church', *Orientalia Christiana Periodica* 39: 191–215, 418–444.

Neusner, J. (trans.) (1971) *Aphrahat and Judaism: The Christian-Jewish Argument in Fourth Century Iran*, Studia Post-Biblica 19, Leiden: E.J. Brill.

Nock, A.D. (1933) *Conversion: The Old and the New in Religion from Alexander the Great to Augustine of Hippo*, Oxford: Oxford University Press.

Norris, R.A. (1966) *God and World in Early Christian Theology: A Study in Justin Martyr, Irenaeus, Tertullian and Origen*, London: Adam & Charles Black.

Osborn, E.F. (1973) *Justin Martyr*, Beitrage zur Historischen Theologie Heraus gegeben von Gerhard Ebeling 47, Tübingen: J.C.B. Mohr (Paul Siebeck).

—— (1981) *The Beginning of Christian Philosophy*, Cambridge: Cambridge University Press.

Oulton, J.E.L. and Lawlor, H.J. (1973) *Eusebius: The Ecclesiastical History, vol 2*, LCL 265, Cambridge, Massachusetts: Harvard University Press.

Pagels, E.H. (1972) 'The Valentinian claim to esoteric exegesis of Romans as basis for anthropological theory', *VChr* 26: 241–258.

—— (1974) '"The Mystery of the Resurrection": A Gnostic Reading of 1 *Cor* 15', *JBL* 93: 276–288.

—— (1979) *The Gnostic Gospels*, New York: Random House.

—— (1985) 'Christian Apologists and "The Fall of the Angels": an attack on Roman Imperial power?', *HThR* 78: 301–325.

—— (1992) *The Gnostic Paul: Gnostic Exegesis of the Pauline Letters*, Philadelphia: Trinity Press International.

Pearson, B.A. (1983) 'Philo, Gnosis and the New Testament', in A.H.B. Logan and A.J.M. Wedderburn (eds), *The New Testament and Gnosis: Essays in Honour of Robert McL. Wilson*, Edinburgh: T & T Clark Ltd.

—— (1984) 'Philo and gnosticism', in W. Haase (ed.), *ANRW* II.21.2: 295–342.

Petersen, E. (1949) 'Einige Bemerkungen zum Hamburger Papyrus Fragment der Acta Pauli', *VChr* 3: 160.

Petersen, W.L. (1986) 'New evidence for the question of the original language of the Diatessaron', in W. Schrage (ed.), *Studien zum Text und zur Ethik des Neuen Testaments: Festschrift Heinrich Greeven*, Berlin: Walter de Gruyter, pp. 325–343.

—— (1990) 'Textual evidence of Tatian's dependence upon Justin's ΑΠΟΜΝΗΜΟΝΕΥΜΑΤΑ', *NTS* 36: 512–534.

—— (1994) *Tatian's Diatessaron: Its Creation, Dissemination, Significance, and History in Scholarship*, Suppl. VChr 25, Leiden: E.J. Brill.

Pétrement, S. (1991) *A Separate God: The Christian Origins of Gnosticism*, trans. C. Harrison, London: Darton, Longman & Todd.

Plooij, D. (1923a) 'Eine enkratitsche Glosse im Diatessaron', *ZNTW* 22: 1–15.

—— (1923b) *A Primitive Text of the Diatessaron*, Leyden: A.W. Sijthoff's Uit-geversmaatschappij.

Poirier, P.-H. (1981) *L'Hymne de la Perle des Actes de Thomas*, Homo Religiosus 8, Louvain-la-Neuve: Centre d'Histoire des Religions de Louvain-la-Neuve.

Price, R.M. (1988) '"Helenisation" and Logos Doctrine in Justin Martyr', *VChr* 42: 18–23.

Puech, A. (1903) *Recherches sur le Discours aux Grecs de Tatien*, Bibliotheque de la Faculté des Lettres 17, Paris: Félix Alcan.

—— (1912) *Les Apologistes Grecs*, Paris.

Radice, R. (1991) 'Observations on the theory of the Ideas as the thoughts of God in Philo of Alexandria', *The Studia Philonica Annual* 3: 126–134.

Radice, R. and Runia, D.T. (1988) *Philo of Alexandria: An Annotated Bibliography (1937–1986)*, Suppl. VChr 8, Leiden: E.J. Brill.

Rich, A.N.M. (1954) 'The Platonic Ideas as the thoughts of God', *Mnemosyne* IV 7: 123–133.

Ritter, A.M. (1987) 'Die Entstehung des neutestamentlichen Kanons: Selbst-durchsetzung oder autoritative Entscheidung?', in A. and J. Assman (eds), *Kanon und Zensier: Beiträge zur Archäologie der literarischen Kommunikation II*, München: Wilhelm Fink Verlag, pp. 93–99.

Robillard, E. (1989) *Justin, L'itinéraire philosophique*, Collections Recherche, Nouvelle série 23, Paris: Les Éditions du Cerf.

Robinson, J.M. (ed.) (1977; 4th edn 1996) *The Nag Hammadi Library in English*, Leiden: E.J. Brill.

Robinson, J.M. and Koester, H. (1971) *Trajectories Through Early Christianity*, Philadelphia: Fortress Press.

Robinson, T.A. (ed.) (1993) *The Early Church: An Annotated Bibliography of Literature in English*, ATLA Bibliographies Series 33, London: The Scarecrow Press Inc.

Roth, N. (1978) 'The "Theft of Philosophy" by the Greek from the Jews', *Classical Folia* 32: 53–67.

Rowland, C. (1982) *The Open Heaven: The Study of Apocalyptic in Judaism and Early Christianity*, London: SPCK.

Rudolph, K. (1987) *Gnosis: The Nature and History of Gnosticism*, New York: Harper San-Francisco.

Ruether, R.R. (1974) *Faith and Fratricide: The Theological Roots of Anti-Semitism*, New York: The Seabury Press.

Runia, D.T. (1990) *Exegesis and Philosophy: Studies on Philo of Alexandria*, Aldershot: Variorum.

—— (1993) *Philo in Early Christian Literature: A Survey*, Compendia Rerum Iudaicarum ad Novum Testamentum, Sec 3: Jewish Traditions in Early Christian Literature 3, Minneapolis: Fortress.

—— (1995) *Philo and the Church Fathers: A Collection of Papers*, Suppl. VChr 32, Leiden: E.J. Brill.

Sanders, E.P. (ed.) (1980) *Jewish and Christian Self-Definition, vol 1: The Shaping of Christianity in the Second and Third Centuries*, London, SCM Press Ltd.

—— (1981) *Jewish and Christian Self-Definition, vol 2: Aspects of Judaism in the Graeco-Roman Period*, London: SCM Press Ltd.

—— (1982) *Jewish and Christian Self-Definition, vol 3: Self-definition in the Graeco-Roman World*, London: SCM Press Ltd.

Sanders, J.T. (1993) *Schismatics, Sectarians, Dissidents, Deviants: The First 100 Years of Jewish-Christian Relations*, London: SCM Press Ltd.

Schoedel, W.R. and Wilken, R.L. (eds) (1979) *Early Christian Literature and the Classical Intellectual Tradition: In Honorem Robert M. Grant*, Théologie Historique 53, Paris: Éditions Beauchesne.

Segal, A.F. (1977) *Two Powers in Heaven: Early Rabbinic Reports about Christianity and Gnosticism*, Studies in Judaism in Late Antiquity 25, Leiden: E.J. Brill.

Sharples, R.W. (1983) *Alexander of Aphrodisias: On Fate*, Duckworth Classical, Medieval and Renaissance Editions, London: Duckworth.

Shotwell, W.A. (1965) *The Biblical Exegesis of Justin Martyr*, London: SPCK.

Simon, M. (1986) *Verus Israel: A Study of the Relations between Christians and Jews in the Roman Empire (135–425)*, The Littman Library of Jewish Civilisation, Oxford: Oxford University Press.

Skarsaune, O. (1976) 'The conversion of Justin Martyr', *STh* 30: 53–73.

—— (1987) *The Proof from Prophecy, A Study in Justin Martyr's Proof-Text Tradition: Text-type, Provenance, Theological Profile*, Leiden: E.J. Brill.

Stead, G.C. (1969) 'The Valentinian myth of Sophia', *JThS (NS)* 20: 75–104.

Stempel, H.A. (1980) 'Der Lehrer in der *Lehre der Zwölf Apostel*', *VChr* 34: 209–217.

Swain, S. (1996) *Hellenism and Empire: Language, Classicism and Power in the Greek World AD 50–250*, Oxford: Clarendon Press.

Tabbernee, W. (1997) *Montanist Inscriptions and Testimonia: Epigraphic Sources Illustrating the History of Montanism*, North American Patristic Society – Patristic Monograph Series 16, Macon: Mercer University Press.

Taylor, A.E. (1926) *Plato: The Man and His Work*, London: Methuen & Co. Ltd.

Trakatellis, D.C. (1976) *The Pre-Existence of Christ in the Writings of Justin Martyr: An Exegetical Study in Reference to the Humiliation and Exaltation Christology*, Harvard Dissertations in Religion 6, Missoula: Scholars Press.

Trapp, M.B. (trans.) (1997) *Maximus of Tyre: The Philosophical Orations*, Oxford: Clarendon Press.

Trevett, C. (1996) *Montanism: Gender, Authority and the New Prophecy*, Cambridge: Cambridge University Press.

Turner, H.E.W. (1954) *The Pattern of Christian Truth: A Study in the Relations between Orthodoxy and Heresy in the Early Church*, London: A.R. Mowbray & Co. Ltd.

Unger, D.J. (trans.) (1992) *St Irenaeus of Lyons Against the Heresies Book 1*, ACW 55, New York: Paulist Press.

van den Broek, R. (1983) 'The Present State of Gnostic Studies', *VChr* 37: 41–71.

van den Hoek, A. (1988) *Clement of Alexandria and His Use of Philo in the Stromateis: An early reshaping of a Jewish model*, Suppl. VChr 3, Leiden: E.J. Brill.

van Winden, J.C.M. (1970) 'Le Christianisme et la Philosophie', in P. Granfield and J.A. Jungmann (eds), *Kyriakon: Festschrift Johannes Quasten, vol 1*, Münster: Verlag Aschendorff.

—— (1971) *An Early Christian Philosopher: Justin Martyr's Dialogue with Trypho Chapters 1–9*, Philosophia Patrum, Interpretations of Patristic Texts 1, Leiden: E.J. Brill.

Vogels, H.J. (1913) 'Lk. 2,36 im Diatessaron', *Biblische Zeistschrift* 11: 168–171.

von Campenhausen, H. (1972) *The Formation of the Christian Bible*, Philadelphia: Fortress Press.

von Engelhardt, M. (1878) *Das Christenthum Justins des Märtyrers: Eine Untersuchung über die Aufänge der Katholischen Glaubenslehre*, Erlangen: A. Deichert.

Vööbus, A. (1951) *Celibacy, A Requirement for Admission to Baptism in the Early Syrian Church*, Papers of the Estonian Theological Society in Exile 1, Stockholm: Estonian Theological Society in Exile.

—— (1958) *History of Asceticism in the Syrian Orient, A Contribution to the History of Culture in the Near East, vol 1: The Origin of Asceticism. Early Monasticism in Persia*, Louvain: Corpus Scriptorium Christianorum Orientalum.

—— (1960) *History of Asceticism in the Syrian Orient, A Contribution to the History of Culture in the Near East, vol 2: Early Monasticism in Mesopotamia and Syria*, Louvain: Corpus Scriptorium Christianorum Orientalum.

—— (1961) 'The institution of the Benai Qeiama and the Benat Qeiama in the Ancient Syrian Church', *ChHist* 30: 19–27.

—— (1988) *History of Asceticism in the Syrian Orient, A Contribution to the History of Culture in the Near East, vol 3*, Louvain: Corpus Scriptorium Christianorum Orientalum.

Walden, J.W.H. (1912) *The Universities of Ancient Greece*, London: George Routledge and Sons Ltd.

Walton, R.L. (1988) 'The pursuit of spiritual man in the second century', unpublished thesis, University of Birmingham.

Waszink, J.H. (1964) 'Bemerkungen zu Justins Lehre vom Logos Spermatikos', in *Mullus Festschrift Theodor Klauser*, Jahrbuch für Antike Christentum Ergänzungsband 1, (1964) Münster: Aschendorffsche Verlagsbuchhandlung, pp. 380–390.

Wedderburn, A.J.M. (1973) 'Philo's 'Heavenly Man'', *NovTest* 15: 301–326.

Whittaker, J. (1987) 'Platonic philosophy in the early centuries of the Empire', in W. Haase (ed.), *ANRW* II.36.1: 81–123.

—— (1990) *Alcinoos: Enseignement des doctrines de Platon*, Collection des Universités de France (Budé), Paris: Société d'Édition 'Les Belles Lettres'.

Whittaker, M. (1966) 'Some textual points in Tatian's *Oratio ad Graecos*', *SP* 7: 348–351.

—— (1975) 'Tatian's educational background', *SP* 13: 57–59.

—— (1982) *Tatian Oratio ad Graecos and Fragments*, Oxford Early Christian Texts, Oxford: Clarendon Press.

Widengren, G. (1945) *inter alia, The Great Vohu Manah and the Apostle of God: Studies in Iranian and Manichaean Religion*, Uppsala Universitets arsskrift 5, Uppsala Leipzig: A.-b. Lundequistska Bokhandeln, O. Harrassowitz.

—— (1946) *Mesopotamian Elements in Manicheism*, Uppsala Universitets arsskrift 3, Uppsala Leipzig: A.-b. Lundequistska Bokhandeln, O. Harrassowitz.

Wilken, R.L. (1971) 'Collegia, philosophical schools, and theology', in S. Benko and J.J. O'Rourke (eds), *The Catacombs and the Collosseum: The Roman Empire as the Setting of Primitive Christianity*, Valley Forge: Judson Press, pp. 268–291.

Wilson, R.McL. (1958) *The Gnostic Problem: A Study of the Relations between Hellenistic Judaism and the Gnostic Heresy*, London: A.R. Mowbray & Co. Ltd.

Winston, D. (1990) 'Judaism and hellenism: hidden tensions in Philo's thought', *The Studia Philonica Annual* 2: 1–19.

Wolfson, H.A. (1947a) *Philo: Foundations of Religious Philosophy in Judaism, Christianity and Islam, vol 1*, Cambridge, Massachusetts: Harvard University Press.

—— (1947b) *Philo: Foundations of Religious Philosophy in Judaism, Christianity and Islam, vol 2*, Cambridge, Massachusetts: Harvard University Press.

—— (1956a) *The Philosophy of the Church Fathers, vol 1*, Cambridge, Massachusetts: Harvard University Press.

—— (1956b) *The Philosophy of the Church Fathers, vol 2*, Cambridge, Massachusetts: Harvard University Press.

—— (1967) 'Philo Judaeus' in P. Edwards (ed.), *The Encyclopedia of Philosophy, vol 6*, London: Collier-Macmillan, pp. 151–155.

Yamauchi, E.M. (1973) *Pre-Christian Gnosticism: A Survey of the Proposed Evidence*, London: Tyndale Press.

Young, F.M. (1979a) 'The God of the Greeks and the nature of religious language', in W.R. Schoedel and R. Wilken (eds), *Early Christian Literature and the Greek Intellectual Tradition: Festscrift for R. M. Grant*, Théologie Historique 53, Paris: Éditions Beauchesne, pp. 45–74.

—— (1979b) *The Use of Sacrificial Ideas in Greek Christian Writers from the New Testament to John Chrysostom*, Patristic Monograph Series 5, Cambridge, Massachusetts: The Philadelphia Patristic Foundation Ltd.

—— (1982) 'Did Epiphanius know what he meant by heresy?', *SP* 18: 199–205.

—— (1991) "Creatio ex Nihilo': a context for the emergence of the Christian doctrine of creation', *Scottish Journal of Theology* 44: 139–151.

—— (1994) *The Theology of the Pastoral Letters*, New Testament Theology Series, Cambridge: Cambridge University Press.

—— (1997) *Biblical Exegesis and the Formation of Christian Culture*, Cambridge: Cambridge University Press.

—— (1999) 'Greek Apologists of the second Century', in M. Edwards, M. Goodman and S.R.F. Price (eds), *Apologetics in the Roman Empire: Pagans, Jews, and Christians*, Oxford: Clarendon Press, pp. 81–104.

Zahn, T. (1891) *Forschungen zur Geschichte des neutestamentlichen Kanons, I: Tatian's Diatessaron*, Erlangen.

Zeller, E. (1892) *The Stoics, Epicureans, and Sceptics*, London: Longmans, Green & Co.

Zintzen, C. (1981) *Der Mittelplatonismus*, Wege der Forschung 70, Darmstadt: Wissenschaftliche Buchgesellschaft.

INDEX